CORRUPTION AND THE

Corruption and the Secret of Law
A Legal Anthropological Perspective

Edited by

MONIQUE NUIJTEN
Wageningen University, The Netherlands
and
GERHARD ANDERS
University of Zurich, Switzerland

ASHGATE

© Monique Nuijten and Gerhard Anders 2007

First printed in paperback 2008.

All rights reserved. No part of this publication may be reproduced, stored in a retrieval system or transmitted in any form or by any means, electronic, mechanical, photocopying, recording or otherwise without the prior permission of the publisher.

Monique Nuijten and Gerhard Anders have asserted their moral right under the Copyright, Designs and Patents Act, 1988, to be identified as the editors of this work.

Published by
Ashgate Publishing Limited
Wey Court East
Union Road
Farnham
Surrey GU9 7PT
England

Ashgate Publishing Company
Suite 420
101 Cherry Street
Burlington,
VT 05401-4405
USA

www.ashgate.com

British Library Cataloguing in Publication Data
Corruption and the secret of law : a legal anthropological
　perspective. - (Law, justice and power series)
　I. Nuijten, Monique II. Anders, Gerhard
　340.1'15

Library of Congress Cataloging-in-Publication Data
Corruption and the secret of law : a legal anthropological perspective / edited by Monique Nuijten and Gerhard Anders.
　　　p. cm. -- (Law, justice and power)
　Includes index.
　ISBN: 978-0-7546-7110-7
　1. Corruption. 2. Corruption--Cross-cultural studies. 3. Culture and law. 4. Law and anthropology. I. Nuijten, Monique. II. Anders, Gerhard.
　HV301.P67 2007
　364.1'323--dc22

2007021824

ISBN: 978-0-7546-7110-7 (Hardback)
ISBN: 978-0-7546-7682-9 (Paperback)

Printed and bound in Great Britain by MPG Books Ltd, Bodmin, Cornwall.

Contents

List of Contributors	*vii*
Acknowledgments	*xi*

1 Corruption and the Secret of Law: An Introduction 1
   Gerhard Anders and Monique Nuijten

SYSTEMATIC CORRUPTION AND BUREAUCRATIC ITINERARIES

2 Hidden Acts, Open Talks. How Anthropology Can "Observe" and Describe Corruption 27
   Giorgio Blundo

3 Deep Corruption in Indonesia: Discourses, Practices, Histories 53
   Heinzpeter Znoj

THE INDETERMINACY OF THE LAW AND THE LEGAL PROFESSION

4 Corruption Judgments in Pre-war Japan: Locating the Influence of Tradition, Morality, and Trust on Criminal Justice 77
   Andrew MacNaughton and Kam Bill Wong

5 Corrupted Files: Cross-fading Defense Strategies of a Vesuvian Lawyer 99
   Livia Holden and Giovanni Tortora

CORRUPTION ACCUSATIONS AND POLITICAL IMAGINARIES

6 Corruption Narratives and the Power of Concealment: The Case of Burundi's Civil War 125
   Simon Turner

7 The Orchestration of Corruption and Excess Enjoyment in Western Mexico 143
   Pieter de Vries

STATE OFFICIALS IN THE TWILIGHT ZONE

8 Corruption or Social Capital? Tact and the Performance of *Guanxi* in Market Socialist China 167
   Alan Smart and Carolyn L. Hsu

9 Corruption in the US Borderlands with Mexico: The "Purity" of
  Society and the "Perversity" of Borders 191
  Josiah McC. Heyman and Howard Campbell

Index *219*

List of Contributors

Gerhard Anders is a lecturer at the Institute of Social Anthropology at the University of Zurich, Switzerland. His research focuses on the anthropology of the postcolonial state, the anthropology of development, and international criminal justice. Recent publications include "Follow the Trial: Some Notes on the Ethnography of International Criminal Justice" (*Anthropology Today*, 2007) and "Good Governance as Technology: Toward an Ethnography of the Bretton Woods Institutions" in D. Mosse and D. Lewis (eds) *The Aid Effect: Global Governance and the Ethnography of International Aid* (Pluto Press, 2005).

Giorgio Blundo is *maître de conferences* at the centre for Sociology, History and Anthropology and Cultural Dynamics (SHADYC), *Ecole des Hautes Etudes en Science Sociales*, in Marseille. He is member of the editorial board of *Politique Africaine* and has published extensively on corruption, public services, and the state in West Africa. Among his recent publications is "Dealing with the Local State: The Informal Privatization of Street-level Bureaucracies in Senegal" (*Development and Change*, 2006). He co-edited with J.-P. Olivier de Sardan *Everyday Corruption and the State: Citizens and Public Officials in Africa* (Zed Books, 2006).

Howard Campbell is Professor of Anthropology at the University of Texas at El Paso. He is the author of "Drug Trafficking Stories: Everyday Forms of Narco-Folklore on the US-Mexico Border" (*The International Journal of Drug Policy*, 2005), "Slantwise: Beyond Domination and Resistance on the Border" with Josiah McC. Heyman (*The Journal of Contemporary Ethnography*, 2007), and numerous books, articles, chapters, and essays on indigenous peoples in Mexico and the United States and on US-Mexico border society and culture (see http://faculty.utep.edu/hcampbel). He is currently writing a book on the drug smuggling along the US-Mexico border.

Josiah McC. Heyman is Professor of Anthropology and Chair of the Sociology and Anthropology Department at the University of Texas at El Paso. He is the editor of *States and Illegal Practices* (Berg, 1999) and author of numerous scholarly articles, chapters, books, and essays focusing on borders, class, and power (see http://faculty.utep.edu/jmheyman). Much of this work concerns the US state and the process of undocumented migration across the US-Mexico border. His current work addresses state governance of the movement of people and goods, both at and beyond borders and applied research on access and barriers to health care for immigrants in the El Paso region.

Livia Holden (MA and MPhil, Paris; PhD, London) is an anthropologist of law affiliated to the Freie University in Berlin, and to the Socio-Legal Research Centre at Griffith University in Queensland. She is interested in the processes of social ordering through structured communication, and especially in the manipulation of legal discourse through extra-systemic networks. She carries out extensive and longitudinal fieldwork in South Asia, Southern Italy, and Australia. Her publications focus on family law, criminal law, gender, traditional jurisdictions, and lawyers' praxis. She has co-authored various collaborative multimedia projects with local informants. Her monograph on Hindu divorce is forthcoming with Ashgate.

Carolyn L. Hsu is Associate Professor of Sociology at Colgate University in Hamilton, New York. She conducts research in the People's Republic of China on organizational transformation, stratification, entrepreneurship, social capital, culture and narratives, and political corruption. Her publications include "Political Narratives and the Production of Legitimacy: The Case of Corruption in Post-Mao China" (*Qualitative Sociology*, 2001) and *Creating Market Socialism: How Ordinary People are Shaping Class and Status in China* (Duke University Press, 2007).

Andrew MacNaughton lectures in the School of Modern Languages and Cultures at The University of Hong Kong where he recently submitted his PhD thesis toward a degree in anthropology and Japanese studies. His research has produced an original company ethnography from the English conversation school industry in Japan. Forthcoming publications will address the relevance of corporate ideology to methods of control and identity among staff, company, and clientele. A co-authored monograph on the anthropology of Japanese corporate ideologies is planned for 2008. He has also published in the areas of legal anthropology and the management of natural resource rights systems.

Monique Nuijten is Associate Professor at the Rural Sociology Group of Wageningen University and Research Center, the Netherlands. In Mexico and Peru she conducted extensive research on agrarian reform and communal land tenure institutions. A special focus in her work has been the law and relations between peasants and the state. At present she directs a research project about the social organization and politics of space in urban slums in Recife, Brazil. She is author of the book *Power, Community and the State; the political anthropology of organisation in Mexico* (Pluto Press, 2003) and numerous articles, including "Between Fear and Fantasy: governmentality and the working of power in Mexico" (*Critique of Anthropology*, 2004).

Alan Smart (PhD, University of Toronto, 1986) is Professor at the Department of Anthropology, University of Calgary. His research has focused on urban issues, housing, foreign investment, and social change. He is author of *Making Room: Squatter Clearance in Hong Kong* (Hong Kong University Press, 1992) *Petty Capitalists and Globalization* co-edited with Josephine Smart (SUNY Press,

2005), *The Shek Kip Mei Myth: Squatters, fires and colonial rule in Hong Kong, 1950–1963* (Hong Kong University Press, 2006), and numerous articles. He is also co-investigator on projects on "The Social and Economic Impact of BSE in Alberta".

Giovanni Tortora (MA in Law, Naples University) was born in Pompei (Naples). He is a criminal lawyer specialized in cases of organized crime. He is interested in the inner motivations of his clients as members of local crime syndicates. He recently obtained the acquittal of a person affiliated with the clan of Torre Annunziata—an outcome that can potentially revise the past conviction of an ancient Mafia boss.

Simon Turner is Senior Researcher at the Danish Institute for International Studies where he is Head of the Research Unit on Migration, Conflict and Development. He has worked on politics, governance and gender identities in refugee camps. He is presently working on long-distance nationalism among the Burundian diaspora in Europe and East Africa. A central theme in his work has been rumours, conspiracy theories and secrecy. His publications include "Under the Gaze of the 'Big Nations'—refugees, rumour and the international community in Tanzania" (*African Affairs*, 2004) and "The Tutsi are Afraid We Will Discover their Secrets: On Secrecy and Sovereign Power in Burundi" (*Social Identities*, 2005).

Pieter de Vries is a development sociologist/anthropologist and teaches at Wageningen University, the Netherlands. He has conducted research in Costa Rica (on planned development interventions), Mexico (on the role of *cacique* strongmen in the imagination of power), French Polynesia (on the socio-medical consequences of nuclear testing), and Peru (on the cultural construction of community). Currently he is engaged in a research project in Brazil on "cultural politics and alternative economies in slums". His publications include "Don't Compromise Your Desire for Development!" (*Third World Quarterly*, 2007), and "The Managerialization of Development" in S. Dar and B. Cooke (eds) *The New Development Management* (Zed Press, 2007).

Kam Bill Wong is a civil servant in the Hong Kong SAR government. He holds seven university degrees including an MA in public order from the University of Leicester and an MA (distinction) in criminology from The University of Hong Kong. He recently completed a PhD program in Sociology at The University of Hong Kong with research on bureaucratic corruption in pre-war Japan. He is currently working on an MA in human rights law at the Law Faculty of The University of Hong Kong with research planned on the subject of *burakumin* and human rights issues in Japan.

Heinzpeter Znoj is Professor at the Institute for Social Anthropology at the University of Bern, Switzerland. His research in Indonesia focuses on economic, legal and political anthropology as well as the anthropology of work. The following publications particularly relate to the topic of this volume: *Tausch und*

Geld in Zentralsumatra. Zur Kritik des Schuldbegriffs in der Wirtschaftsethnologie (Berner Sumatra-Studien, Reimer, 1995) and "Hot Money and War-Debts: Transactional Regimes in Southwestern Sumatra" (*Comparative Studies in Society and History*, 1998).

Acknowledgments

This book originated in the panel "Corruption and States of Illegality" that we organized for the conference "Law, Plural Society, and Social Cohesion" in Fredericton NB, Canada in August 2004. Thanks are due to the Commission of Folk Law and Legal Pluralism that planned this XIVth International Congress, especially to Melanie Wiber, Professor of Anthropology at the University of New Brunswick, for her skilful organizing of this event.

Our panel on corruption resulted in stimulating discussions that we continued after the conference with several of the participants. This is how the idea for this volume was born. We did not, however, want to jump on the bandwagon of a "sexy" topic: we aimed at a volume that seriously investigated hidden connections between corruption and the law. Therefore, the authors took great effort and time in writing and rewriting their chapters with the common themes in mind that emerged during our discussions.

We are grateful to Josiah Heyman and Howard Campbell who did not participate in the conference but enthusiastically followed our invitation to contribute a chapter on the US borderlands with Mexico. Special words of appreciation should go to Luisa Steur who worked on the revision of the manuscript and did an excellent job in editing.

Chapter 1

Corruption and the Secret of Law: An Introduction

Gerhard Anders and Monique Nuijten

> Only his own heart-beats told him he was guilty—that he had joined the ranks of the corrupt police officers—Bailey who had kept a safe deposit in another city, Crayshaw who had been found with diamonds, Boyston against whom nothing had been definitely proved and who had been invalided out. They had been corrupted by money, and he had been corrupted by sentiment. Sentiment was the more dangerous, because you couldn't name its price. A man open to bribes was to be relied upon below a certain figure, but sentiment might uncoil in the heart at a name, a photograph, even a smell remembered.
>
> Graham Greene (1948: 45)

There is more to corruption than the mere transgression of rules governing the conduct of public officials. The word may also refer to the individual feeling of moral depravity and perversion or to the moral decay of whole societies. To define corruption primarily in moral rather than legal terms has a long tradition in Occidental thinking and today's legal prohibitions of bribery, theft, embezzlement, and the misuse of public property for private gains constitute the secular avatars of ethical principles once formulated by moral philosophers and theologians. Graham Greene was keenly aware of the moral as well as legal dimensions of corruption. In the novel *The Heart of the Matter*, set in a West-African British backwater possession during World War II, he addresses the connection between bribery in public office and moral decadence. The novel traces the entanglement of a scrupulous Catholic police officer, Major Scobie, in a web of corrupt colonial officials, Syrian diamond smugglers, and an adulterous affair. This police officer, the novel's anti-hero, is not corrupted by bribes but by sentiment, locked in a vicious circle of desire to break out of a dull marital routine and the intense feelings of guilt triggered by this desire. He becomes enmeshed in a web of lies, deceiving his wife and his superiors, and all his efforts to cover up his missteps only bring him closer to his fatal end. Greene's novel is instructive since he astutely observes the ethical dilemmas arising from an environment characterized by widespread bribe taking and moral depravity. Using Major Scobie's demise as a case study of sorts, Greene reveals the manifold connections between personal ethics, legal prohibitions, and morality.

Although the social-scientific study of corruption has attracted considerable attention from anthropologists in recent years, it is surprising that few efforts have been made to develop an ethnographic approach that situates corruption within discussions on law and morality. *Corruption and the Secret of Law* addresses this lacuna by presenting fine-grained ethnographic case studies dealing with corruption's hidden connections with morality and the law of the nation-state. In this book we take a stance that differs in three fundamental ways from current perspectives in academic and public debates about corruption. First, we do not treat the global anti-corruption industry and dominant social-scientific approaches as frameworks of analysis but rather as subjects of anthropological study. In doing so we aim to reveal the moralistic and ethnocentric undertones of what we deem is essentially a political project. Second, we do not conceive of corruption as an individual act but as a phenomenon that is institutionalized and embedded in the wider matrix of power relations in society. The contextualization of individual acts reveals the systemic and structural dimensions of corruption. Third, and most important, we take distance from the commonly held view that corruption is simply the law's negation, a vice afflicting the body politic. Instead, we argue that corruption and the law are not opposites but constitutive of one another. Thus, we propose an approach that transcends binary oppositions and explores the hidden continuities between corruption and its antonyms law and virtue.

This introductory chapter is divided into two parts. The first part discusses the current prominence of corruption in academic literature and international policy circles. We present an overview of dominant social-scientific approaches and their limitations, arguing for an anthropological perspective. The introduction argues that the current debate about corruption is shaped by the division between the state and society and a corresponding public–private dichotomy. The second part of this chapter suggests ways to go beyond these dichotomies. A perspective that does not conceptualize law and corruption as opposites allows us to investigate the moral and legal complexities pertaining to practices that are often simply dismissed as illegal. In many situations people distinguish behavior that is justifiable on moral grounds but prohibited by the law of the nation-state. This is due to the existence of alternative sets of social and moral norms that either condone illegal behavior or criticize perfectly legal practices as being immoral. A legal pluralist perspective helps to elucidate the contingent nature of official prohibitions of corruption and to understand that rules of tact and etiquette exist even within the realm of the illicit. This introductory chapter further argues that the study of corruption cannot be an end in itself but should rather be a field of inquiry to understand power relations in society at large. Even the pettiest forms of corruption reflect structural power relations. Finally, the last section addresses often neglected but crucial aspects of corruption, namely the importance of performance, the meaning of different discursive registers, the prevalence of conspiracy theories and fantasies surrounding corrupt practices, and the role of corruption accusations.

The C-word and the Social Sciences

The Global Anti-Corruption Consensus

The "South" and the "East" have become the main targets of the global coalition against corruption, spearheaded by Transparency International, the NGO founded in 1993 by the former World Bank manager Peter Eigen. Transparency International has played a crucial role in advancing corruption as one of the main issues in the global political arena and claims that it serves the sole purpose of furthering transparency by exposing corruption. The former World Bank president Wolfensohn then swiftly read the sign of the times and identified the fight against corruption as crucial to poverty reduction. In 1996 he introduced the "c-word" in his address to the annual meeting of the World Bank:

> Let's not mince words: We need to deal with the cancer of corruption. In country after country, it is the people who are demanding action on this issue. They know that corruption diverts resources from the poor to the rich, increases the cost of running businesses, distorts public expenditures, and deters foreign investors. They also know that it erodes the constituency for aid programs and humanitarian relief. And we all know that it is a major barrier to sound and equitable development.

Since the 1990s transparency has become one of the key political concepts worldwide. Governments, international organizations, and corporations strive for improved governance and management by means of new accounting and auditing standards. Politicians, policy makers, bureaucrats, CEOs, and lobbyists all emphasize the need to be more transparent and open. Recent anthropological studies (West and Sanders 2003), however, argue that the burgeoning global talk about transparency has not resulted in more openness in the exercise of power. On the contrary, it seems that the operations of powerful global players have become less transparent. Paraphrasing Das and Poole (2004: 9f.) it could be argued that international organizations and multi-national corporations are more "illegible" than ever to citizens and consumers, in spite of their proclamations to strive for greater transparency.

The fight against corruption has Orientalist overtones. Endemic corruption is thought to bedevil bureaucracies and represents the evil and primitive Other of the global rhetoric about transparency and "good governance." Especially in the countries of the "South" and the "East," corruption seems to frustrate economic development and urgently needed foreign direct investment. Of course, as the crusaders against the curse of corruption will readily admit, Western liberal democracies are also afflicted by corruption. There is, however, a tendency to treat corruption in the more developed parts of the world as incidental, as at worst a few rotten apples—not like the structural and widespread corruption in less developed parts of the world.[1]

---

1   Italy is something of a special case. Although it has become one of the leading economic powers in the world, in northern Europe it is still regarded as a hotbed of

Taussig draws attention to this common dualism, which represents "north as honest and industrious and repressed, the south as anything but" (1999: 78). According to Taussig "it must be a deep thing, this secret of the secret, in which the south in its dishonesty mirrors the dissimulation of dissimulation in the north" (1999: 79). The juxtaposition of the honest, hardworking, and sober North with the image of a decadent, deceptive, and savage South is ubiquitous. If social capital and corruption are just two perspectives on the same phenomenon, as Smart (1993) argues, social capital would be an attribute of an entrepreneurial North whereas corruption would characterize a decadent South or East. Taussig emphasizes exactly this connection when he states, "there can be no south without a north" (Taussig 1999: 80). The image of a thoroughly corrupted South seems to be necessary to uphold the idea of an efficient and transparent North. This volume, therefore, also includes a case study of the US border regime that subverts this common distinction (Heyman and Campbell).

The Anthropology of Corruption

The subject of corruption is also *en vogue* in academic circles. Economists, political scientists, sociologists, and anthropologists have rediscovered the subject and one need not be a conspiracy theorist to see the connection between the agenda of the global coalition against corruption and the burgeoning scientific literature on corruption. Though corruption has been on the agenda of social scientists for a long time, its social-scientific study has experienced a veritable boom since the 1990s.[2]

Unlike their peers in political science and economics, anthropologists used to be reluctant to refer to corruption explicitly.[3] This does not mean that anthropologists have not studied social phenomena that would qualify as corruption. Anthropology has a long and rich tradition of studying hidden practices and illegal or semi-legal exchanges. A host of anthropological studies in the 1960s and 1970s addressed patronage and brokerage (see, for example, Blok 1969, 1974; Boissevain 1974; Gellner 1977) or described bribery in terms of reciprocity and gift-giving practices (see Moore 1973). The virtual absence of the word corruption in these earlier studies is, however, striking. It seems that anthropologists, steeped in a strongly relativist tradition, were reluctant to pass implicit judgment by using such a normative concept and tended to adopt a more apologetic stance.

In recent years a considerable change has occurred and anthropologists no longer hesitate to use the term corruption. Panels on corruption have become a common sight at conferences and several anthropological studies on the subject

---

corruption. But because of its economic prowess it is not a prime target of the global anti-corruption coalition.

2 For an extensive overview of the literature on corruption see Heidenheimer and Johnston (2002). See also the studies of Bayart (1993), Chabal and Daloz (1999), Della Porta and Mény (1997), Harris (2003), Reno (1995), and Rose-Ackerman (1999).

3 One of the few exceptions is Wertheim's work on corruption (1961, 1964).

have been published. In August 2002, for example, Shore and Haller organized a well-attended panel on corruption at the conference of the European Association of Social Anthropologists (EASA) and in December that year the Amsterdam School for Social Science Research (ASSR) chose corruption as the theme of its Jubilee Conference. The rate of publications using the term corruption or related concepts such as bribery also seems to have picked up considerably since the 1990s. During the 1990s, publications by anthropologists on the subject were scant—with a few notable exceptions (for example, Gupta 1995; Lomnitz-Adler 1995; Smart 1993). Since the late 1990s, however, a growing number of anthropological studies has been published explicitly on corruption (for example, Blundo and Olivier de Sardan 2001, 2006; Haller and Shore 2005; Hasty 2005; Olivier de Sardan 1999; Ries 2002; Schneider and Schneider 2003, 2005).

So why have anthropologists joined the ranks of scientists using the c-word? We see three main influences at work in the context of international developments in politics and academia. First, during the 1980s funding agencies and academic institutes have become more assertive in setting the agenda for research with a strongly applied character. Both "applied" and "academic" scientists have found it hard to resist the pressure to present evidence for the usefulness of their work. In combination with a growing concern among policy makers and politicians for transparency and "good governance," this has led to a favorable climate for research projects explicitly addressing corruption, transparency, and governance.

As important as funding policy is, it is not sufficient to change research agendas on its own. There is a second trend that explains anthropologists" growing interest in the subject and that is the ubiquity of the talk about corruption, which has become an important feature of anthropologists" fieldwork sites. This is mainly due to the diffusion of the global corruption discourse that has introduced the campaign against corruption to the localities studied by anthropologists at an unprecedented scale. Third, there has been a growing convergence of anthropologists" and political scientists" fields of study as anthropologists have started to research the state (Blom Hansen and Stepputat 2001; Das and Poole 2004; Fuller and Bénéï 2000; Gupta 1995) but also the global scale (Appadurai 1996; Comaroff and Comaroff 2001; Geschiere and Meyer 1999; Trouillot 2003).

Anthropology, with its focus on the social construction of typologies and dichotomies and its distrust of the promises of scientific positivism, has the potential to elucidate the social processes that shape the binary opposition between transparency and corruption. From such an angle definitions of the boundary between public office and private life, between illegality and legality, virtue and vice, may turn into objects of study, keywords of local and global ideoscapes, in Appadurai's sense (1996), employed and reflected upon by the actors themselves. Therefore, the global anti-corruption consensus driving most national policies in the countries of the East and South is an important subject of research in its own right (cf. Haller and Shore 2005; Sampson 2005; West and Sanders 2003).

The ethnography of sites where the anti-corruption consensus is instantiated entails the blurring of the boundaries between the researcher and the subject of research. In her study of global networks of women's rights activists, Riles (2001) points out that the contemporary anthropologist is confronted with sites where research subjects continually reflect on their actions using the same terms and concepts used by the anthropologist in her analysis. Such an insight entails a different approach to the corruption indices and country reports that are churned out by Transparency International and the World Bank at a dazzling rate. From Riles' perspective these reports and indices do not represent scientific data, which can be verified or falsified. Instead we would be well advised to conceptualize them as cultural artifacts embedded in the context of global politics and contested meanings.

Defining an Elusive Phenomenon

As mentioned above, so far the study of corruption has been mainly a domain of political scientists and economists. From their perspective the most important shortcoming of legal and moral characterizations of corruption is their temporally and spatially contingent nature and failure to meet the standards of scientific rationality since they do not generate quantifiable and comparable data sets. For that reason they directed their efforts toward the development of universal definitions and reliable methods of measuring corruption and its effects (Friedrich 1972; Heidenheimer and Johnston 2002; Huntington 1968; Klaveren 1957; Klitgaard 1988; Leys 1965; Myrdal 1968; Nye 2002; Rose-Ackerman 1999; Scott 1979).

Although the authors of this volume do not share the view that the primary aim should be the formulation of a universal definition of corruption, they do not deny that classifications and typologies can provide useful points of departure and much-needed orientation in a field that seems prone to get grounded in juicy stories and anecdotes, as Blundo argues in his chapter. He reminds us that basic differentiations, such as between grand and petty corruption or between political and bureaucratic corruption, provide preliminary guidance for any inquiry into corruption. Blundo emphasizes the need for methodological rigor and the writing of ethnographies that go beyond the anecdotal register. Instead he suggests writing "bureaucratic itineraries" as a device to track corrupt practices through the bureaucratic machinery.

The differentiation of various types of practices sharpens the focus of the empirical study of corruption. In an earlier study Blundo and Olivier de Sardan (2001) distinguish seven forms of petty corruption: first, the "commission" paid for illicit favors, such as kickbacks for the award of government tenders; second, the "gratuity" as the reward for a civil servant who has executed his or her official duty; third, "having connections" with civil servants; fourth, the informal payment for services rendered as opposed to official fees; fifth, the private use of government property, in French *"perruque"*—and, sixth, its appropriation; and finally, the more severe form of everyday corruption, namely extortion, when public officials, usually police or army personnel, demand the payment of a "fine" for fictive violations of regulations and threaten to use force if the "fine" is not paid.

Obviously, types of corruption differ according to the nature of the political and economic regime. It would be wrong to assume that there is a type of political order that is immune to corruption and in spite of the widely held view among the proponents of "good governance" and transparency there is no evidence that multi-party democracies are less prone to corruption than other types of political regimes.[4] On the contrary, evidence presented by empirical studies suggests otherwise (Anders 2005; Krastev 2003; Roitman 2005). Olivier de Sardan rightly states that "each type of regime develops its own particular form of corruption: electoral corruption is linked to democracy, in the same way that the black market is linked to bureaucratic forms of exchange control" (1999: 34).

Whereas anthropologists prefer to work with a more loosely defined field of inquiry, the issue of a universal definition continues to dominate political science and to a lesser degree economic approaches. Generally three definitions are distinguished: public office centered, public-interest centered, and market definitions (Heidenheimer and Johnston 2002; Philps 2002). Nye's definition is usually cited as representative of a public office centered definition. He defines corruption as "behavior which deviates from the formal duties of a public role because of private-regarding (personal, close family, private clique) pecuniary or status gains; or violates rules against the exercise of certain types of private-regarding influence" (Nye 2002: 284). Public-interest centered definitions started with Friedrich who already in the 1970s wrote one of the most important studies on corruption emphasizing the threat to public interest in his definition of corruption as "deviant behavior associated with a particular motivation, namely that of private gain at public expense" (Friedrich 1972: 127).

Market-centered definitions do not focus on norms or public interest but on the office as business, the income of which the corrupt bureaucrat strives to maximize. Market-centered definitions claim moral and legal neutrality but they fail to break free from the notion of a more or less clearly defined set of rules or principles. Philps (2002), for instance, states: "the view that they can offer an alternative definition ... is itself conceptually muddled. Market-centered definitions are certainly one way of *understanding* corruption, they may also provide a fruitful model for the explanation of the incidence of corruption, but they are not a way of defining it" (Philps 2002: 50). It is impossible, therefore, to apply market-centered definitions without reference to a set of rules demarcating the boundary between proper and improper use of the office as a unit to maximize profit (cf. Smart 1993).

Thus none of the countless attempts to arrive at a universally acceptable definition can really forego the notion of deviation from an ideal or norm. Public-office centered, public-interest centered, and market-centered definitions are all hampered by the same problem as legal or moral definitions are and do not, therefore, offer a viable alternative. The authors of this volume, therefore, do not aim at contributing to the quest for a universal and cross-cultural definition

---

4 This also applies to totalitarian regimes. In spite of their anti-corruption rhetoric, there is often widespread corruption in these regimes—as ample empirical evidence has indicated in the case of Nazi Germany, for example (Angermund 2002).

of corruption but rather call for the careful investigation of the socio-political context of both practices labeled as corrupt and the talk about corruption.

Corruption and "State Thought"

It has not gone unnoticed that the present global agreement on corruption has highly moralistic undertones (Krastev 2003; Sampson 2005). On the surface the new science of corruption promoted by Transparency International and the Bretton Woods institutions relies on quantifiable data and scientific strategies to stamp out the "cancer" of corruption, but underneath it is driven by a zealous belief in the necessity and possibility of cleansing and strengthening the body politic. According to the current global consensus corruption primarily affects "weak" states, with only rudimentary democratic structures, in Africa, Asia, Latin America, and Eastern Europe. Its proponents unequivocally identify corruption as one of the main causes for poverty and underdevelopment. Corruption is said to lead to great economic losses for the developing world as it makes business contracts insecure, leads to uncertainty and lack of trust among the citizenry, and causes great delays in the discharge of bureaucrats' duties (for example, de Soto 2000).

This view harks back to a debate of the 1960s and 1970s when a whole range of studies on the influence of corruption on the development of newly independent states in Africa and Asia challenged the moralistic view that corruption was evil and harmful to development (Huntington 1968; Leys 1965; Scott 1979; Wertheim 1961). These studies advanced the functional argument that corruption could also be considered to facilitate development in nation-states characterized by transplanted bureaucracies, which were not yet adjusted to the needs of society. Leys (1965), for example, argued that it "is natural but wrong to assume that the results of corruption are always both bad and important ... Where bureaucracy is both elaborate and inefficient, the provision of strong personal incentives to bureaucrats to cut red tape may be the only way of speeding the establishment of a new firm" (ibid.: 222). Huntington (1968), in an earlier life, made a similar point when he argued that "modernization breed[s] corruption" (ibid.: 60). He compares corruption to violence in that regard since during a period of rapid modernization these are both "means by which individuals and groups relate themselves to the political system in ways which violate the mores of the system" (ibid.: 63).

In the light of the crisis of the modernization paradigm the functionalist approach appears to be anachronistically naïve and optimistic, but the idea of the dysfunctionality of state institutions remains at the core of policymaking as well as part of the academic debate on development. Although both theoretical approaches seem to be fundamentally opposed to each other they share the basic premise of the division between state and society. The new science of corruption draws on neo-liberal thinking and identifies bloated and inefficient state bureaucracy riddled by widespread corruption as the main cause for underdevelopment since it impedes the expansion of the private sector, which is rooted in society. The World Bank, for example, in its report on sub-Saharan Africa in which the term "governance" was introduced for the first time, blamed "bad governance" for the failure to create the necessary "enabling environment" for a dynamic informal sector that would form a "seedbed" for the market (World Bank 1989: 135-47). De Soto makes a similar argument about the informal market that is denied the potential to transform into capital by corrupted bureaucracies (de Soto 2000). The earlier view advanced by Huntington, Leys, and Scott also assumes the absolute division of state and society but they argue that the dysfunctionality of the state, due to the gap with society, is only a problem of adaptation that will eventually disappear as modernization progresses.

In the academic debate about the nature of the postcolonial state in Africa the notion of "dysfunctionality" is often employed to describe the relation between the state bureaucracy and society (Bayart 1993; Chabal and Daloz 1999; Cohen 1980; Diamond 1987; Mbembé 1992, 2001; Médard 1982, 2002). Early studies of the state in Africa usually adopted a Weberian approach. Cohen (1980), Diamond (1987), Ekeh (1975), and Médard (1982), for example, measure the bureaucracies in Africa against criteria derived from Weber's ideal type of rational-legal power and find that African state institutions are "dysfunctional" and "corrupted" by patronage and tribalism—in other words by "primordial" ties of affection. Médard adopted Eisenstadt's (1973) concept of neo-patrimonialism to describe the hybrid nature of the African state. In the neo-patrimonial state, "the bureaucratic logic was artificially applied to a patrimonial logic" based on "primordial sentiments" (Médard 1982: 179). The concept of neo-patrimonialism is essentially social-pathological since it is based on the deviation from an ideal model of rational-bureaucratic order usually equated with the advanced Western democracies.

The studies by Chabal and Daloz (1999), Bayart (1993), and Mbembé (1992, 2001) are also informed by the social-pathological paradigm but instead of blaming the dysfunctionality of the bureaucracy on clientelism they conceptualize the subversive and creative appropriation of the bureaucracy by ethnic and tribal networks as a distinctly African creation stemming from the colonial experience. Due to their focus on the rational-legal model of the state, however, these researchers usually do not differentiate the so-called clientelistic relations that usurp the state institutions. Thus they unwittingly reproduce the dualism between the Weberian legal-rational order and African society by lumping all types of social relationships, ranging from kinship to various voluntary forms of association, under the latter.

Studies on Asia and Latin America also highlight the importance of patron-client relationships and usually point to their influence on the working of the state bureaucracy as the main cause of corruption (Camp 1996; DaMatta 1991; Evers 1987). In this context, several authors have discussed the conflicting principles that inspire the work of bureaucrats (Grindle 1977; Lomnitz-Adler 1992). Lomnitz-Adler (1992), for example, addresses the coexistence of legal bureaucratic rationalism and personalism in the Mexican bureaucracy. He argues that "there has been a tremendous tension between rational-bureaucratic practices and practices that are founded on other kinds of principles, such as friendship, kinship, and personal loyalty" (1992: 297). In the same way, DaMatta (1991) describes the complex dialectic in Brazilian society and the state apparatus between on the one hand the impersonal world of laws, decrees, and rules and on the other hand the principles of reciprocity, loyalty, and charity. Most of these works see corruption as an important cause of the ineffective and unjust working of the state but also mention the positive sides of corruption in terms of mutual support and flexibility in circumventing rigid rules.

The analytical divide between state and society is closely related to the distinction between public office and private sphere, the main hallmark of rational bureaucratic order according to Weber (1990). Weber's ideal-type of rational-bureaucratic rule, however, fails to address the manifold ways in which these spheres that he so rigidly divides at the conceptual level are actually, as anthropological studies of state functionaries show, connected to each other. Herzfeld (1992), for example, argues that the appearance of indifference, which is so central to rational-bureaucratic order, is the outcome of contested and ambivalent historical processes of state formation rather than the linear progressive rationalization suggested by Weber. According to Herzfeld, the boundary between bureaucrat and client is not fixed but continuously redrawn and renegotiated. Purportedly fixed boundaries between the public office and the private sphere are unstable and contested in everyday encounters between government representatives and citizens as empirical research on civil servants amply shows (Anders 2005; Benda-Beckmann and Benda-Beckmann 1998; Blundo and Olivier de Sardan 2001, 2006; Gupta 1995; Lipsky 1980; Maynard-Moody and Musheno 2003).

The fuzziness of the boundaries between state and society and between the public office and the private sphere underlines the necessity of overcoming what Bourdieu dubbed "state thought," "the state categories of thought produced and guaranteed by the state" (Bourdieu 1994: 1). By adopting the absolute division between state and society that is at the heart of the self-representation of the state it becomes difficult to transcend "state thought." We ought to therefore adopt state categories of thought as subjects of study rather than as a conceptual framework. Indeed, recent studies have tried to overcome the common division between state and society by drawing on Foucauldian notions of power and governmentality (Blom and Stepputat 2001; Das and Poole 2004; Mitchell 1991, 2002), focusing on both the practices and discourses constituting the state. Gupta (1995), for example, contributed to the anthropology of the post-colonial state by analyzing both the everyday practices of petty bureaucrats and street-level officials and the popular discourse about corruption in everyday conversations and the mass media. Nuijten (2003, 2004) uses a similar approach in her work on the Mexican state. According to Nuijten the talk of corruption is inextricably linked with the operation of state power. In rural Mexico Kafkaesque fantasies about ways to influence corrupt state officials are the products of a fervid popular imagination obsessed by the state. By drawing on these attempts to transcend seemingly "natural" dichotomies this introduction calls for the study of the hidden continuities between the opposite poles of law and virtue, on the one hand, and vice and corruption, on the other.

Law and Corruption: Beyond Binary Oppositions

The Secret of Law

The current debate about corruption is shaped by thinking in binary oppositions: corruption and the law are seen as each other's opposite. This book, however, adopts a different position and zooms in on the hidden continuities between the law and its negation. We will start with a vignette to illustrate the epistemological shift we deem necessary to understand the nature of corruption. Enlightenment in the eighteenth century promoted thinking in terms of binary oppositions such as rational/irrational and modern/traditional. Many manifestations of Enlightenment thinking, however, also in fact hint at hidden continuities between opposites and their inherently ambiguous character. Francisco Goya's etching entitled *The Sleep of Reason Produces Monsters* (1797–1798),[5] for example, is usually read as exemplary of Enlightenment thinking and the artist's individual angst. It is a self-portrait of the sleeping artist, his head resting on his arms, surrounded by demonic-looking animals resembling bats and owls and with a lynx sitting at the artist's feet. Usually *The Sleep of Reason* is interpreted as warning that Enlightenment is a continuous struggle and that we are constantly threatened by a relapse to the irrationality of an earlier age. This chapter suggests a less evolutionary interpretation. If the title is taken quite literally, the monsters are the product of the sleep of reason. If they are produced by sleep they do not exist completely independent from reason but are rather the distorted products of reason. According to this more apocryphal reading it would not be the absence of reason that allows the monsters to enter our dreams but it would be reason itself that spawns monsters when we are asleep.

If we apply this interpretation of *The Sleep of Reason* to law a promising line of inquiry opens up. Bataille (1987) draws attention to the hidden continuities between law and transgression in his study of eroticism and taboo. Grappling with the connection between eroticism and death, he addresses "the profound complicity of law and the violation of law" (Bataille 1987: 36). Bataille argues that prohibitions and their transgressions are not separate phenomena. On the contrary "a transgression ... suspends a taboo without suppressing it" (ibid.). According to Bataille, then, prohibition and transgression constitute each other, one demanding the other. Here the analogy with Schmitt, another Catholic maverick, does not seem too far-fetched. It is well known that for Schmitt (1985) the state of exception, the suspension of the legal order, defines the concept of sovereignty. Like Bataille, therefore, he does not see the suspension of the legal order as the negation of law but rather as its very foundation (cf. Agamben 1998, 2005).

In a similar vein, Taussig (1999) argues that the act of defacement or desecration of the sacred is actually not the negation but rather the very origin of sacredness. He argues that the act of defacement is already "hidden" or "inscribed" as "tabooed possibility" in that which is sacred (Taussig 1999: 52). For him "'law'

---

5   First published in 1803 as plate 43 of *Los Caprichos*.

defines *taboo* not simply as prohibition ...but as the prohibition that, illicitly, so to speak, secretly, so to speak, contains hidden yearning, an appeal, even a demand, within itself to transgress that which it prohibits: this, its secret" (ibid: 53). Taussig draws our attention to the subtle and hidden ways by which order constitutes disorder and by which the law already contains the possibility of its violation or desecration. Seen from this angle, binaries such as virtue/vice or legal/illegal are not opposites excluding one another but rather two dimensions of a whole co-joined in an ambivalent relationship. Heyman and Smart illustrate this clearly in their work, stating that, "state law inevitably creates its counterparts, zones of ambiguity and outright illegality" (Heyman and Smart 1999: 1). This, according to Taussig, is the secret, which is "inaccessible to analysis by means of binary distinctions or contradictions" (Taussig 1999: 63).

Roitman (2005) maps these zones of ambiguity between the state and criminal networks in her ethnography of the secret collusion between state officials and clandestine criminal networks in the Chad Basin, the border region between northern Cameroon, Chad, Nigeria, and the Central African Republic. Here the shadow economy and lawlessness are thriving; unemployed youth, smugglers, highway robbers, and corrupt soldiers roam the roads and the "bush," crisscrossing national boundaries, striving to escape dire living conditions in a context of civil war, high unemployment, and economic crisis. The informalization of the economy and the prevalence of criminal networks do not, however, imply the breakdown of order, as Roitman argues. She takes issue with approaches that imagine an absolute divide between two opposites such as informal/formal, official/unofficial, and legal/illegal and argues that the parallel economy is neither residual nor unregulated. Instead she draws attention to the multifarious ways in which the legal and the illegal economy are connected and constitute one another. She discovered that the smugglers and highway robbers collude with army officers, wealthy businessmen, local party officials, and traditional leaders who finance their criminal operations and are the main beneficiaries. Roitman coins the term "military-commercial nexus" to denote these networks. The state's entanglement with the shadow economy implies, according to her, that "the state is at the very heart of the proliferation of unregulated economic exchanges as well as the pluralization of regulatory authority" (Roitman 2005: 204).

Corruption is thus at the very core of order, inscribed into the law of the nation-state. As we will show, it is because of this close and contradictory relationship with the formal legal order that corruption is surrounded by gossip, rumors, conspiracy, and accusations. Drawing on the insight that law and its negation are opposites that are constitutive of each other and for that reason cannot exist without each other avoids the reification of the dualism between the legal and the illegal, transparency and secrecy. The possibility of its transgression or perversion is always already inscribed into the law as hidden possibility. This, then, is the secret of law.

Legal Plurality

Whilst we argue that the possibility of its violation is already inscribed into the law, it would be misleading to assume the exclusivity of the law of the nation-state. Several alternative and even conflicting normative orders exist within a specific domain of social interaction. Such a situation is referred to as legal pluralism in legal anthropological scholarship (Benda-Beckmann 1992; Griffiths 1986; Melissaris 2004; Merry 1988; Wilson 2000). Legal pluralism acknowledges the co-existence of multiple sets of rules that influence people's actions: the law of the nation-state, indigenous customary rules, religious decrees, moral codes, and practical norms of social life often apply to the same situation thereby creating complex configurations of legal plurality within a social setting. Such a perspective focuses on the interrelation between norms and actual practices, a phenomenon referred to by de Sousa Santos (1995) as "interlegality." Classic studies in legal anthropology reveal the emergence of social fields with their own forms of regulation and informal norms, many of which contradict official regulations (Moore 1978). Other studies have shown the complex interaction between different normative systems (Griffiths 1996; Nader 1990). So, from a legal pluralist perspective it is hardly surprising that what is defined as corrupt according to one legal order conforms to another set of rules. Practices are never per definition corrupt, they are labeled as corrupt by reference to a set of legal or other norms that draw a boundary between conformity and transgression. Smart and Hsu (this volume) describe the salience of an alternative set of rules in contemporary China where people differentiate between actions officially labeled as corrupt but morally justified in terms of solidarity and trust, on the one, and actions rejected as immoral and selfish, even though not necessarily illegal, on the other hand.

Another reason for being careful in taking the legal system of the nation-state as the standard against which practices are judged as corrupt or not corrupt is that in many situations the state apparatus itself seems to be implicated in and endorse corruption. As Haller and Shore show, in many cases "politicians (such as Italy's premier, Silvio Berlusconi) change the law so that their previously illegal practices of book-keeping, are reclassified as legal" (Haller and Shore 2005: 4). Even in states considered to be less prone to corruption the boundary between the law and corruption is often far from clear. In the Netherlands, for example, the government refrained from supporting people who had lost all their savings at the hands of a fraudulent investment company. Although in the words of the minister of justice the company had been corrupt, he also declared that he did not see it as his responsibility to protect citizens against the immoral activities of the company. The maneuvers remained within the "letter of the law" and thus there was no reason for the state to interfere.

Anthropology of law, legal realism, and the law and society movement have demystified the claims to efficacy of the law and demonstrated its socially and historically contingent nature that is as much shaped by social practice as it shapes everyday experience. From such an angle the law of the state loses much of its appeal as modern myth (Fitzpatrick 1992). The judiciary, so it seems, is often not suitable to tackle corruption. The reason for the susceptibility of the legal system to illegal and corrupt practices partly lies in the law itself. The meaning of legal rules is never determinate and always remains subject to interpretation. The indeterminacy of the law and the gap between abstract legal rules and actual real life situations open a wide margin readily exploited by legal experts. Sally Falk Moore once remarked that the "making of rules and social symbolic order is a human industry matched only by the manipulation, circumvention, remaking, replacing, and unmaking of rules and symbols in which people seem almost equally engaged" (Moore 1978: 1).

Therefore, it is important to study the legal profession, not only because this group is particularly prone to corruption (in many countries, for example, Indonesia, Sierra Leone, Yemen, the judiciary is seen as the most corrupt branch of government) but also because judges and lawyers define and interpret the scope of the law, thereby exploiting its indeterminacy. The room for maneuver inherent to the legal order is described in Holden and Tortora's portrait of a lawyer rendering legal services to members of the *camorra* in Naples. Their ethnography of the lawyer's mundane decisions and the dilemmas he faces when dealing with clients who belong to Naples's omnipresent crime syndicates exemplify the consequences of the law's indeterminacy and what it means to operate in an environment where the law is superseded by a deeply entrenched parallel order.

MacNaughton and Wong describe another possible consequence of the law's indeterminacy. Because the difficulty of proving corruption in a court of law hampered the prosecution of many cases, the Japanese Supreme Court in the 1920s introduced an extra-legal moral principle, *taikasei*. According to this principle the mere "possibility" of using the public office for private ends constituted a violation of the duties of a civil servant. By invoking the moral principle of *taikasei* the Supreme Court was relieved of the necessity to establish an actual connection between a gift received and the misuse of the public office.

The fact that the law is notoriously indeterminate and ambivalent and that its interpretation and application is fraught by discretion and manipulation is at odds with the image painted by the proponents of the rule of law who uphold the notion of determinacy, the possibility that the law can induce desirable behavior and eventually—in spite of all its imperfections—constitutes an instrument to realize social change, the notion of "legal engineering." Hence, although great powers are often attributed to the law in steering social processes and inducing change, its rules and procedures can always be used and abused in different ways, serving the interests of economic classes or groups in society—a view that can be traced back to Marxist interpretations of law.

The demystification of claims concerning the efficacy of the law of the nation-state in steering the behavior of people and processes in society implies skepticism about the use of the law in the fight against corruption. We argue that the failure of the law to reduce levels of corruption is not always attributable to the well-known imperfections of law (availability of evidence and indeterminacy of the law), but rather to the secret endorsement of corrupt practices by state authorities. Often the clamorous rhetoric of transparency seems to hide the more opaque operation of power (West and Sanders 2003; Heyman and Campbell, and

Znoj in this volume) and it is striking how some governments collaborate with criminal networks (Heyman 1999).

Corruption and the Exercise of Power

Corrupt practices cannot be dissociated from the operation of power. Following Lemke (2003) and adapting some of his ideas, we think it useful for the study of corruption to identify three perspectives on power at different levels of abstraction: power in interaction, institutional power, and structural power. A similar view of power is also advanced by Lukes (2005). With a "three-dimensional view of power" he seeks to account for situations in which conflict might only be latent and decision-making is covertly manipulated. Individual acts of exercising coercion, influence, and authority have to be situated in "socially structured and culturally patterned behaviour of groups, and practices of institutions" (Lukes 2005: 26). The first perspective focuses on a single or a series of connected transactions between individuals, such as bribes paid in exchange for administrative services. As Lemke points out, "power as strategic games is a ubiquitous feature of human interaction, insofar as it signifies structuring possible fields of action of others. This can take many forms, for example ideological manipulation or rational argumentation, moral advice or economic exploitation" (Lemke 2003: 5). Hence, individual transactions need to be situated in the context of institutional and structural power.

The second perspective focuses on institutional power and refers to more or less systematized and regulated modes of operation that go beyond the individual interactive exercise. It refers to the regulation of conduct through institutionalized practices. These common practices are related to the emergence of specific discursive fields. We can think here, for example, about established ways of addressing police officers to negotiate a traffic fine. Not only personal skills are drawn upon in this interaction, but also a general body of knowledge about how to address police officers in cases of infliction, which words to use and which to avoid, and how much approximately to pay. So, institutional power refers to the social patterns that go beyond the spontaneous performance of the participants. It is through these discursive and performative rituals in corrupt interactions that particular subjectivities, for example those of "the briber" and "the bribed," are created.

Finally, power is analyzed in structural terms with regard to relationships that are stable and hierarchical over a longer period of time, positions that seem rather fixed and difficult to reverse. It refers to those asymmetrical relationships of power over which the subordinated persons have little room for maneuver (Lemke 2003: 5). We use a structural perspective when we show that the scope for corrupt activities and the possibility to gain from them are obviously not evenly distributed among the population. Wealthy and politically well-connected captains of industry have more possibilities for illegal personal enrichment and protection from legal prosecution than small peasants. Hence, a structural perspective addresses the relation of corruption to the unequal distribution of resources in society.

An important consequence of this approach to power and corruption is that individual corrupt transactions need to be analyzed in the context of broader institutionalized practices and structural perspectives. As other authors have also stressed, corrupt acts "are not merely selfish and private but profoundly social, shaped by larger sociocultural notions of power, privilege, and responsibility" (Hasty 2005: 271). The quote from Graham Greene's novel with which we started this chapter also reminds us of the ethical challenges and political predicaments individuals are often confronted with. Corruption is like a web in which even well-meaning individuals can become entangled, unable to resist the institutional and structural operation of power.

In their chapter on corruption on the US side of the US-Mexico border, Heyman and Campbell reveal how individual acts of corruption in drug trafficking, smuggling, and unauthorized immigration are grounded in dense webs of multiple relationships among people living in the border zone. The authors argue that the systemic nature of corruption in the border zone can only be explained by taking into account the reliance of the US economy on cheap labor from Mexico and the dependence of US law enforcement agencies on crime and its revenues to justify their own institutional survival and budgets. In their daily working environment law enforcement officers quickly learn that strict application of the rules at the border is impossible and undesirable. They soon get skilled in the ritualized ways to negate and negotiate the official rules. However, the room for individual discretion in these spheres of illegality makes that borderland officials constantly have to negotiate between the ideological fetish of law and order in the US and the practical demands of the environment in which they operate.

The fact that individual transactions form part of institutionalized practices embedded within larger structures of power implies that corruption is not a "cancer" that can simply be localized and surgically removed from an infected body politic. This has been aptly described by Waquet (1991) in his perceptive study of corruption in Florence during the seventeenth and eighteenth century. He concludes his analysis with the wry observation that the sovereign rulers of Florence had considerable difficulties in pursuing an unequivocal policy with regard to corrupt public servants. Most of the senior positions in the administration were held by Florentine noblemen, many of whom used their public office for personal enrichment, but any effective action against them threatened the precarious and tacit understanding between nobility and monarch. Most rulers, therefore, chose a path of appeasement and even those who had the intention of stamping out all forms of misconduct by officials were not able "to decree the reign of virtue" on the elite on which their authority ultimately depended (Waquet 1991: 193).

Some authors argue that the discrepancy between public denouncement and secret endorsement should even be seen as a manifestation of the fact that the public fight against corruption is necessary for the reproduction of the murky corrupt underworld (Žižek 1996). According to Žižek, the shadowy realm in which the brutal exercise of power takes place needs the civilized gentle public appearance of the rule of law and order. As he argues, "this obscene shadowy realm, far from undermining the civilized semblance of the public power, serves as its inherent support" (Žižek 1996: 100). According to Žižek, people are only able to benefit from public official life if they follow the unwritten rules of the shadowy realm. This becomes clear in the fact that the penalty for breaking these unwritten, murky rules is much harsher than for breaking the public rules. So, in his view, the formal legal system is only able to operate and survive because of the multiple informal networks and corrupt transactions taking place outside the formal arenas. From his argument follows that social scientists should not only analyze corruption but also the fight against corruption in relation to the exercise of power in society at large.

Performance, Conspiracy, and Fantasy

So far, we have argued that corruption cannot be reduced to the violation of a moral or legal rule and that there are multifarious connections between the law and its violation. This entails a much closer look at a much neglected—though essential—dimension of corruption: the significance of performance. Because of its contentious nature corruption demands a great deal of performative qualities, embodied in tact, for instance. The specific qualities required are culturally codified and there are multiple shades and nuances within matters of tact and tacit agreement. It is well known that the uninitiated's attempt to bribe will be disgustedly rejected by even the most corrupt of public officials. The foreign researcher especially may need some time to come to grips with these specific culturally codified manners and words, and their meanings. Adherence to certain forms of tact and etiquette is a prerequisite for corrupt transactions. Smart and Hsu present an instructive example of the importance of tact in transactions in their study of *guanxi*, networks of friendship and gift exchange in China that tend to be defined as corruption in state declarations. In general, corruption tends to be accompanied by secret idioms, symbols, and codes. In individual transactions, the subtlety of the wording is very important and to call something "corrupt" instead of a "gift" is considered to be very rude and impolite and would end the transaction immediately since *guanxi* is described in terms of disinterested friendship and amity.

Often several different discursive repertoires can be used in a specific cultural context to talk about these matters. One may change the way of talking about corrupt practices according to the audience addressed. This is well illustrated by Znoj in his chapter on corruption in Indonesia, according to the corruption index of Transparency International, one of the most corrupt countries in the world. His chapter explores the hidden connections between the public denouncements of corruption by government officials and politicians and the secret endorsement of corrupt practices. He shows how within the same conversation a civil servant can vehemently argue against corruption and the next moment laughingly and proudly tell about his own "corrupt" transactions, which are expressed in a different idiom. Znoj shows how the rigid division between official anti-corruption rhetoric and the ritualized justifications of corruption in everyday language serves to sustain a parallel system of non-budgetary finance.

But discursive scripts are not only important in private settings or in the transactions themselves. The popular imagination often has an impressive and evocative vocabulary pertaining to practices labeled corrupt. In Mexico people refer to *mordida* or "bite," while in Indonesia they talk about *uang lelah* or "tired money." In Africa corruption is widely expressed in terms of eating and bodily fluids (Bayart 1993; Hasty 2005; Mbembé 2001). Hasty, for example, observes "another corporeal metaphor used to understand the practices of corruption in Ghana is that of blood flow and circulation" (2005: 276). Too much corruption is consequently discursively expressed as "hemorrhage." Both in Latin America (de Vries 2002) and in Africa (Mbembé 2001) the idiom of corruption tends to be very sexualized and cast in terms of male virility. By using sexualized languages and metaphors to describe the phenomenon it is obvious that corruption is not necessarily considered to be bad but is also a manifestation of strength and audacity. Especially men known to be corrupt are often in a certain way envied because of their wit, seductiveness, and virility.

These issues warrant a closer look at those who corrupt and those who are corrupted. Corruption is shrouded in gossip, rumors, and conspiracy theories in which the protagonists tend to be ambivalent, liminal characters who stage spectacles to show off their power and diligence in "playing with the system." In his chapter, de Vries presents a case study of a regional Mexican strongman who gets involved in the political struggle around a water users' association, a struggle in which accusations of corruption play a prominent role. By analyzing the festivities this man organizes at home for his political allies, de Vries shows how he manipulates the discourse and imagery of corruption so as to pursue his own personal projects. The fantastic speculations about his corrupt activities—that the man himself encourages—feed into the imaginations and fantasies about his incredible powers.

The pleasures derived from being corrupt also pertain to the forms of bonding between the participants in corrupt transactions. Although generally the negative, selfish, and unpleasant aspects of corruption are emphasized, several authors to this volume also stress the positive elements for those involved. These rewards not only include financial gains but also, equally important, aspects of care for others and enjoyment (de Vries 2002; Lomnitz-Adler 1992). It is also important to keep in mind that corruption is often characterized by the establishment of enduring networks of trust and exchange with an eye on the future.

Returning to Greene's novel we are reminded of the power of corruption accusations, which—whether justified or not—can be more threatening to an ambitious public servant or daring entrepreneur than the actual involvement in corrupt activities. In *The Heart of the Matter*, Greene constructs a very claustrophobic setting in which everybody is being watched. The secrecy of corruption—surreptitious conversations, secret deals, and implicit understandings—appears to be one of the main reasons for the popular fascination, fuelling rumors and resulting in scandals. Hence, it seems the act of concealment is crucial to the understanding of corrupt practices. Greene masterfully shows that it is this clandestine and elusive character of corruption that never fails to arouse the popular fascination.

Often accusations succeed in forcing politicians and public officials to resign regardless of there being evidence whereas a smoothly running corruption racket can operate for decades without ever being detected. Corruption accusations can develop a life of their own and public denial usually only succeeds in reinforcing the impression that the accusations are true. Gossip about corrupt practices often takes the form of conspiracy theories that quickly absorb contrary evidence into a conspiracy of even grander proportions. The public imagination quickly substitutes a lack of tangible proof with gossip and rumors. The difficulty of observing corrupt transactions and producing legal evidence of acts of bribery, embezzlement, and fraud provides fertile ground for stories about the corruption of those in power peddled by the "little people."

Corruption then is characterized by this paradoxical relationship between the legal and illegal, secrecy and publicity, condemnation and fascination. In this sense corruption shares several characteristics with witchcraft. De Vries argues in his chapter that corruption in Mexico plays the same role as witchcraft does in contemporary African politics (Comaroff and Comaroff 1999; Geschiere 1997). Like witchcraft in Africa, he argues, Mexican discourses and images of corruption make it possible to represent and thematize political conflicts and social contradictions. Turner follows the same line of thought in his chapter on the role of corruption accusations and conspiracy theories in imaginaries of the nation and politics in the civil war in Burundi. Turner shows how Burundians morally evaluate politics and politicians through narratives about corrupt practices and secret deals. He compares these narratives to witchcraft accusations, with which they share many characteristics, and argues that both witchcraft and corruption are crucial for the operation of power. It is important to underscore another similarity between witchcraft accusations and corruption allegations. They both tend to be directed toward people who have suddenly and inexplicably increased their wealth or power. Both types of accusations are surrounded by conspiracy theories, while practices take place in the hidden and are never completely revealed. In addition, if practices are revealed, one never knows why a secret has been disclosed and whether something remains hidden. As Žižek puts it: "The phantasmatic logic of conspiracy effectively hinders the public revelation of actual conspiracies, corruption cases, etc. The efficiency of the phantasmatic logic of conspiracy demands that the enemy remains an unfathomable entity whose true identity can never be fully disclosed" (Žižek 1996: 120). This explains the secret world of obscure rituals that forms the background of power, the underneath of corruption that permeated by enjoyment and structured in fantasies.

The following chapters address the ambivalent dialectics of concealment and publicity and the hidden continuities between the illegal and the legal, and the moral and the immoral. We hope that the fine ethnographic case studies contribute to an anthropology of corruption that transcends the normative binary thinking characterizing economic and political science approaches. We propose an approach that does not assume the binary opposition as a given but sees it rather as the product of ongoing processes of social construction. As such it needs to be unpacked and disentangled in careful, ethnographically grounded inquiries. By revealing the secret of law this volume aims at contributing to a better understanding of a phenomenon that only exists by virtue of its opposite.

References

Agamben, G. (1998) *Homo Sacer: Sovereign Power and Bare Life*. Stanford, CA: Stanford University Press.
—— (2005) *State of Exception*. Chicago, IL: University of Chicago Press.
Anders, G. (2005) Civil Servants in Malawi: Cultural Dualism, Moonlighting and Corruption in the Shadow of Good Governance. PhD thesis. Rotterdam: Erasmus University Rotterdam.
Angermund, R. (2002) Corruption under German National Socialism. In: A.J. Heidenheimer and M. Johnston (eds) *Political Corruption: Concepts and Contexts*. 3rd ed. New Brunswick, NJ: Transaction Publishers: 605–20.
Appadurai, A. (1996) *Modernity at Large: Cultural Dimensions of Globalization*. Minneapolis, MN: University of Minnesota Press.
Bataille, G. (1987) *Eroticism*. London: Marion Boyars.
Bayart, J.-F. (1993) *The State in Africa: The Politics of the Belly*. London: Longman.
Benda Beckmann, F. von (1992) Changing Legal Pluralism in Indonesia. No. 4. *Tahun* VII, July–August: 1–23.
—— and K. von Benda-Beckmann (1998) Where Structures Merge: State and Off-state Involvement in Rural Social Security in Ambon, Indonesia. In: S. Pannell and F. von Benda-Beckmann (eds) *Old World Places, New World Problems: Exploring Resource Management Issues in Eastern Indonesia*. Canberra: The Australian National University, Centre for Resource and Environmental Studies: 143–80.
Blok, A. (1969) Variations in Patronage. *Sociologische Gids* 16(6): 365–78.
—— (1974) *The Mafia of a Sicilian Village, 1860–1960: A Study of Violent Peasant Entrepreneurs*. Oxford: Blackwell.
Blom Hansen, T. and F. Stepputat (eds) (2001) *States of Imagination: Ethnographic Explorations of the Postcolonial State*. Durham, NC: Duke University Press.
Blundo, G. and J.-P. Olivier de Sardan (eds) (2001) La corruption quotidienne en Afrique l'Ouest. *Politique Africaine* 83.
—— (2006) *Everyday Corruption and the State: Citizens and Public Officials in Africa*. London: Zed Books.
Boissevain, J. (1974) *Friends of Friends: Networks, Manipulators and Coalitions*. New York: St Martin's.
Bourdieu, P. (1994) Rethinking the State: Genesis and Structure of the Bureaucratic Field. *Sociological Theory* 12(1): 1–18.
Camp, R. (1996) *Politics in Mexico*. Oxford: Oxford University Press
Chabal, P. and J.-P. Daloz (1999) *Africa Works: Disorder as Political Instrument*. Oxford, Bloomington and Indianapolis: James Currey and Indiana University Press.
Cohen, R. (1980) The Blessed Job in Nigeria. In: G.M. Britan and R. Cohen (eds) *Hierarchy and Society: Anthropological Perspectives on Bureaucracy*. Philadelphia, PA: Institute for the Study of Human Issues: 73–88.

Comaroff, J. and J. Comaroff (1999) Occult Economies and the Violence of Abstraction: Notes from the South African Postcolony. *American Ethnologist* 26: 279–301.

—— (eds) (2001) *Millenial Capitalism and the Culture of Neoliberalism.* Durham, NC: Duke University Press.

DaMatta, R. (1991) *Carnivals, Rogues, and Heroes: An Interpretation of the Brazilian Dilemma.* Notre Dame, IN: University of Notre Dame Press.

Das, V. and D. Poole (eds) (2004) *Anthropology in the Margins of the State.* Santa Fe and Oxford: School of American Research Press and James Currey.

Das, V. and D. Poole (2004) State and its Margins: Comparative Ethnographies. In: V. Das and D. Poole (eds) *Anthropology in the Margins of the State.* Santa Fe and Oxford: School of American Research Press and James Currey: 3–33.

Della Porta, D. and Y. Mény (eds) (1997) *Democracy and Corruption in Europe.* London: Cassell.

Diamond, L. (1987) Class Formation in the Swollen African State. *Journal of Modern African Studies* 25(4): 567–96.

Eisenstadt, S.N. (1973) *Traditional Patrimonialism and Modern Neo-Patrimonialism.* London: Sage.

Ekeh, P. (1975) Colonialism and the Two Publics in Africa: A Theoretical Statement. *Comparative Studies in Society and History* 17: 91–112.

Evers, H.-D. (1987) The Bureaucratisation of Southeast Asia. *Comparative Studies in Society and History* 29: 666–85.

Fitzpatrick, P. (1992) *The Mythology of Modern Law.* London: Routledge.

Friedrich, C.J. (1972) *The Pathology of Politics: Violence, Betrayal, Corruption, Secrecy and Propaganda.* New York: Harper and Row.

Fuller, C. and V. Bénéï (eds) (2000) *The Everyday State and Society in Modern India.* New Delhi: Social Science Press.

Gellner, E. (1977) Patrons and Clients. In: E. Gellner and J. Waterbury (eds) *Patrons and Clients in Mediterranean Society.* London: Duckworth.

Geschiere, P. (1997). *The Modernity of Witchcraft: Politics and the Occult in Postcolonial Africa.* Charlottesville, VA: University of Virginia Press.

—— and B. Meyer (eds) (1999) *Globalization and Identity: Dialectics of Flow and Closure.* Oxford: Basil Blackwell.

Greene, G. (1948) *The Heart of the Matter.* London: Vintage.

Griffiths, A. (1996) Between Paradigms: Differing Perspectives on Justice in Molepole Botswana, *Journal of Legal Pluralism* 36: 195–214.

Griffiths, J. (1986) What is Legal Pluralism? *Journal of Legal Pluralism* 24: 2–55.

Grindle, M. (1977) *Bureaucrats, Politicians, and Peasants in Mexico: A Case Study in Public Policy.* Berkeley, CA: University of California Press.

Gupta, A. (1995) Blurred Boundaries: The Discourse of Corruption, the Culture of Politics, and the Imagined State. *American Ethnologist*, 22(2): 375–402.

Haller, D. and C. Shore (eds) (2005) *Corruption: Anthropological Perspectives.* London: Pluto Press.

Harris, R. (2003) *Political Corruption: In and Beyond the Nation State.* London: Routledge.

Hasty, J. (2005) The Pleasures of Corruption: Desire and Discipline in Ghanaian Political Culture. *Cultural Anthropology* 20(2): 271–301.

Heidenheimer, A. and M. Johnston (eds) (2002) *Political Corruption: Concepts and Contexts.* New Brunswick, NJ: Transaction Publishers.

Herzfeld, M. (1992) *The Social Production of Indifference: Exploring the Symbolic Roots of Western Bureaucracy.* New York and Oxford: Berg.

Heyman, J. McC. (ed.) (1999) *States and Illegal Practices*. Oxford: Berg.

—— and A. Smart (1999) States and Illegal Practices: An Overview. In: J. McC. Heyman (ed.) *States and Illegal Practices*. Oxford: Berg: 1–24.

Huntington, S.P. (1968) *Political Order in Changing Societies*. New Haven, CT: Yale University Press.

Klaveren, J. (1957) Die historische Erscheinung der Korruption, in ihrem Zusammenhang mit der Staats- und Gesellschaftsstruktur beachtet. *Vierteljahresschrift für Sozial- und Wirtschaftsgeschichte*, 44(4): 294–302. Translation under the title Corruption as Historical Phenomenon. In: A.J. Heidenheimer and M. Johnston (eds) (2000) *Political Corruption: Concepts and Contexts*. 3rd ed. New Brunswick, NJ and London: Transaction Publishers: 83–94.

Klitgaard, R. (1988) *Controlling Corruption*. Berkeley, CA:University of California Press.

Krastev, I. (2003) When "Should" Does Not Imply "Can:" The Making of the Washington Consensus on Corruption. In: W. Lepenies (ed.) *Entangled Histories and Negotiated Universals: Centers and Peripheries in a Changing World*. Frankfurt: Campus: 105–26.

Lemke, T. (2003) *Foucault, Governmentality and Critique*. Paper presented at the Staff Seminar of the Amsterdam School for Social Science Research, 16 September 2003, Amsterdam UVA/ASSR.

Leys, C. (1965) What is the Problem about Corruption? *Journal of Modern African Studies* 3(2): 215–30.

Lipsky, M. (1980) *Street-Level Bureaucracy: Dilemmas of the Individual in Public Services*. New York: Russell Sage Foundation.

Lomnitz-Adler, C. (1992) *Exits from the Labyrinth: Culture and Ideology in the Mexican National Space*. Berkeley, CA:University of California Press.

—— (1995) Ritual, Rumor and Corruption in the Constitution of Polity in Mexico. *Journal of Latin American Anthropology* 1(1): 20–24.

Lukes, S. (2005) *Power: A Radical View*. 2nd ed. Houndmills: Palgrave Macmillan.

Maynard-Moody, S. and M. Musheno (2003) *Cops, Teachers, Counselors: Stories from the Front Lines of Public Service*. Ann Arbor, MI: University of Michigan Press.

Mbembé, A. (1992) Provisional Notes on the Postcolony. *Africa* 62(1): 3–37.

—— (2001) *On the Postcolony*. Berkeley, CA:University of California Press.

Médard, J.-F. (1982) The Underdeveloped State in Tropical Africa: Political Clientelism or Neo-Patrimonialism? In: C. Clapham (ed.) *Private Patronage and Public Power: Political Clientelism in the Modern State*. London: Frances Pinter: 162–92.

—— (2002) Corruption in the Neo-Patrimonial States of Sub-Saharan Africa. In: A.J. Heidenheimer and M. Johnston (eds) *Political Corruption: Concepts and Contexts*. New Brunswick, NJ: Transaction Publishers: 379–402.

Melissaris, E. (2004) The More the Merrier? A New Take on Legal Pluralism. *Social and Legal Studies*. 13(1): 57–79.

Merry, S.E. (1988) Legal Pluralism. *Law and Society Review* 22: 869–901.

Mitchell. T. (1991) The Limits of the State: Beyond Statist Approaches and their Critics. *The American Political Science Review* 85(1): 77–96.

—— (2002) *Rule of Experts: Egypt, Techno-Politics, Modernity*. Berkeley, CA:University of California Press.

Moore, S.F. (1973) Law and Social Change: The Semi-autonomous Social Field as an Appropriate Subject of Study. *Law and Society Review* 7(3): 719–46.

—— (1978) *Law as Process: An Anthropological Approach*. Oxford: Oxford University Press.

Myrdal, G. (1968) *Asian Drama: An Enquiry into the Poverty of Nations*, vol. II. New York: Twentieth Century.

Nader, L. (1990) *Harmony Ideology: Justice and Control in a Mountain Zapotec Village.* Stanford, CA: Stanford University Press.

Nuijten, M. (2003) *Power, Community, and the State: The Political Anthropology of Organisation in Mexico.* London: Pluto Press.

—— (2004) Between Fear and Fantasy. Governmentality and the Working of Power in Mexico. *Critique of Anthropology* 24 (2): 209–30.

Nye, J.S. (2002) Corruption and Political Development: A Cost-Benefit Analysis. In: A.J. Heidenheimer and M. Johnston (eds) *Political Corruption: Concepts and Contexts.* 3rd ed. New Brunswick, NJ and London: Transaction Publishers: 281–300.

Olivier de Sardan, J.-P. (1999) A Moral Economy of Corruption in Africa? *Journal of Modern African Studies* 37(1): 25–52.

Philps, M. (2002) Conceptualising Political Corruption. In: A. J. Heidenheimer and M. Johnston (eds.) *Political Corruption: Concepts and Contexts.* 3rd ed. New Brunswick, NJ and London: Transaction Publishers: 41–57.

Reno, W. (1995) *Corruption and State Politics in Sierra Leone.* Cambridge: Cambridge University Press.

Ries, N. (2002) "Honest" Bandits and "Warped People:" Russian Narratives about Money, Corruption and Moral Decay. In: C. Greenhouse, K. Warren and E. Mertz (eds) *Ethnography in Unstable Places: Everyday Lives in Contexts of Dramatic Political Change.* Durham, NC: Duke University Press: 276–315.

Riles, A. (2001) *The Network Inside Out.* Ann Arbor: Michigan University Press.

Roitman, J. (2005) *Fiscal Disobedience: An Anthropology of Economic Regulation in Central Africa.* Princeton, NJ: Princeton University Press.

Rose-Ackerman, S. (1999) *Corruption and Government: Causes, Consequences and Reform.* Cambridge: Cambridge University Press.

Sampson, S. (2005) Integrity Warriors: Global Morality and the Anti-Corruption Movement in the Balkans. In: D. Haller and C. Shore (eds) *Corruption: Anthropological Perspectives.* London: Pluto Press: 103–30.

Schmitt, C. (1985) *Political Theology: Four Chapters on the Concept of Sovereignty.* Cambridge, MA: MIT Press.

Schneider, J. and P. Schneider (2003) *Reversible Destiny: Mafia, Antimafia, and the Struggle for Palermo.* Berkeley, CA:University of California Press.

—— (2005) Mafia, Antimafia and the Plural Cultures of Sicily. *Current Anthropology* 46: 501–20.

Scott, J.C. (1979) The Analysis of Corruption in Developing Nations. In: M.U. Epko (ed.) *Bureaucratic Corruption in sub-Saharan Africa: Toward a Search for Causes and Consequences.* Washington, DC: University Press of America: 29–61.

Smart, A. (1993) Gifts, Bribes and Guanxi: A Reconsideration of Bourdieu's Social Capital. *Cultural Anthropology* 8(3): 388–408.

Soto, H. de (2000) *The Mystery of Capital: Why Capitalism Triumphs in the West and Fails Everywhere Else.* New York: Basic Books.

Sousa Santos, B. de (1995) *Toward a New Common Sense: Law, Science and Politics in the Paradigmatic Transition.* London: Routledge.

Taussig, M. (1999) *Defacement: Public Secrecy and the Labor of the Negative.* Stanford, CA: Stanford University Press.

Trouillot, M.-R. (2003) *Global Transformations: Anthropology and the Modern World.* Houndmills: Palgrave Macmillan.

Vries, P. de (2002) Vanishing Mediators: Enjoyment as a Political Factor in Western Mexico. *American Ethnologist* 29(4): 901–27.

Waquet, J.-C. (1991) *Corruption: Ethics and Power in Florence, 1600–1770*. Pennsylvania, PA: Pennsylvania State University Press.

Weber, M. (1990) *Wirtschaft und Gesellschaft: Grundriss der verstehenden Soziologie*. 5th ed. Tübingen: Mohr.

Wertheim, W.F. (1961) *Corruptie*. Assen: Van Gorcum and Comp. N.V.

—— (1964) *East-West Parallels: Sociological Approaches to Modern Asia*. The Hague: Van Hoeve.

West, H.G. and T. Sanders (eds) (2003) *Transparency and Conspiracy: Ethnographies of Suspicion in the New World Order*. Durham, NC: Duke University Press.

Wilson, R.A. (2000) Reconciliation and Revenge in Post-apartheid South Africa: Rethinking Legal Pluralism and Human Rights. *Current Anthropology* 41(1): 75–98.

World Bank (1989) *Sub-Saharan Africa: From Crisis to Sustainable Growth*. Washington, DC: The World Bank.

Žižek, S. (1996) "I Hear you with my Eyes:" Or, the Invisible Master. In: R. Saleci and S. Žižek (eds) *Gaze and Voice as Love Objects*. Durham, NC: Duke University Press: 90–126.

Systematic Corruption and Bureaucratic Itineraries

Chapter 2

Hidden Acts, Open Talks.
How Anthropology Can "Observe" and Describe Corruption

Giorgio Blundo

In this chapter, I will focus on the methodological challenges and ethical dilemmas involved in an anthropological study of phenomena such as corruption that are at the same time hidden and diffuse, concealed and openly discussed, justified and stigmatized in daily conversations.[1] Even in its more commonplace and routine forms, corruption remains difficult to observe, still less to film.[2] If ethnographic description is a kind of "writing of the visible," a process by which the gaze is transformed into language,[3] how can one then describe an object like practices of corruption, which are sometimes hidden and sometimes undetected, as such, by the social actors? What forms does description take in the absence of observation? What is one really describing when one works on the phenomenon of corruption? What are one's sources and terms of inquiry? What is the argumentative status of descriptions that are constructed more from discursive data than from direct observations, the latter remaining for the most sporadic and fortuitous? What can be said of the typical character of these descriptions?

I will start with a discussion of the properties of the object of corruption and suggest that they determine, at least partially, the forms of its observation and its description. Next, I will discuss the nature of descriptive sources produced during an empirical research on the phenomenon of corruption by outlining the objective constraints and the strategies that can be envisaged in the field. Finally, I will present some recent examples of ethnographic description of the phenomenon in publications and highlight the principal descriptive registers at work. In this way, I will try to show how each of these procedures allows us to "see" corruption in a different way. I will conclude by noting that through the study of corruption—a fairly new subject for anthropology—we can improve our understanding of social and political issues such as local representations of citizenship and the state and its bureaucracies; we can also better understand

---

    1   This chapter is the modified and shortened English version of an article published in French (Blundo 2003).
    2   In the sense given to this expression by Olivier de Sardan (2003).
    3   According to the terms of Laplantine (1996: 8).

how norms and rules really work in different political and social settings (see also Shore and Haller 2005: 8).

The Properties of Corruption

At the very outset, it must be said that corruption does not lend itself easily to analysis in the social sciences: of awkward definition, it presents some problems to the researcher, as much of an ethical as of a methodological nature. I will here only take up those problems that concern the question of observation/description in anthropology and qualitative sociology. Proceeding by analogy, I suggest that the anthropology of corruption presents features that bring it close to the anthropology of deviant phenomena, to the anthropology of witchcraft, and to the anthropology of transactions.

Corruption as Deviance

The notion of corruption is theoretically inseparable from the transgression of a set of norms (juridical or ethical). Its definition is therefore dependent, explicitly or implicitly, on a particular conception of what an uncorrupted administration or political system should be (Philp 1997)—in other words on normative judgments on the appropriate nature of politics: "the other face of a discourse of corruption … is a discourse of accountability" (Gupta 1995: 388).

It must be stated that most of the scholarly definitions—which are not far removed from a legal definition—consider corruption essentially as a deviation in relation to norms that govern public service[4] or that, more generally, define the safeguard of public interest (Rogow and Lasswell 1966: 132). But if it is possible, with the help of a penal code, to characterize what is corrupt in a given society, the task is complicated when it comes to adopting an emic approach.[5] The reduction of corruptive practices to their essentially legal and penal dimension leads to losing sight of the fact that they are strongly embedded in ordinary forms of sociability (Blundo and Olivier de Sardan 2006a). Corruption does not exist in the abstract but is measured "according to public opinion's capacity of absorption" (Morice 1991: 157) or at the level of "the cultural acceptability of corruption" (Olivier de Sardan 1996: 109). Perceptions and evaluations of corrupt practices are culturally embedded. The corruptive phenomenon therefore invites questions similar to those raised by the sociology of deviance.

In the first place, corruption is similar to deviance with respect to the definition of the phenomenon and the demarcation of its frontiers. The theme of corruption

---

4 Corruption is then "behaviour which deviates from the formal duties of a public role because of private-regarding (personal, close family, private clique) pecuniary or status gains; or violates rules against the exercise of certain types of private-regarding influence" (Nye 1967: 419).

5 That is, focusing on discursive data that give access to the representations of "native" actors (for a recent discussion about this concept, see Olivier de Sardan 1998).

has given birth to unending and sometimes sterile controversies of definition centered on the substance of the act (Williams 1999). It is possible to avoid the dead end of definition by concentrating on the processes of qualification of behaviors termed deviant or transgressive from an emic point of view: in a Beckerian optic, corruption would then be "an act to which this label was successfully applied."[6] In this perspective, the discourses and representations of corruption refer more to "a negotiated classification of behavior rather than ... an inherent quality of behavior" (Chibnall and Saunders 1977: 139). In a given social or professional universe, actors can adopt a "situational morality" that coincides with their aims and the criteria of informal interpretation common to their universe of belonging. Most often, they would recognize the illegal or immoral character of such actions but they will simply decide to ignore it or to underestimate it (ibid.: 141). What is common practice, for example, in the relation between contractors of public works and municipal decision makers (an exchange of favors and gifts, meetings outside the place of work, and so on) will become unacceptable only when it is subjected to an examination in a courtroom.

Although definition remains difficult the exercise cannot be dismissed too quickly: it is the definition of an object "that permits its isolation as a unit of observation" (Weber 2000: 93). The eternal question of definition ceases to be a simple exercise of style and erudition when it comes to "observing" the phenomenon. This is the second way in which an empirical socio-anthropology of corruption that deals with strongly normative representations and takes an interest in clandestine or hidden practices, faces problems that are similar to those encountered by criminal sociology or the sociology of deviance. While it is difficult to define these practices, it is equally problematic to observe them. The researcher is generally confronted with clandestine or concealed acts. We can here think of inquiries into petty or large-scale delinquency, parallel or "informal" commercial circuits, prostitution, deviant sexual practices, the economy of drugs, or even sects or secret societies. These fields are not easily accessible and are closed to the uninitiated. They require the mobilization of appropriate methods, which are not without problems of an ethical and deontological character.

A risk and a dilemma can be evoked here. The risk is of transforming the sociological inquiry into a police inquiry, in other words, of excessively "criminalizing" the practices observed. The dilemma concerns the empirical study of generally clandestine practices and raises in a troubling way the question of the researcher's insertion and the disclosing of the aims of the study to his or her informants. In certain circumstances the concealed observation will be the only means of producing the facts.[7]

---

6 As Pierre Lascoumes (1999: 49) suggests, drawing inspiration from Howard S. Becker (1963).

7 In the middle of the 1950s, Festinger and his team (Festinger, Riecken, and Schachter 1956) studied an American sect prophesying the end of the world by themselves becoming unsuspected adepts of the organization. Investigating the anonymous relations between homosexuals in the United States, Laud Humphreys (1970) adopted a role recognized by the informal rules governing conduct in public toilets: that of the lookout,

An additional dilemma in such a situation of inquiry is that the observation of corruption often coincides with its disclosure. By their descriptions, researchers reveal acts, which had previously been hidden. How then, can the information collected in the field be conveyed, when their revelation can have negative consequences for the informants? How can the theme be approached without the risk of destroying the relation of confidence between researcher and informant and without giving the impression of searching for confessions, given the nearly always illegal character of most corruptive behaviors? How can the truth of the stories one hears be verified, without slipping into a police inquiry?[8] How, when confronted with a field that is hidden from observation, can the imperative of the exactness of the stories that are proposed to the researcher be taken up, without borrowing strategies contrary to the professional ethic: infiltration, dissimulation of research aims, and predation (Punch 1989: 197)?

Methodological questions add themselves to the ethical problems: if it is the researcher who has discovered the affair, on the basis of which criteria can he or she label specific practices as corruption? On the other hand, if they are working on cases of registered corruption, researchers' descriptions will depend upon the determination of the seriousness of the act by institutions guarding norms of public honesty.

Corruption as Witchcraft

The universe of corruptive practices is an initiatory, opaque space crossed by the secret.[9] This representation of the phenomenon is also found in popular expressions, when one examines the semantic field of words that designate corruption: to the familiar "under the table" echoes the term *mbuuxum* in Wolof,[10] which is derived from the verb *buux*, signifying "to give discretely," and is used to indicate a bribe (Blundo and Olivier de Sardan 2006b). In this respect, corruption does evoke the phenomenon of magic practices and witchcraft, with which it shares some principal properties.

First, corruption, like witchcraft, constitutes what Michael Taussig (1999: 2) calls a "public secret," for which the stake is "knowing what not to know." As a "family crime," most corruptive behaviors are manifested in private between consenting actors, producing no direct victims who would be interested in

---

both Peeping Tom and guard in case of public controls. On the other hand, confronted with problems of observation, the research conducted by Philippe Bourgois on the drug trade at Harlem (Bourgois 1995) or that of Jean-François Werner on prostitution and the consumption of drugs in the suburbs of Dakar (Werner 1993) opted for a less concealed approach.

8   Cynthia Werner (2000: 15f.) asks similar questions in her work on petty corruption in post-Soviet Kazakhstan.

9   The Italian political scientist Donatella Della Porta (1992) talks of "hidden exchange," and the most important non-governmental organization for the fight against the phenomenon, Transparency International, defines itself by the antonym of one of the features of corruption.

10 Wolof is the most widely spoken language in Senegal.

bringing the facts to the knowledge of the authorities. The actors, moreover, are constantly subjected to different euphemisms and denials according to particular political cultures. These factors of "social invisibility" (Lascoumes 1999: 15f., 24) ensure that the majority of the corruptive facts, and the magic practices, far from being visible, present themselves to the researcher essentially in the form of diffuse accusations or allegations without proof, conveyed by rumor and gossip.[11] But when these facts *are* publicly revealed this usually takes place through the particular style of mediatic revelation of illicit political or administrative practices that is the scandal. The event that is the object of the scandal is dramatized and at the same time reduced to its stigmatized dimension: it is a question of designating a responsible, whose condemnation "is supposed to re-establish the symbolic order of values and socially protected interests" (Lascoumes 1999: 69). The spectacular and ritualized revelation of the moves of the corrupted, or of the sorcerer, is generally inscribed in a context of emergent movements of moralization of politics or anti-witchcraft struggles: changes of government in Africa, for example, are privileged occasions for witch hunts, in both the literal and the figurative sense of the term.

Second, if the empirical evidence of corruption and sorcery is constituted above all by a discourse that crystallizes around rumors rather than around facts that could be easily documented, one is led to question the nature of rumors (accusatory or justificatory) and what it is that they actually convey. Corruption, just as much as sorcery, functions in a system of circular beliefs that are private and feed themselves, and that can explain unhappiness, disgrace, the failure of an administrative step, and the loss of a case in court. In Africa, in order to explain the trajectories of quick wealth, someone can be suspected just as easily of corrupt behavior as of having recourse to magic and/or witchcraft.[12] Corruption and witchcraft are thus mechanisms to interpret, explain, and attempt to manipulate the world.[13]

Moreover, the "belief" that corruption is omnipresent and endemic leads to its generalization. Everyone considers its practice as a preventive measure: one defends oneself from the corruption of "others" by taking recourse to the same style of political protection, of acquaintance with mercenary and accommodating officers, of "anticipatory" gifts, and so on. It is the same with magical practices applied to counteract witchcraft and evil magic. Corruption and witchcraft are thus reproduced within the same space of uncertainty and suspicion.

Third, corruption, as much as witchcraft and the actors involved in it, are dependent on ambivalent representations that oscillate between stigmatization and indulgence and between fascination and rejection. This ambivalence is reflected

---

11 Cf. Alex Kondos (1987: 16), who establishes an explicit parallel between the accusations of corruption and the accusations of witchcraft.

12 On the "witchcraft of riches," see Geschiere (2000).

13 This aspect is not only the preserve of Africa: according to a specialist of post-Soviet societies, "corruption is for the Lettons what witchcraft is for the Azande" (Sedlenieks 2002: 8).

in the paradox, pushed to the extreme in the African context, of corruption being ubiquitously condemned while practiced everywhere on a daily basis.

Fourth, similarly to inquiries on witchcraft, the claim to be undertaking an ethnography of corruption with an essentially informative objective is something of an illusion. To paraphrase Favret-Saada (1977: 26), one could say that "to speak of corruption, is never for the purpose of informing." Our informants, when aware that corrupting practices occur, never show themselves neutral: either they denounce and perhaps complain at the same time, or they justify themselves, or they dodge the issue, but in any case, they never expect their words to receive a "neutral" and "scientific" treatment. Though on the one hand abstaining from any moral condemnation and normative judgment appears an essential imperative for the success of a study on corruption, on the other hand it would be awkward—entrenched behind the presupposition of neutrality characteristic of research in the social sciences—to brush aside the axiological dimension of the phenomenon.

Corruption as Transaction

In order to "decriminalize" corruption, it is appropriate to reintegrate it into a more ordinary space, by looking at the nature of social and political relations that are at stake, as well as the resources (symbolic and material) mobilized in the corruptive exchange. At heart, the corruptive exchange is only one of the possible modalities of interaction between state and citizens, or between public services and users, and for this reason must be reinserted into a larger movement of social relations based on exchange, reciprocity, and negotiation. The gaze slides here from transgression to transaction "in which one party exchanges wealth—or trades on more durable assets such as kinship ties—for a measure of influence over the authoritative decisions of government" (Scott 1969: 321). The corrupting relation declines under several forms that are situated schematically in a continuity going from extortion (imposing an informal "toll" for every user of the administration or soliciting payments for free services) to mutually favorable transactions (sometimes taking the form of commissions, sometimes of bonus, and sometimes of an exchange of favors), through forms of personal appropriation of public goods (like the classic embezzlement of funds or the well-known practice of "moonlighting" or *travail à la perruque*).[14]

But the meaning of a transaction is not given once and for all. It varies according to the stakes, positions, and perceptions of different partners. Scott's classic typology, distinguishing between "parochial corruption," which mobilizes symbolic resources like friendship, family bonds, or ethnic references, and "market corruption," which is immediate and concerns socially anonymous partners, therefore merits some nuances.

As Florence Weber has clearly shown, in a market relation the exchanged good is not evaluated according to the relation between exchanging partners and the

---

14 For a deeper discussion of these "elementary forms of corruption," see Blundo and Olivier de Sardan (2006a).

transfer and counter-transfer are practically simultaneous. In other words, it is a question of an instantaneous relation, lacking affective connotations and not involving a succession of interactions such as double transfers of the kind "gift and counter-gift" described by Mauss (Weber 2000: 87). A number of corrupting interactions are therefore not to be integrated into a market transaction because they are characterized by an important gap between transfer and counter-transfer (many anticipatory gifts do not foresee an immediate return). Moreover, what monetary equivalence can one establish for an administrative decision taken contrary to norms when it is provided in the name of friendship or family solidarity, or when the sum of the bribe is incommensurate with the benefits drawn by the user? Besides, a market relation can be non-monetary and conversely, a personal relation can mobilize money, without being characterized as a market relationship. In addition to these topics, the focus on corruption as a transaction leads to two central questions addressed to ethnographic description.

In the first place, from a synchronic angle the performative aspects of interaction are important for describing corruption. Negotiations do not all happen in the same way. It is a question of competencies which, far from being concentrated on the simple determination of the sum to pay or to offer, concern the temporality of the process, the hidden or implicit codes, the gestures, and the language adopted. During a corrupting transaction, the partners measure their own capacities of negotiation, their cleverness, and their power and relative status (Ruud 2000: 289). Learning to progress in the universe of corrupt practices thus demands a kind of socialization—of learning—as much on the part of the officer as on the part of the user. In other words, "the informal procedures for successfully engaging in corrupt activities are also embedded in the local culture" (Werner 2000: 16). It is a question of etiquette: who is ready to accept a bribe? What and how much to give? Where and when? What must be said to open the transaction (ibid.: 18)?

In the second place, by privileging the diachronic dimension, corruption can be described as a process. In fact, it only rarely manifests itself as an isolated and isolable action, as some stereotypical descriptions of the corrupted exchange would indicate (a building contractor slips an envelope into the hands of a public officer to obtain a service contrary to the norms governing the administrative space). On the contrary, it concerns a complex process unfolding in time in which, most of the time, the transaction is indirect (that is to say, implying the intervention of intermediaries) and occupies only one step in a series of events that precede or follow it. In fact, describing a corrupting transaction implies identifying a before and an after, which are contained in the biography of the actors of the exchange, their professional experiences, the history of the administrative service concerned or, again, in the evolution of public policies put in place by the state and its different governments to fight against corruption (or, more often, to conceal it and leave it unpunished). In describing a given corruptive practice, one cannot isolate it from the individual and collective context in which it has arisen.

Once again, challenging problems come up as to the forms of observation and description of corrupting exchanges; while a market transaction can perhaps be observed in its entirety (where in principle the gap is non-existent between the transfer and the counter-transfer), how can the long process of a non-economic transaction be observed, where it is difficult, even impossible to identify the spatio-temporal facts of the counter-gift or the counter-transfer (Weber 2000: 97)?

The Properties of Corruption and the Implications for its Description

What then are the principal properties of the corrupting phenomenon that affect its descriptivity? The first property concerns the observability of the phenomenon, which we partly discussed above. The observability of corruption is structured by a constant tension between occultation and visibility and between the spectacular and the commonplace. The social invisibility of practices associated with corruption actually proceeds from some different mechanisms, according to the extent of the phenomenon (is it sector-based or generalized?), the levels on which it is manifested ("large-scale" or "petty" corruption), and its degree of acceptance in a given socio-political context. The sphere of "black corruption"—that is, acts publicly stamped with the seal of the illicit—is hardly visible because its protagonists hide the facts. But when corruption is commonplace and practiced daily, when it becomes one of the—and sometimes the only—possible ways to access state services (a situation that we have encountered during our inquiries on the functioning of the local state in West Africa, cf. Blundo and Olivier de Sardan 2006c), one is confronted with this paradox: it is so visible that it stops being considered deviant behavior and is submerged within other morally acceptable social practices and even largely encouraged. Where the jurist (or the researcher) will see an illicit commission or a bribe, the protagonists of the exchange will see a small bonus for a service satisfactorily rendered. In such a context, it is honesty that constitutes the deviation: the formal norms are replaced in daily life by practical norms, which privilege negotiation, bargaining, and "arrangements" at the cost of rules emptied of their substance.

The risk then for the observer/describer is of being attracted only by the spectacular dimension of "visible" corruption, by sensational affairs, or by scandals that make it into the newspaper headlines. A good description of the practices of corruption must, on the contrary, restore them to their triteness, their daily character, their ordinary dimension, and their ambivalence.

A related problem with the weak visibility of corruption is that observations are generally not very repetitive and standardisable, and could not in any case lead to a sufficiently precise measurement of the phenomenon. If "the knowledge of its scale depends upon the social and political conditions of its revelation" (Médard 2001: 65), how then can the total of the sums exchanged or embezzled, the frequency of practices, or the degree of their expansion in the social and political body be determined? And to what extent will the descriptions provided be representative of the phenomenon taken in its globality?

Secondly, if first-hand description is difficult, one then has recourse to second-hand or "emic" descriptions, resulting from discursive interactions with informants. These emic descriptions vary according to the many different points of view on corruptive practices and, as we have seen, are often strongly ambivalent. One can then either describe the phenomenon by adopting one of these possible points of view (for example, that of the corrupted or that of the institutions who pursue them), or seek to reconstruct the various points of view of the different groups involved. A description of a corrupting practice will most often combine direct and second-degree observations and present contradictory discourses on the practice. One can no doubt affirm that every description of corruption, which is always preceded (explicitly or implicitly) by an evaluation and qualification of the observed behaviors, is a negotiated description, in the sense that the actors, according to their position with respect to the corrupting act (victim, corrupter, corrupted, magistrate, and so on), characterize it with the help of systems of norms, moral values and processes of justification that can diverge considerably. Descriptions of corruption are therefore strongly interpretative and evaluative.

A third implication of the properties of corruption for its description is that while one can only observe isolated acts, the description must not ignore the procedural dimension of corrupting acts. Observation-description must then be related to listening-description, that is to say, the use of other techniques of data production (case studies, interviews, biographies, life histories, and so on—see below).

Fieldwork's Different Sources of Descriptive Data

"Observing" Corruption

The point here is not to take up an analysis of different types of empirical sources on corruption already sketched elsewhere (Blundo and Olivier de Sardan 2000) but to highlight the crucial dilemmas in observing corruption. All descriptive work is based on sources, whether they are the anthropologist's field notes or the historian's archives. In the study of corruption, the most common sources are either documentary researches (press analyses, judicial archives), or quantitative inquiries taking the form of opinion polls.[15] The domination of the archival document and the questionnaire is due to the empirical tradition of the disciplines that have monopolized research on corruption, that is to say, political science and economics. Borrowing a typology common in criminal sociology,[16] one can say that these disciplines give their attention principally to "legal corruption" (that is, acts punished by institutions controlling legality) and "apparent corruption" (the offences known to judicial institutions). One then understands the ironical optimism of an economist according to whom corruption is "like an elephant, even though it may be difficult to describe, it is generally not difficult to recognize when

---

15 As Jean-Michel Chapoulie reminds us in his preface to the French version of Becker's *Outsiders (Outsiders. Etudes de sociologie de la déviance*, Paris, Métailié, 1985: 15), in this field of study, the situation presents analogies with those against which the sociology of deviance, renewed by Becker at the beginning of the 1960s, would assert itself for some time: sociologists working essentially with archival materials, official statistics, and juridical texts.

16 Cf. J.M. Bessette (1989: 496), cited by Dartigues and de Lescure (2000: 326).

observed" (Tanzi 1998: 564). It is obvious that economists and political scientists observe elephants—or corruption—in a way different from anthropologists. If the former are interested only in the acts which have led to a penal procedure and have been reported by the press, the latter focus their attention on "real corruption" (the set of offences committed, which do not necessarily become known to institutions of suppression).

However, the newspaper, the judicial archives, and the polls should not be neglected under the influence of an excessive inclination toward oral inquiry and participant observation. The analysis of a corpus of the press reflects the level of mediatization of corrupting phenomena but also constitutes an irreplaceable source of information on the visible dimension of the phenomenon ("scandalous corruption") and represents "the most important mechanism in public culture for the circulation of discourses on corruption" (Gupta 1995: 385). Newspaper articles provide raw material for a "thick description" of a trans-local phenomenon like the State. Indeed, a corrupt system is not only made of practices that can be grasped at the local level but also represents "a discursive field that enables the phenomenon to be labeled, discussed, practiced, decried, and denounced" (ibid.). Access to judicial archives in turn allows us to appreciate the effectiveness of mechanisms of suppression and punishment of the phenomenon and their variations according to historical and social context. Moreover, dockets from court hearings describe the details of the acts judged and reveal the stories and testimonies of the actors involved. Finally, the polls can provide a measure, albeit vague, of the perceptions of public opinion as to the importance of the corrupting phenomenon and its qualification as a social problem.

But these sources only reveal the points at which the underground river of corruption is exposed to the light. Observation, in its different forms and modalities, then becomes an unavoidable method for the exploration of the river of illicit political practices. Not only does observation enable an awareness of the gap between formal and pragmatic norms, it also gives access to practices that remain in the sphere of the implicit, the unsaid, and the inadmissible.

In anthropology one can generally distinguish two postures with respect to observations in the field: participant observation, which follows from the prolonged insertion of the researcher in the social milieu studied, and more systematic and detailed observations. Corruption often reveals itself to the researcher in personal experiences. If researchers are working in a country where petty corruption is commonplace and daily, they will no doubt sometimes find themselves in the position of the victim of extortion on the part of the forces of order or local administration; or at other times in the situation of the corrupter, when they learn the art of accelerating a procedure of visa renewal or getting their goods cleared by customs, or when they acquire the skill of negotiating the reduction of a fine with a member of the police force. These daily interactions, which constitute the universe of "petty corruption," are of course ideal moments to impregnate oneself in local practices and learn to juggle with the administration. Yet these are sporadic and occasional events that can leave the major part of corrupting practices unexamined. The majority of anthropological texts on corruption fall into the category of accidental observations. Their authors "discovered" corruption by induction. Gupta (1995) notes the frequency of the theme of corruption in the daily conversations of villagers of northern India; Werner, working on gift and economic exchange in Kazakhstan, affirms: "It was probably to my advantage that I did not intend to study bribery and corruption. ... Only in the process of doing this research did I become interested in bribery" (Werner 2000: 16); Smith (2003) familiarized himself with bribes while investigating a family planning program in Nigeria.

Observations of corrupting practices also often surface on the margins of participant observation centered on other themes. For example, during the course of inquiries dealing with the investment activities of a Senegalese municipality (Blundo 2001b), I had been struck by the recurrence in local debate of the theme of bad management. Very different informants (local representatives, members of cooperatives or of associations of gardeners, administrative officers, peasants, stockbreeders, and so on) offered systematic criticism of a series of practices that one could easily refer to under the notion of corruption: embezzlement of public funds, abuse of social goods, the establishment of fictive bills, irregularities in the allotment of a public market, and the illicit borrowing from the safe of an association managing a development project. Unforeseen in an initial phase of research, the themes of embezzlement of public funds and of administrative corruption were in a way imposed on me by my informants. It is thus a continued insertion in a given social space that permits one to perceive practices and discourses linked to corruption. It must be recognized that these observations are not systematic; they take place through chance encounters and luck and are strongly oriented toward what the locals say about the phenomenon.

Participant observation on corrupt practices—outside or on the margins of other inquiries—is thus generally an "involuntary" observation of the researcher. This is why most anthropological studies based on empirical material focus on "petty" corruption, which characterizes relations between users and interface or street-level bureaucracies (Lipsky 1980). Yet, one can wonder whether these practices—which researchers have observed directly or in which they have taken an active part—are representative of the phenomenon. The researcher's origins for example, certainly influences the nature of their exchanges with the administration: perceived as the possessor of large sums of money and lacking—at least in the first phases of the fieldwork—links in local society, they can be the object of the most extreme forms of corruption, that is, extortion, just as they can be excluded from forms of corruption that are based upon the exchange of favors and refer to local norms of politeness and well-being. Through the direct involvement in corrupting interactions the researcher himself or herself does, however, learn the subtle art of corruption.[17] It is also at this price that they will then be capable of describing it.

It is also possible to carry out more deliberate and systematic observation. During his doctoral research in Northern Nigeria in the years 1949–1951, Smith made experimental sales of cotton on several markets "employing local agents who were asked to guarantee the exactitude of their relations by swearing on

---

17 As Sean Cush McNamara's (1986) experience shows.

the Koran" (Smith 1964: 187). "In the first test, my agents were permitted to offer bribes to secure prompt entry to the market and high grades from the Hausa 'cotton mallams' in charge; all cotton sold in the experiment that year received the highest grade. In the second test, bribes were forbidden, no cotton received top grade, and access proved difficult and slow" (ibid.). So, the agents practicing corruption sold off their cotton faster and at a better price than their honest collaborators did. In our research on petty corruption in West Africa, we too undertook systematic observation at specific sites, such as roadblocks, customs posts, buses, bush taxis, hospitals, or state offices. In some cases, when the researcher was too visibly "foreign," the work of observation was "delegated" to collaborators merging more discretely with the environment. It was thus only after a day spent in a state office of the city of Tahoua in Niger that it was possible to see the department employees share the fruits of their small "arrangements" with the public, and this with the greatest simplicity, without even wanting to hide this from us.

Every observation *in situ* must thus ideally be linked to other spaces that resist the researcher's gaze. In order to penetrate the heart of corrupting transactions themselves within the professional circle of a given administration, a more systematic "participant" posture is then necessary: the temporary adoption of an ad hoc professional role. To take an example, some German researchers were able to gather around 40,000 documents proving cases of corruption within European pharmaceutical companies, thanks to the role played by two members of the research team: one was a former employee in the sector, the other got himself recruited as a representative in a firm.[18] One can also evoke the works of Chambliss (1971), who between 1962 and 1969 conducted field investigations on the networks of organized crime in Seattle by adopting the method of participant observation.[19]

This position is not without its specific problems: it demands a particularly high investment of time and energy because the submersion in the daily rhythm of a given professional group does not guarantee immediate access to the behaviors that this group recognizes as deviant and which it hides from strangers for this very reason. Maurice Punch's experience speaks for itself on this count: at the end of two years of practically continuous participation in the activities of a police patrol in an Amsterdam neighborhood, he was astonished by the apparent absence of deviant behavior on the part of the policemen. Some time later, however, the news of a scandal within the very police station he studied led him to understand that in fact the deviation "was going on around me, almost literally under my nose, but I did not see it (and, perhaps unconsciously, may not have wanted to see it)" (Punch 1989: 179).

Besides, if researchers gain the confidence of their informants and are finally allowed to view deviant activities within an administration, they are then confronted with questions of an ethical order: must they take an active part?

---

18 Cf. K. Langbein et al., *Gesunde Geschäfte: Die Praktiken des Pharma-Industrie*, Köln, Kiepenhener and Witsch, 1981, quoted in Van der Geest (1984).

19 For a more detailed presentation of this study, cf. Lascoumes 2000.

Should they communicate to the hierarchical supervisors, knowing that silence could lead to their punishment (for having covered up for the officials involved) and that denouncement could mean the end of the fieldwork (Punch 1989: 184)? Additionally, the more one climbs the administrative hierarchy, the more doors are closed, mouths are shut, and opaqueness installs itself. The visibility of corrupt acts decreases as one reaches the top of a bureaucratic organization, as I noted while studying decentralization, local revenue, and public procurements in Senegal.

Finally, even when one claims to adopt a research posture based on participant observation within an administrative service, the use of this term could be imprecise, as Punch (1989: 184) admits: "to a large extent I never actually witnessed the phenomenon I was studying—corruption." Besides, concentrating the observations exclusively on administrative sites can prove itself to be the wrong track, to the extent that a lot of corrupt transactions take place far from the bureaucratic space: "It's toilets and bars that have to become more transparent, not just boardrooms and office cubicles."[20] In order to appreciate a phenomenon whose generality no longer needs to be shown, one must therefore use everything, multiplying the sites of observation and combining lucky and casual observations with more systematic and programmed observations.

For the rest, participant observation also consists of chatter and informal discussion, through which gossip, stories, and rumors are exchanged. Through nastiness and gossip people talk of the corruption of others, describe or mark their acts, and pronounce judgments. Although the literature on corruption generally rejects rumor as a source of information in favor of the "truth" of facts and proofs,[21] the analysis of the contextualized corpus of rumors gives access to a set of discourses and representations on corruption: it is thus possible to analyze the terms and expressions used to designate these practices, but also to reconstitute the channels of transmission of accusations of corruption, and to distinguish acts that become the object of denouncements, accusations, and eventually punishments from those that are justified and tolerated. In other words, it is a matter of including in the inquiry perspectives that offer an inventory of the different social uses of rumor, that underlie the expression of a conflict in situations of social proximity, constitute a means of political struggle for groups and/or individual contractors, and convey a criticism of power and of social and economic inequalities.

---

20 A.F. Robertson, "Corporate Decay," paper presented at the *15th Anniversary Conference on Corruption*, 12–13 December 2002, Amsterdam School for Social Science. My very first contact with the universe of illicit exchanges took place in the toilets of Dakar airport where I had been called by an employee of the airline company to negotiate a reduction of excess weight of my baggage. And it was in a bar of the Senegalese city of Kaolack that solid links were established between building contractors and the public decision makers.

21 Cf. for example Miller, Koschechkina, and Grodeland (1997: 201). Narrating the inquiries conducted in the Czech Republic and in Ukraine, these authors sought to clearly distinguish the statements founded on rumours of corruption and those issuing from a direct experience or lived in the circle of the informant.

At the same time, it is not a matter of opposing the truth of the researcher's direct observations with the construction of experiences recounted and practices narrated. Ethnographic description reports a social reality seized from "seeing" but transforms it into language, the latter registering itself in a relation of intertextuality (things said or written) (Laplantinc 1996: 28). On the one hand, I have sufficiently underlined that what is observable often remains at an anecdotal level and cannot therefore constitute the only descriptive support to explain the phenomenon in its complexity; these anecdotes are probably not sufficiently "typical" to describe the practices which have remained hidden. On the other hand, any observation on corruption is necessarily "filtered" (and then constructed) by discursive interactions which themselves have an observational component (one can note the hesitations, the postures, and so on). These discursive interactions constitute a reservoir of emic descriptions and, because of this, represent the principal corpus of descriptive facts in an empirical inquiry on corruption. Here the interview is not only a complement to participant observation, but sometimes becomes the only way of "observing" corruption.

The Descriptive Narratives

The interview gives access to descriptive narratives or emic descriptions. Through the interview, it will be a question of seeing with the other's eyes that which is unobservable, or of seeking to correct the deformations of an insufficient gaze. These emic descriptions can take various forms, according to the position or the role played by the interviewee. The latter will, in certain circumstances, be led to express more or less shared knowledge on the mechanisms, actors, places, or the temporalities of corruption, in a rather impersonal manner: he will be adopting the posture of *consultant* (see explanation below of the different roles that informants may take on during an interview). In other cases, the interviewee will provide testimony of a precise incident of corruption by quoting cases drawn from personal experience or casual observations or by quoting situations experienced by a member of his circle. We will then be dealing with descriptions constructed from the posture of the *narrator*.[22]

It goes without saying that this distinction does not correspond to diametrically opposed types of interviews. In fact, the corpus of around 920 interviews constituted by our research team[23] shows a constant slide within a given interview

---

22 This distinction between consultation and narrative in an interview comes from Olivier de Sardan (1995).

23 From 1999 to 2001, a team of six researchers of six different nationalities and 14 research assistants carried out field and documentary studies in Benin, Niger, and Senegal on petty everyday corruption. The research focused on the following specific areas and sectors: transport and customs (in the three countries), the legal system (in the three countries), health (in Benin and Niger), public procurements (in Benin and Senegal), the local tax system (in Senegal), the way corruption is dealt with by the press (in the three countries), development-aid projects (based on the example of the scandal surrounding Italian-Senegalese development cooperation), and the policies adopted to fight corruption

between these two postures. Judges invited to describe phenomena that they fight as "experts" have often also narrated personal experiences in which they suffered political pressure or offers of corruption. Conversely, contractors preferred to disguise their direct knowledge of the discrete world of bribes by stories staging anonymous colleagues.

But one can attribute different characteristics to the two postures. The posture of the consultant expresses itself in the first place by general statements, which aim at describing the phenomenon in its globality:

> I am ashamed to say this to you, but in this country ... I think there are more corrupt people than honest people. People, they are like that, it is their daily life, they get up early in the morning to go find opportunities to enrich themselves and that is regrettable. (Inspector in the Finance Ministry, Dakar)

It also portrays ideal, hypothetical situations, whose plausibility is as high as the informant's specific knowledge of the sector of activity described, as it appears in this extract of an interview with a Senegalese contractor in the construction field (Blundo 2001a: 80):

> He who sees himself given a procurement and who "forgets" those who had selected him at the time of payment, will not have the benefit of help a second time. Such an attitude would be equivalent to "beating the tam-tam with an axe" (*in Wolof: tegg dênd yi ak tel yi*).

The words spoken while mainly playing the role of consultant refer, however, to degrees of competence that differ greatly: if the majority of studies of the phenomenon of corruption focus on the views of "experts" in the proper sense of the term (journalists, judges, politicians, auditors) and possibly of professionals (transporters, shopkeepers, constructors), it is necessary, with a concern to diversifying the points of view, to simultaneously grasp the vision of people from below, simple users of the administration.

When an informant chooses to play the narrator, their words will refer to concrete situations, lived or witnessed, and generally be richer in detail and in information on the corrupt transaction that has taken place. This level of statement, in the first person, will principally present the actors themselves as victims of corruption or extortion.

But in the context of ordinary political and administrative corruption, the actors involved sometimes express themselves without reticence on the meaning of their own practices.[24] In order to equip oneself to confront forms of unbridled corruption, it is better to seek to formalize the illicit exchange. Corruption

---

in the three countries. This was the first detailed and systematic anthropological study to be carried out in a group of countries on the specific topic of everyday corruption in Africa (Blundo and Olivier de Sardan 2006c).

24 As the pioneering work of de Le Vine (1990) showed, former dignitaries of the Ghanian regime described without embarrassment their criminal activities (which were legitimate in their eyes).

can then be admitted, as by this contractor in the construction field in Dakar, according to whom corruption allows private and public partners to maintain egalitarian relations:

> It is as dangerous to deal with corrupt officers as it is with honest officers. When I follow the works of the hospital of Kedougou, the engineer of town planning who is to supervise us comes in the car and arrives covered with dust, while I go in a plane. He has problems finding a place to stay, while I have my hotel. My architect has touched 7 percent while the engineer of town planning, his minister gives him nothing. And it is he who will have to approve my account! In order to avoid these hurdles, I propose to pay him 800,000 FCFA during the work, the same as my engineer. With corruption, I re-establish a correct relation of equality ... I myself am comfortable with corruption. (Blundo 2001a: 94)

Certainly, most often the passage to the stance of the narrator-corruptor/corrupted is accompanied by well-known mechanisms of auto-defense and justification, as the embarrassed words of this Senegalese policeman show:

> It happens that people pay me with cola, cigarettes, but there too, I work with them ... I chew cola, I smoke cigarettes. When they give me cola, it is to satisfy themselves ... this too, it is so that they make my job easier. I am obliged to take it, even if I do not want to, I am obliged to take .... When I am given money, I do not take ... but when the person gives me a cigarette ... that, to be honest and direct with you, I take. I could as well not answer this question. But we are Africans, I am with them.

Incontestably, the richest story would ideally be the one collected in the form of a witness or a confession, with the exception perhaps that in a court, the "interview" aims to establish the existence or not of a criminal act and determine the weight of the punishment. The declarations in corruption trials, like those obtained in the context of inquiries of "Clean Hands" in Italy, no doubt represent an unequaled source for the researcher (Della Porta 1992).

Whether they testify from personal experience or evaluate acts committed by another, or whether they come from corruptors or corrupted, victims or extortionists, moral entrepreneurs or simple citizens, the facts and words related to corruption unmask its ideological, argumentative, and symbolic landscape. On the one hand, this "popular semiology of corruption" (Blundo and Olivier de Sardan 2006b) contains the vocabulary of corruption, that is, the language codes and gestures used in the corrupt transactions, as well as the terms and expressions that designate different practices. We thus have access to the semantic field of corruption. On the other hand, it assembles the discourses and arguments by which corruption is sometimes marked, sometimes legitimized, sometimes explained. We then enter the ideological configurations around corruption, which are constructed in a constant tension between practical norms and official norms.[25]

---

[25] Works that seek to analyse the semiological dimension of discourses and the discursive interactions around corruption are rare, not to say nonexistent. Apart from the work of David Gould (1980), where the author proposes a glossary of words and local

Sometimes precise, technical, and detailed, often disillusioned and cynical, always coated with a good dose of humor, emic stories about corruption inextricably mix descriptions of procedures and value judgments, facts and interpretations. They thus have the same character as any ethnographic fact in which, according to Lenclud's portrayal, facts and values are as inseparable as the yellow and white of a beaten egg (Lenclud 1996: 11). One cannot therefore do without the specific context of their enunciation or the strategies that underlie the discourse of accusation and justification.[26]

We now come to the third part of our analysis, which concerns the staging of observational and discursive sources of description, that is, the description of corruption in the context of a scientific publication.

Writing about Corruption

For Van der Geest (1984: 88), the anthropological approach, armed with participant observation and a holistic posture, would be the best way to grasp the complex phenomenon of corruption because of the restitution of corruption in its broader social context. However, Caplan's statement (1971: 266) on the strange silence of anthropologists on a phenomenon that is widespread in most of the states in which they conduct their studies remains, with some exceptions, topical.[27] And the rare anthropological works dealing with corruption astonish by their weak recourse to fine descriptions of practices grasped in the field and by their limited variety of descriptive registers. As was mentioned above, for a large part the reason for this is that these works base themselves, as Ruud puts it, "on ethnographic data that mostly came (his) way in an incidental fashion" (Ruud 2000: 272).

One can identify four major descriptive registers in the anthropological literature on corruption: the personal anecdote, the biographical trajectory, the polyphonic case study, and the bureaucratic itinerary. Each of these registers corresponds to empirical sources of a different nature and translates levels of increasing complexity in the problematization of the object of research.

---

expressions, one can cite the analysis of content dealing with a corpus of 136 interviews with the citizens of East European countries: Ukraine, Czech Republic, Slovakia, and Bulgaria (Miller et al. 2001). But the analysis made use of extracts of interviews in an exclusively illustrative manner. The terms used by the informants are rarely left in their original language. One generally gets a synopsis constructed by the interviewer more than a verbatim quote; the result is an obvious and deplorable impoverishment of the original corpus and of its possibilities of analytical exploitation.

26 In my Senegalese field, driven by factional struggles, one always had to ask oneself whether the information on such or such an embezzlement aimed at denigrating the faction in power or the political adversary, whether it had been completely invented or whether one could attribute some basis to it. Gradually, the denunciations could thus furnish the cartography of rival political groups.

27 The same assertion of the absence of anthropological reflection on corrupting practices is made by Kondos (1987: 15).

The Anecdotal Register

The simplest descriptive figure is the one based on the anecdote lived by the researcher himself. In an ambitious text aiming to prove the porosity of frontiers between bribe and gift in Kazakh society, Cynthia Werner provides only one actual description, a personal anecdote that, from all evidence, seems greatly removed from the central theme of her article:

> I will never forget the first time I got off a plane in Kazakhstan. I was dreading the long and infamous process through passport control, customs, and baggage claim, when I jealously noticed a fellow traveler, a well-dressed Kazak, go no more than 10 steps from the bottom of the jet's stairway, across the tarmac, and into a foreign, chauffeur-driven automobile. Assuming this man must be somebody important to get around airport security and customs procedures, I asked the European businessman who sat next to me on the flight if he had any idea who this man might be. He had already spent several months in Kazakhstan, and in his opinion, the man was probably not an important political figure. Most likely, his driver had simply bribed the guards in exchange for easy tarmac access, as Kazakhstan was a place where "nothing is allowed, but everything is possible." (Werner 2000: 18)

The reason for this passage—which says more about the stereotypes of Westerners on Central Asia than about the reality of corruption in this region—could be found in the deontological preoccupations of the author, who affirms having taken the precaution of carefully hiding all information that could permit the identification of her informants. But let us not be mistaken: this anecdote, isolated in a text of mainly theoretical ambitions, reveals not so much an excess of self-censorship as an empirical inconsistency of the analysis proposed, because Werner admits: "I never directly observed any bribe-giving or bribe-receiving, and all the second-hand accounts I did manage to collect are limited to relatively small forms of corruption" (2000:15).

Biographical Trajectories

The second form of description identified stages individual trajectories. In this case, the anthropologist selects a biographical sequence that he considers of ideal value. The "heroes" of these descriptions are diverse; people in search of a job, like the Bengalis, Uttam and Kalo, one hoping for a teaching job in a primary school and the other aspiring to an administrative post in a local hospital (Ruud 2000: 275–6, 278–81), or parents coveting the admission of their young daughter to a school with a high reputation (Smith 2001: 352–3), the head of a firm who obtains a public contract thanks to the support of a relative who is director of a program in the World Bank (ibid.: 355–6), or again, a businessman who experiences the ungratefulness of a politician whose candidature he had openly supported (ibid.: 356–7). These biographical trajectories have the ambition of illustrating the "everyday forms ... of the widespread petty corruption that involves ordinary people" (Ruud 2000: 272) by showing the importance of social networks for successful access to state resources, by underlining the diffusion of local forms of political clientelism, and by reminding how norms of reciprocity are at the heart of corrupt transactions. Despite their evident relevance in retracing the strategies of actors to their social context and temporality, these descriptions remain focused on one single point of view, that of the protagonist of the story, who in most cases is a user, sometimes winner, sometimes victim, in his relations with the administration. Their "monophonic" character, it seems to me, makes the typical or ideal character of these stories problematic. This is even more so when the heterogeneity of the cases reported in a text appears to be not so much a desired strategy of diversification of experiences as a choice imposed by the limited chances of observation of cases in the researcher's circle (friends and informants).[28] Here one finds the anecdotal character of the descriptions examined above, with the only difference that the latter examples concern the locals (and not the researcher) and retrace the processes rather than focus on isolated cases, frozen in the ethnographic present. Let us note, incidentally, that despite the poor density and the unsystematic nature of data presented, the authors pretend to describe the system of corruption (even if they confine themselves to "petty corruption") on the scale of countries as vast and complex as India or Nigeria. Let us think for a moment of the welcome that would be reserved for an essay on a "noble" theme of the anthropological discipline, which would base the essentials of its analysis on hearsay and on lucky and sporadic observations.

The "Polyphonic" Case Studies

Case studies represent the third descriptive register at work in ethnographic studies of corruption. One of the most accomplished essays, that of Gupta, stages situations of interaction, the fruit of observations and interviews with the concerned actors. In one of the case studies presented, two young cultivators go to the office of a small officer, Sharmaji, responsible for issues concerning landed property in a district of Northern India. Gupta describes the context of Sharmaji's life and work with precision:

> Sharmaji lived in a small, inconspicuous house deep in the old part of town. ... The lower part of the house consisted of two rooms and a small-enclosed courtyard. One of those rooms had a large door that opened on the street. This room functioned as Sharmaji's "office." (Gupta 1995: 379)

> Two of the sidewalls of the office were lined with benches; facing the entrance toward the inner part of the room was a raised platform, barely big enough for three people. It was here that Sharmaji sat and held court, and it was here that he kept the land registers for the villages that he administered. (ibid.)

---

28 Ruud admits that Kalo "was a close friend of mine" (2000: 278) and in one of the cases reported by Smith it was he himself who was called, as a friend of the family, to intercede with the principal of the school for the admission of the young girl (2001: 352).

Surrounded by two collaborators—of whom one, Verma, is presented by Gupta as the Sharmaji's alter ego—Sharmaji manages several transactions at the same time and poses rhetorical questions to the postulants who are packed into the narrow room: "Have I said anything wrong?," "Is what I have said true or not?" (Gupta 1995: 379). It is to be noted that Gupta does not hide that Sharmaji takes advantage of the prerogatives linked to his work, particularly that of deciding land disputes: "Of course, these things "cost money," but in most cases the "rates" were well-known and fixed" (ibid.).

The static description of the decor and the actors inaugurates a second description, more dynamic, centered on what Gupta calls "a botched bribe." Two young peasants arrive at Sharmaji's house to add their name to the land deed. At first they seem decided to undertake their work without the help of Verma, Sharmaji's right arm. But Sharmaji's initially aggressive and defiant attitude—he proposes that they try and obtain their paper all by themselves: in case of failure, he will be there to help them—as well as the advice of the users present, who sing Sharmaji's praises ("a very well-connected person"—Gupta 1995: 380), end up convincing the inexperienced peasants to solicit the help of the minor official. The youth will have to "pay for it" the latter noisily announces. Meanwhile, the unfortunate do not know how much to give and Sharmaji hands over their question to Verma who plays his role of intermediary to perfection: "Give whatever amount you want to give" (ibid.). The weak offer of the poor peasants, decidedly ignorant of the world of Indian bureaucracy invites the hilarity of those present: the proposed sum, 10 rupees, is nothing compared to the official cost of the work, retorts Sharmaji. "Go and find out the cost of putting your name in the land register ... and then give Verma exactly half of that," he adds (ibid.). As no one gives them the information on the "real administrative costs," they leave the place giving up the idea of pursuing their move.

This descriptive case illustrates, according to Gupta, the central point of his argument:

> The "practice" of bribe giving was not, as the young men learned, simply an economic transaction but a cultural practice that required a great degree of performative competence. When villagers complained about the corruption of state officials, therefore, they were not just voicing their exclusion from government services because they were costly .... More important, they were expressing frustration because they lacked the cultural capital required to negotiate deftly for those services. (Gupta 1995: 381)

Unlike the individual biographical trajectories, the study of a case of interactions puts several actors on stage. It is, so to say, "polyphonic." The conditions and limits of observation are clearly stated: "when I arrived on the scene, negotiations seemed to have broken down already" (Gupta 1995: 380); "I never did find out why they wanted to add a name to the land records" (ibid.). The accent is put on the details deemed to be significant. For example, the description of the clothes worn and the aspect of the helpless peasants reinforce the impression of inadequacy before the overall power of the local State reinforced by Sharmaji:

"Their rubber slippers and unkempt hair," "Clothes that had obviously not been stitched by a tailor," and so on (ibid.). This detailed description also gives access to the semiological dimension of corrupting practices when Gupta notes the respectful tone of the peasants begging for Sharmaji's help: "*Tau* [father's elder brother], you know what's best" (ibid.).

This kind of case study, however, only deals with a particular transaction. If Gupta had multiplied his observations at Sharmaji's office, or if he had made the same observations in other administrative sites, he would no doubt have witnessed successful transactions and would have perhaps appreciated to what extent the weight of the social status of postulants determines the conclusion of the transaction or the sum to be paid. In crossing his observation notes with emic descriptive stories, he would have been capable of constructing archetypal or modal descriptions (Olivier de Sardan 2003), in this way synthesizing several singular descriptions.

Bureaucratic Itineraries

We finally come to what could be called "bureaucratic itineraries," which correspond to the fourth type of description offered by the anthropological literature on corruption. While studying the port authorities of Cotonou, envisaged as an "institutional digest of different sectors of national life considered to be sectors with a high propensity for corruption," Nassirou Bako Arifari (2001: 38f.) chose a place of observation "where it is possible to follow all forms of corruption, from high to petty, passing through intermediary forms, as well as a good part of the different networks that cross the State and society thanks to the involvement of a large number of actors from the summit to the base." On the basis of an inquiry combining loose observation and systematic observations, documentary research and non-directive interviews of a large variety of actors (customs officers, formal and informal agents, shopkeepers, importers, policemen, and so on), he offers an ideal-typical description of the steps necessary to "get a merchandise out of the port" (ibid.: 44). This itinerary consists of "nineteen steps: three in the societies of transit and deposit, five in unions and para-public structures of control and eleven inside the port customs" (ibid.: 44). Each of these steps corresponds to different sites and actors and requires the handing over of "fictive charges" (*faux frais*), a euphemism that, in the port slang, designates recourse to corruption to get the file for customs payment moving on. These successive scenes seize the individuals in full action ("operator of confiscation, … also called, …, comes forward to encash the tip, before whispering the number of his file to the user, which, in principle he should not know"—ibid.: 45). Often, the author enriches the "modal description" through the use of emic descriptions:

> For a vehicle worth 1.3 million, I declared 900,000 francs CFA. I was forced to give 100,000 francs to the visiting chief. The inspector, he did not manage to see this. So, I won 300,000 francs CFA on a vehicle. (D., itinerant customs broker—ibid.: 46)

Finally, a constant parallel is established between the steps such as they should be and the steps as they really are. This comparison, indispensable to judge the illegality of the acts without for all that, prejudging their legitimacy in the eyes of the port actors, was made possible thanks to a long documentary work on the official rules and procedures.

This last descriptive register is no doubt the most complete before the problems raised by anthropological writing about "the properties of corruption": ambivalence, concealment, and their commonplace character or processual dimension. However, here the gaze is certainly once more that of the user (potential corruptor) who meets the representatives of the local state (potentially corrupt) directly or through intermediaries. This world, the world of minor officials, bureaucrats, uniformed persons, administrative intermediaries, remains more opaque, sometimes constituting the decor, sometimes the corridors of the principal scene. The ideal would be to approach the state agent not when he is enthroned in the courtroom or crouching at the bottom of a cell, but in his specific social universe.

Conclusion

The journey proposed, between the torments of observation and the limits of the description of an object like corruption, must not conceal the fact that there are other social facts—not necessarily subjected to social or juridical reprobation—which lend themselves to this kind of methodological questioning: the experience of illness and therapeutic itineraries, the decision processes within the firm, the corridors of an electoral campaign, or even the number of livestock held by a Sahelian nomad. The example of corruption, which combines in itself alone most of the difficulties of observation and description which an empirical inquiry presents, played the role here of a magnifying glass, enlarging problems that come up commonly for an anthropology of hidden phenomena. In the instance of corruption, these objects, we have seen, raise questions about the descriptive anthropological posture, as mainly stemming from a "direct observation of behavior" (Lahire 1998: 172).

But as a specific mode of accession to the state, the universe of corruption offers to anthropological reflection a fertile perspective of exploration of concrete forms of public space, popular representations of forms of government, and daily intrusions of public power in the life of citizens. By this nature, it is a hard test for the myth of the ethnographic method based on participant observation, the unicity of the place of observation, and the practice of the native language ("tent and language," according to Jarvie's terms[29]): a "comprehensive" study of transversal phenomena, between the local and the global, asks for a multi-sited anthropology (Marcus 1995); it requires one to go from a courtroom to the corridors of an

---

29 "A tent down among the native houses so that the observer is physically close to the native life; and learning the language, not using pidgin or interpreters, so that the observer can participate in the life he wishes to observe just as it is lived" (Jarvie 1969: 505).

administrative office, from the esplanade of a port to a roadblock, and to speak different languages (that of the jurists, the slang of policemen, the unspoken words of the contractors, the proverbs and the popular maxims). Every study of corruption is therefore by definition comparative, even the most "micro" or the most sectoral: comparison between different points of view, between diverse logics of actions. Fine descriptions such as fieldwork anthropology alone is able to produce, despite the limits referred to, can unmask the ambivalence of corrupting acts and their embeddedness in daily life, which is difficult to fathom. If one of the principal functions of description is to produce the unrecorded, the unobvious, and the uncommon (Reuter 1998: 56), then the unmasking of the hidden face of the facts of corruption remains an objective in itself of a political anthropology of the contemporary state. For beyond the ethnographic description of illicit transactions and the ways in which they are locally embedded, the question is above all one of perceiving corruption for what it is, that is, a polysemous and diffused object: one of the ways of acceding to public services, a manner of accusation in politics, a "social problem" at the heart of controversial public debates and beleaguered by a gust of neoliberal reformism, in short one of the contemporary forms of governance.

References

Bako Arifari, N. (2001) La corruption au Port de Cotonou: douaniers et intermédiaires. *Politique Africaine* (83): 38–58.
Becker, H. (1963) *Outsiders: Studies in the Sociology of Deviance*. New York: The Free Press.
Bessette, J.M. (1989) La sociologie criminelle. In: P. Durand and R. Weil (eds) *Sociologie contemporaine*. Paris: Vigot: 491–509.
Blundo, G. (2001a) "Dessus de table." La corruption dans la passation des marchés publics locaux au Sénégal. *Politique Africaine* (83): 79–97.
—— (2001b) La corruption comme mode de gouvernance locale: trois décennies de décentralisation au Sénégal. *Afrique contemporaine* 199:106–18.
—— (2003) Décrire le caché. Autour du cas de la corruption. In: G. Blundo and J.-P. Olivier de Sardan (eds) *Pratiques de la description*. Paris: Editions de l'EHESS: 75–111.
—— (2006) An Ordered Corruption? The Social World of Public Procurement. In: G. Blundo and J.-P. Olivier de Sardan (with N.B. Arifari and M. Tidjani Alou) (eds) *Everyday Corruption and the State. Citizens and Public Officials in Africa*. London: Zed Books: 225–62.
Blundo, G. and J.-P. Olivier de Sardan (2000) La corruption comme terrain. Pour une approche socio-anthropologique. In: G. Blundo (ed.) *Monnayer les pouvoirs. Espaces, mécanismes et représentations de la corruption*. Paris-Geneva: PUF-IUED: 21–46.
—— (2006a) Everyday Corruption in West Africa. In: G. Blundo and J.-P. Olivier de Sardan (with N.B. Arifari and M. Tidjani Alou) (eds) *Everyday Corruption and the State. Citizens and Public Officials in Africa*. London: Zed Books: 69–109.
—— (2006b) The Popular Semiology of Corruption. In: G. Blundo and J.-P. Olivier de Sardan (with N.B. Arifari and M. Tidjani Alou) (eds) *Everyday Corruption and the State. Citizens and Public Officials in Africa*. London: Zed Books: 110–34.

—— (with N.B. Arifari and M. Tidjani Alou) (2006c) *Everyday Corruption and the State. Citizens and Public Officials in Africa*. London: Zed Books.
Bourgois, Ph. (1995) *In Search of Respect: Selling Crack in El Barrio*. Cambridge, MA: Cambridge University Press.
Caplan, L. (1971) Cash and Kind: Two Media of "Bribery" in Nepal. *Man* 6 (2): 266–78.
Chambliss, W.J. (1971) Vice, Corruption, Bureaucracy and Power. *Wisconsin Law Review* 4: 1150–73.
Chibnall, S. and P. Saunders (1977) Worlds Apart: Notes on the Social Reality of Corruption. *British Journal of Sociology* 28(2): 138–54.
Dartigues, L. and E. de Lescure (2000) La corruption, de l'"économie de bazar" au bazar de l'économie? In G. Blundo (ed.) *Monnayer les pouvoirs. Espaces, mécanismes et représentations de la corruption*. Paris-Geneva: PUF-IUED: 315–44.
Della Porta, D. (1992) *Lo scambio occulto. Casi di corruzione politica in Italia*. Bologna: Il Mulino.
Favret-Saada, J. (1977) *Les mots, la mort, les sorts*. Paris: Gallimard.
Festinger, L., H. Riecken and S. Schachter (1956) *When Prophecy Fails. A Social and Psychological Study of a Modern Group that Predicted the Destruction of the World*. Minneapolis, MN: University of Minnesota Press.
Geest, S. van der (1984) Anthropology and Pharmaceuticals in Developing Countries—II *Medical Anthropology Quarterly* 15(4): 87–90.
Geschiere, P. (2000) Sorcellerie et modernité: retour sur une étrange complicité. *Politique Africaine* 79: 17–32.
Gould, D. (1980) *Bureaucratic Corruption and Underdevelopment in the Third World: The Case of Zaire*. New York: Pergamon.
Gupta, A. (1995) Blurred Boundaries: The Discourse of Corruption, the Culture of Politics, and the Imagined State. *American Ethnologist* 22(2): 375–402.
Humphreys, L. (1970) *Tearoom Trade: Impersonal Sex in Public Places*. Chicago, IL: Aldine.
Jarvie, I.C. (1969) The Problem of Ethical Integrity in Participant Observation. *Current Anthropology* 10(5): 505–8.
Kondos, A. (1987) The Question of "Corruption" in Nepal. *Mankind* 17(1): 15–29.
Lahire, B. (1998) Décrire la réalité sociale? Place et nature de la description en sociologie. In: Y. Reuter (ed.) *La description. Théories, recherches, formation, enseignement*. Lille: Presses Universitaires du Septentrion: 171–9.
Laplantine, F. (1996) *La description ethnographique*. Paris: Nathan.
Lascoumes, P. (1999) *Corruptions*. Paris: Presses de Sciences Po.
—— (2000) Analyse des corruptions, construction d'un champ de recherche. L'exemple des Etats-Unis (1902–1980). In: G. Blundo (ed.) *Monnayer les pouvoirs. Espaces, mécanismes et représentations de la corruption*. Paris-Geneva: PUF-IUED: 47–64.
Lenclud, G. (1996) The Factual and the Normative in Ethnography. Do Cultural Differences Derive from Description? *Anthropology Today* 12(1): 7–11.
Lipsky, M. (1980) *Street-level Bureaucracy. Dilemmas of the Individual in Public Services*. New York: Russell Sage Foundation.
Marcus, G.E. (1995) Ethnography in/of the World System: The Emergence of Multi-Sited Ethnography. *Annual Review of Anthropology* 24: 95–117.
McNamara, S.C. (1986) Learning How to Bribe a Policeman. *Anthropology Today* 2(2): 2–3.

Médard, J.-F. (2001) L'évaluation de la corruption: approches et problèmes. In: J.-F. Baré (ed.) *L'évaluation des politiques de développement. Approches pluridisciplinaires*. Paris: L'Harmattan: 53–90.

Miller, W.L., A.B. Grodeland, and T.Y. Koshechkina (2001) *A Culture of Corruption? Coping with Government in Post Communist Europe*. Budapest: Central University Press.

——, Koschechkina, T.Y. and Grodeland, A. (1997) How Citizens Cope with Post communist Officials: Evidence from Focus Group Discussions in Ukraine and the Czech Republic. In: P. Heywood (ed.) *Political Corruption*. Oxford: Blackwell: 181–209.

Morice, A. (1991) Les maîtres de l'informel: corruption et modèles mafieux d'organisation sociale. In: B. Lautier, C. de Miras, and A. Morice (eds) *L'Etat et l'informel*. Paris: L'Harmattan: 143–208.

Nye, J.S. (1967) Corruption and Political Development: A Cost-Benefit Analysis. *American Political Science Review* 61(2):417–27.

Olivier de Sardan, J.-P. (1995) La politique du terrain. Sur la production de données en anthropologie. *Enquête* 1:71–109.

—— (1996) L'économie morale de la corruption en Afrique. *Politique Africaine* 63: 97–116.

—— (1998) Emique. *L'Homme* 147: 151–66.

—— (2003) Observation et description en socio-anthropologie. In: G. Blundo and J.-P. Olivier de Sardan (eds) *Pratiques de la description*. Paris: Editions de l'EHESS: 13–39.

Philp, M. (1997) Defining Political Corruption. In P. Heywood (ed.) *Political Corruption*. Oxford: Blackwell: 20–46.

Punch, M. (1989) Researching Police Deviance: A Personal Encounter with the Limitations and Liabilities of Field-Work. *The British Journal of Sociology* 40(2): 177–204.

Reuter, Y. (1998) La description en questions. In: Y. Reuter (ed.) *La description. Théories, recherches, formation, enseignement*. Lille: Presses Universitaires du Septentrion: 33–59.

Robertson, A.F. (2002) Corporate Decay. Paper presented at the *15th Anniversary Conference on Corruption*, 12–13 December, Amsterdam School for Social Science.

Rogow, A.A. and H.D. Lasswell (1966) *Power, Corruption and Rectitude*. Englewood Cliff, NJ: Prentice Hall.

Ruud, A.E. (2000) Corruption as Everyday Practice. The Public-Private Divide in Local Indian Society. *Forum for Development Studies* 2: 271–94.

Scott, J.C. (1969) The Analysis of Corruption in Developing Nations. *Comparative Studies in Society and History* 11: 315–41.

Sedlenieks, K. (2002) Latvian-Azande Parallel. Corruption as Witchcraft for Latvia during Transition. Paper presented at the *Fourth Nordic Conference of Post-Socialism*, April 2002 (http://www.anthrobase.com/Txt/S/Sedlenieks_K_01.htm).

Shore, C. and D. Haller (2005) Sharp Practice: Anthropology and the Study of Corruption. In: D. Haller and C. Shore (eds) *Corruption: Anthropological Perspectives*. London: Pluto Press: 1–26.

Smith, D.J. (2001) Kinship and Corruption in Contemporary Nigeria. *Ethnos* 66(3): 344–64.

—— (2003) Patronage, Per Diems and the "Workshop Mentality": The Practice of Family Planning Programs in Southeastern Nigeria. *World Development* 31(4): 703–15.

Smith, M.G. (1964) Historical and Cultural Conditions of Political Corruption among the Hausa. *Comparative Studies in Society and History* 6(2): 164–94.

Tanzi, V. (1998) Corruption Around the World. Causes, Consequences, Scope, and Cures. *IMF Staff Papers* 45(4).

Taussig, M. (1999) *Defacement. Public Secrecy and the Labour of the Negative*. Palo Alto, CA: Stanford University Press.

Tidjani Alou, M. (2001) La corruption chez les agents de contrôle. In: G. Blundo and J.-P. Olivier de Sardan (eds) *La corruption au quotidien en Afrique de l'Ouest. Approche socio-anthropologique comparative: Bénin, Niger et Sénégal*. EHESS-IUED-IRD, research report.

Vine, V.T. le (1990) Supportive Values of the Culture of Corruption in Ghana. In: A.J. Heidenheimer, M. Johnston, and V.T. le Vine (eds) *Political Corruption. A Handbook*. New Brunswick, NJ: Transaction Publishers: 363–73.

Weber, F. (2000) Transactions marchandes, échanges rituels, relations personnelles. Une ethnographie économique après le Grand Partage. *Genèses* 41: 85–107.

Werner, C. (2000) "Gifts, Bribes, and Development in Post-Soviet Kazakhstan. *Human Organization* 59(1):11–22.

Werner, J.-F. (1993) *Marges, sexe et drogues à Dakar. Enquête ethnographique*. Paris: Karthala-ORSTOM.

Williams, R. (1999) New Concepts for Old? *Third World Quarterly* 20(3): 503–13.

Chapter 3

Deep Corruption in Indonesia: Discourses, Practices, Histories

Heinzpeter Znoj

This chapter presents an analysis of systemic corruption in Indonesia relying on two complementary approaches. On the one hand it proposes an analysis of the discursive field of corruption: the various critical and the various legitimizing discourses about it, the dynamic between them, and the way they relate to practices labeled corrupt. I argue that the specific discursive field of corruption in Indonesia reflects its firm establishment as a systemic practice. On the other hand, the chapter offers a tentative analysis of the institutional development that resulted in systemic corruption. I will show that during the frequent political and economic crises of the young republic parts of the administration—and primarily the armed forces—increasingly relied on "non-budgetary finance," a parallel financial infrastructure drawing on illicitly acquired resources. These finances are linked in many ways to the fragmentation and lack of transparency of the government as well as to everyday forms of corruption. In conclusion I will argue that systemic corruption is a disciplining and rewarding practice that confirms the bureaucratic hierarchies. While it undermines the legitimacy of the administration and the prospects of its democratic control, it does not in itself make the Indonesian bureaucracy unstable or inefficient. Systemic corruption as exemplified by the Indonesian case should therefore be understood as a constitutive element of a specific type of governance system.

Indonesia is today universally considered to be one of the most corrupt countries in the world (Transparency International 2006). The extent of corruption in the administration and its all-pervasive effects in the political, legal, and economic fields have led commentators to look at it not as an occasional lapse in orderly bureaucratic proceedings, but as systemic, that is, as an integral part of the functioning of the administration. In this chapter I follow the definition of systemic corruption offered by Stefes (2005: 6):

> Systemic corruption is characterized by extensive corrupt activities, such as bribery, extortion, and embezzlement, ranging from petty to grand corruption. Corruption becomes the rule rather than the exception. Moreover, systemic corruption is characterized by the presence of rules and norms that are commonly known and adhered to by most officials and citizens most of the time. These rules and norms are informal insofar as they are neither explicitly codified nor externally enforced. They nevertheless shape the interests and strategies of public officials and citizens. In short,

systemic corruption is characterized both by the magnitude of corrupt activities and the presence of rules and norms that inform these activities.

To analyze corruption in Indonesia as systemic means to conceive of it as social practice rather than individual offense. The question must therefore be: what are the structural conditions and the established rules and expectations that make corrupt practices inescapable for Indonesian officials and their clients? This question calls for empirical social scientific and historical investigations into practices that are, as bluntly and routinely as they are carried out, nevertheless illegal. The nature of the available data is for this reason precarious: Rumors, denouncements, and denials abound, but well-documented cases remain scarce. Methodologically, a social anthropological approach seems appropriate to deal with this kind of data. An analysis of the accessible discourses about corruption, combined with a historical study of "non-budgetary" government finance, especially of the military, provides a clear and consistent picture of the social and political logic of systemic corruption in Indonesia.[1]

In 1998, Indonesia, the country hit hardest by the Asian crisis, was on the brink of bankruptcy and political chaos. The breakdown of a number of banks under the burden of immense credits that private and state-owned banks had granted members of the political elite without sufficient security devalued the national currency, the Rupiah, to a fourth of its previous exchange rate and thus instantly impoverished millions of Indonesians. Student activists organized massive protests against the regime of President Suharto whom they held responsible for the crisis. The IMF and the World Bank eventually bailed the country out and refinanced the banking system, but not before urging the president to step down. They insisted on institutional reforms like decentralization and the strengthening of legislative bodies in order to improve governance and fiscal discipline and—specifically—to reduce rampant corruption in the administration, which they saw as the structural cause of the crisis. A few years earlier, a World Bank report had estimated the rate of graft on projects financed by the Bank in Indonesia at 20 to 30 percent (quoted in Goodpaster 2002: 95). International investors were no longer willing to support a regime that had become predatory not only within its own country but also toward its foreign allies and creditors (Jomo 2003).

The dramatic downfall of Suharto in 1998 ended three decades of military dictatorship. Suharto had assumed power in 1965 in a coup against the first president of the Republic, Soekarno. He was backed by the US, which had suspected Soekarno's Indonesia would have become another satellite of the communist side. It was the uncritical support of Suharto's anti-communist "new order" regime by the Western powers and investors that allowed the country to rebuild a run-down economy. Western support continued even as Suharto developed an ever more dictatorial rule, eliminating hundreds of thousands

---

1 The research project "Indonesian corruption in context," 2001–2003, was generously financed by the Swiss Science Foundation. I wish to thank my Indonesian research assistant and collaborators, who prefer not to be quoted under their real names. They carried out most interviews and data-gathering.

of communist leaders and party-members in a gruesome massacre in 1965, systematically suppressing political opposition, leading civil wars in Aceh and West Papua, annexing East Timor, and recklessly enriching himself and his closest followers (Crouch 1988).

The end of Suharto's "new order" opened the stage for a decidedly more democratic period, the "reform era." In short order, four presidents succeeded each other. B.J. Habibie, Suharto's vice-president, lasted one year. Abdurrahman Wahid, the leader of the Muslim mass organization *Nahdatul Ulama*, became the first democratically elected president in 1999. He attempted some daring measures to reduce the still dominant influence of the armed forces and to curb corruption, but after two years was himself chased from office amid charges of nepotism and graft. He was followed in 2001 by Megawati Soekarnoputri, Soekarno's daughter. Under her weak rule, which lasted three years, the old army-based power elite steadily regained control of political life. In 2004, General Susilo Bambang Yudhoyono was democratically elected as her successor.

The alliance of internal opposition leaders and global financial organizations may well have been able to change the rules of Indonesia's political life after 1998, but it was incapable of fundamentally altering the functioning of the bureaucracy in its interaction with the political and economic elite. Within a few months of the "reform era" the democratic reforms stalled due to the deeply entrenched system of corruption (Assegaf 2002). Newly-elected legislators soon turned out to be as susceptible to bribes as the mighty bureaucrats of the former Suharto regime had been. They could design new laws that profited those who paid for them. State capture, which had been the privilege of a circumscribed circle of businessmen and members of the Suharto family, took new, quasi-democratic forms (Bertrand 1999b). And the new semi-autonomous regional governments soon learned such skills as "shopping for money" (*belanga uang*)[2] at the central government's ministry of finance. They would bribe the minister of finance to receive an increase for their city's or province's budget by offering him a kickback on this "bought" money.

All this occurred in an environment of great political openness, public criticism of the administration, and seemingly universal commitment to establishing a clean and accountable government. How is it possible that public criticism of corruption and legal measures against it had so little effect? To answer this question I will next present a short history of public criticism of corruption in Indonesia as well as an analysis of the dynamic between critical and legitimizing discourses about corruption.

The Discursive Field of Corruption

Discourses are answers to political problems—or denials of such problems—and in their rhetoric themselves function as part of politics. Departing from Foucault's

---

2   The term was used in a focus group interview with four young officials carried out by Budi (an alias), a project collaborator, in March 2002.

interest in the relationship of knowledge and power, the question then is: what knowledge and whose knowledge come to be held true in public and political institutions (Foucault 1971; Schwab-Trapp 2001)? The discourse-analytic approach I am using here assumes that a set of discourses within a discursive formation compete with one another—quoting, parodying, superseding, and correcting each other and thereby making power relations visible (Oester 1996). Concretely, I assume that the discursive field of corruption in Indonesia expresses the ways power is yielded in the interactions between state institutions and citizens.

Criticism of corruption in Indonesia is almost as old as the republic that declared independence in 1945. Early in 1950 the first vice-president of the young nation, Mohammad Hatta, declared that Indonesia had developed "a culture of corruption." This should not be understood as a statement that no corruption existed under Dutch rule. For instance, it is known that Dutch officials received lavish retirement gifts from plantation owners. These gifts reflect the generalized collusion between European planters and the ruling Dutch administration on which the colonial state was built. At the same time, the fact that these gifts were given at retirement, when the officials could no longer return the favor, seems to indicate that routine bribery did not figure prominently in the ongoing interaction between state and colonial citizens. Indeed, the Dutch colonial government was criticized by contemporaries primarily as exploitative, racist, and deeply unjust—but not as corrupt in a legal sense. I take it that Hatta perceived that with independence there came a change in the scale, frequency, and style of corruption.

Mohammad Hatta was considered the moral conscience of the country during a period of political factionalism, increasingly authoritarian rule, and abuse of power by President Soekarno's government. Soekarno's successor Suharto appointed him as a member of the Commission of Four, set up in 1970 to propose remedies against corruption (Alatas 1999: 65, 68). Ever since Hatta's famous words, all successive Indonesian presidents have promised to make the fight against corruption a priority of their government. And ever since, critical intellectuals have found ways to expose the contradiction between the proposed ideals and the continued corrupt practices of the country's leaders, and have pointed out the demoralizing effects of this ambiguity on the whole government apparatus. Indonesia's eminent writer Pramoedya Ananta Toer exemplified this mechanism already in his novel *Korupsi* ([1954] 2002) about the moral demise of a petty official. In a similar way, Mohtar Lubis took up the theme in short stories during the 1960s, and later in a scientific book on corruption he co-edited with James C. Scott in 1985 (Lubis and Scott 1985).

Many people persistently and openly criticized Suharto's massively corrupt regime, even if this meant risking their freedom and even their lives. Among these critics were intellectuals like Onghokam (1983); outspoken lawyers like Andy Hamzah (1984) and Baharuddin Lopa (2001), who became, in succession, Attorney General and Minister of Justice after Suharto's downfall; journalists, most prominently the editor of the weekly *Tempo*, Goenawan Mohammad; as well as leaders of religious organizations, such as Amien Rais (1999). Criticism against corruption was so prevalent during Suharto's rule that the dictator was repeatedly forced to silence his most daring critics—most blatantly in 1994 when he closed down a number of periodicals, among which was Goenawan Mohammad's *Tempo*. Apart from suppressing criticism against his regime and the widespread corruption, Suharto's strategy was also to influence and steer this criticism. In the early 1970s, when massive student protests against Suharto's military dictatorship made corruption a central political issue, he set up the aforementioned Commission of Four, and parliament subsequently passed a first series of laws specifically directed against corruption. Apart from occasional show trials against lower bureaucrats, these laws were hardly ever applied. During the 1990s until his downfall in 1998, as a shamelessly kleptocratic inner circle around the President attracted not only increasingly angry comments in the Indonesian press but was singled out in the global debate about good governance, he reacted by leading his own phony anti-corruption campaign (Assegaf 2002).

Eventually, corruption allegations became so strong that they played a significant role in his removal from office. To assess the significance of the critical discourses about corruption in this process it is revealing to follow Amien Rais's political career, which rested on his opinion-leadership, since the demise of *Tempo* in 1994, in the oppositional criticism of corruption. Rais attacked Suharto with the authority of a professor of political science at the Universitas Gajah Mada and as the leader of the Muslim mass organization *Muhammadiyah*. In 1993 he wrote a series of newspaper columns in which he advanced the view that there are three different kinds of corruption, namely corruption proper or extortion, collusion, and nepotism (Rais 1999). This notion gave rise to the popular acronym KKN, which stands for *Korupsi, Kolusi dan Nepotisme*. By thus re-labeling corruption, Rais managed to blend a variety of criticisms and to unite the opposition against Suharto under the banner of the fight against corruption. His prominence as the leading voice of a both differentiating and popular critical discourse about corruption allowed him to gather a large following in Indonesia and at the same time to be taken seriously by the country's international creditors wishing to see Suharto replaced.

Amien Rais's initiative can be traced back to 1993. Early in that year he visited the University of Chicago—where he had received his doctorate—and noticed the rise of the "good governance" paradigm in political science, international policy-making circles, and American foreign policy, which blamed systemic corruption for a lack of government accountability, legal insecurity, and underdevelopment. Drawing his inspiration also from the *Mani Pulite* movement in Italy, which had ended the long-term rule of the *Democrazia Christiana*, he realized the potential of an oppositional anti-corruption campaign against Suharto's decades-old dictatorship. Immediately after this visit to the United States, he presented his views on corruption in newspaper columns, interviews, and public speeches (Rais 1999). True to its Western sources, Rais's analysis of corruption in Indonesia was consistently secular and scientific. But he never forgot also to quote passages referring to corruption from the Qur'an and from the writings of the medieval Persian philosopher al-Ghazali. His blending of a secular and a civic Islamic discourse about corruption made him an accepted mediator between religious and secular critics of the regime. Eventually, he became a key player in bringing down Suharto in 1998 and was rewarded with the post of Speaker of the National Assembly.

Amien Rais's case also points toward the global roots of the 1990's wave of criticism of corruption in Indonesia. Analyzing the manifold manifestations of this wave leads one to recognize that Indonesian political thinking about corruption has essentially adopted ideas that circulate globally and has fused these with local concepts of justice. In the following section I turn to the various critical discourses about corruption that have developed since the 1990s.

Critical Discourses about Corruption

Newspaper editorials, opinion columns, and official reports employ different sets of vocabularies and metaphors in the representation of corruption and display different views about its causes and possible remedies. Broadly speaking, five critical discourses can be distinguished.

First there is what I call the neoliberal discourse, which can regularly be found in, for instance, the economy section of the leading national newspaper *Kompas*. This discourse describes corruption as an informal market in services to circumvent inefficient over-regulation by the state. The less bureaucracy, the less opportunity for corruption, so the general message goes. This opinion and its corresponding economic vocabulary are today promoted by the World Bank and the IMF in their publications and in their policy advice to governments in the East and in the South. In Indonesia it is mostly newspapers and magazines with an entrepreneurial readership that have adopted this discourse.

Second, there is an official state discourse, which can be clearly distinguished from the neoliberal discourse and in contrast demands stronger state institutions, their public auditing and democratic supervision, and their immunity against private lobbying. Rather than promoting economic growth and market liberalization as the most important means to overcome the deep-rooted penchant for state-capture in Indonesia, it pleads for well-paid, professional, and clean personnel who identify with the ideals of democracy, the rule of law, and accountability of all state institutions, above all the armed forces and the legal system. These demands partly overlap with the "good governance" agenda promoted by the international financial institutions.

Third, there is also a well-articulated civic religious discourse, which demands a strong civil society in a secular state and which regards the various religions as indispensable sources of a general moral attitude, out of which civic virtues are expected to grow. It deems a religiously inspired, morally firm civil society the only source of successful resistance against the "social disease" of corruption.

A fourth consistent critical discourse about corruption that can be clearly distinguished from all others is in the register of Islamist mobilization. In this discourse, corruption is described as an "evil" and a "sin," and the only measure against it likely to succeed is believed to be the reorganizing of public life according to religious principles. Islamist movements in Indonesia use the criticism against corruption to call for the introduction of the *sharia* and the promotion of Islam to Indonesia's exclusive state religion.

And finally, there is a popular critical discourse about corruption. Its vocabulary is drastic and vivid: politicians and bureaucrats always "eat" or "steal" ordinary people's money. It offers a simple analysis and, instead of remedies, sheer fatalism: as soon as anyone holds a public office they will take part in enriching themselves. But in the end fate always catches up with these people. They and their family members may get sick or die prematurely. In the afterlife their sins will be weighed against them.

These five critical discourses about corruption are all internally consistent and immediately recognizable by the kinds of examples of corruption they routinely offer, by the theories of the causes and effects of corruption that they refer to, and by their specific vocabularies—their semantics. While often being employed in interpretive conflicts, they do not necessarily contradict each other in every respect. In part, they put forward complementary arguments. The important difference between them is that they emphasize those aspects of corruption that violate the underlying political, social, or religious values of the discourse. The various political groups in the country instrumentalize the criticism of corruption to promote their own values and ideologies. Individual politicians though may engage in various discourses, opportunistically adapting to changing contexts and catering to a heterogeneous audience. Amien Rais, for instance, may typically engage in the official state discourse in the diagnostic first part of a column but end it with a moral conclusion that draws on the register of the civic religious discourse.

Legitimizing Discourses about Corruption

Public political statements on corruption are thus usually consistently critical, clearly reflecting the underlying ideology or ideologies. In contrast, private everyday statements on corruption typically reveal a much higher degree of ambivalence, the speakers incessantly switching between different critical and legitimizing discursive registers or repertoires—as for instance in the following interview.

In August, 2001, my collaborator Laila Khalid and myself talked to Sulfwan,[3] a young, low-level official of the department of religious affairs of one district of Yogyakarta. We discussed the question whether Suharto's downfall had led to a decrease of corruption. Sulfwan first described in detail that his colleagues at the department's fear of negative reports in the press and of legal sanctions was an efficient check on any potential plans to engage in corrupt activities. This fear had markedly increased since the reform era after the fall of Suharto. At least in his department, Sulfwan said, it had led to a considerable decrease in corruption. A little later I asked—in a paradoxical intervention—what would have to happen for corruption to decrease considerably in Indonesia. He replied that it would probably remain on similarly high levels as today for another 50 years.

---

3   Both names are aliases.

The problem could only be overcome if all Indonesians became more religious. They would then act according to moral premises. The idea that corruption could be overcome by paying officials higher salaries or by sanctioning it more severely was wrong, for no institutional changes can check the greed for money, which is the motive for all corruption—only increased religious devotion can help each official overcome his greed. After a while Sulfwan developed the argument, saying that even religious people would often be corrupt—and thus reveal themselves as not religious enough. He even admitted having himself taken from the project money destined for religious educational books for the villages. Such project money would get "tired" in the offices of the department and would hardly leave it again on its destined path. We all laughed at this jocular confession. Since all the others equally took of this "tired" money, he continued, he himself regarded it as only "half-*haram*," half-forbidden money. Finally, on a more serious note, he defended his own embezzling, arguing that even as an official in the department of religious affairs he could not escape the social pressure to pay for expensive status symbols and to help needy relatives out of such additional income.

Analyzing this interview, which lasted about an hour, a variety of discourses can be identified that shaped Sulfwan's answers in succession. He started out with the official state discourse, according to which corruption of government employees means the undermining of the state's legitimacy. As a state official he showed his loyalty to the current administration by denying that corruption is still a contemporary practice. In the context of the interview as a whole, Sulfwan's initial self-imposed taboo on open information about corrupt practices is pivotal. The entire conversation circles around this taboo until it is finally broken. Asked about his own judgment about the future of corruption in Indonesia he first drew on the critical Islamic discourse but immediately switched to a number of legitimizing discourses. The breaking of the taboo announced itself when Sulfwan criticized his own in-group at the department of religious affairs, conceding that even religious people are occasionally corrupt. The actual breaking of the taboo occurs when he admits—euphemistically—that he himself occasionally takes his share of the "tired money"[4] (*uang lelah*) in his office. The laughter of all participants of the conversation sanctions the breaking of the taboo. Adding that such money is only "half-*haram*" he reasserted the validity of Islamic norms in a tongue-in-cheek way. He closes his statement with rationalizing arguments that legitimize corruption with structural constraints, contradicting all his earlier critical statements.

"Tired money" is only one of many euphemistic metaphors Indonesian officials and their clients use in colloquial statements to refer to the widespread practices of graft and extortion, which from a legal point of view fall into the category of corruption. Other metaphors are "mutual help" (*tolong-menolong*), "gift" (*hadiah*), "tip" (*uang rokok*), "understanding" (*pengertian*), "volunteering" (*sukarelah*), "cooperation" (*bekerjasama*), "to take one's share" (*mengambil bagian*), "wet" and "dry" spots (*tempat basah, tempat kering*) with a high or low potential for corrupt income or, in connection with corrupt judges, "knocking money" (*uang*

---

4   The term is here used with the meaning of embezzled project money.

ketok).[5] While some of these euphemisms are commonly understood, others are in-group specific.

Most interviews with officials followed a pattern similar to the one described above. Regularly, after about half-an-hour or three-quarters of an hour, a sudden and complete transition occurred from official and critical discourses to pragmatic and legitimizing ones. Laughing loudly and occasionally clapping our thighs to invite us to laugh with them, our interview partners would then offer a series of euphemistic metaphors for corruption and confess that they took part in such transactions. These three elements mark the group of legitimizing discourses: the euphemistic metaphors; the laughter of the officials that goes along with them—and which contrasts with the unwavering seriousness of the critical discourses; and the excuse of corruption by pointing to structural constraints.

The Intertextuality of Discourses about Corruption

In this section I highlight the intertextual connectedness of the various critical and legitimizing discourses and suggest that this intertextuality reflects an overall ordering of the discursive field that is functional to the establishment of systemic corruption. Critical discourses mostly describe corruption in an abstract code and conceptualize it as an individual—or collective—deviance from an ideal norm. The code of everyday language is conspicuously absent in most of their variants—the only exception being the popular discourse. Conversely, legitimizing discourses do use everyday language and refer in euphemistic ways to what is alternatively called corruption. The use of the concepts of "corruption," "extortion," or "KKN"—although implicitly evoked by their conspicuous avoidance—would be deemed "impossible" in a legitimizing statement.

This intertextuality of critical and legitimizing discourses about corruption is constantly reproduced by the "linguistic habitus" (Bourdieu 1987) that Indonesian bureaucrats and, to various degrees, the Indonesian public as a whole, have internalized and that involves the practical knowledge as to what may properly be said about corruption, with what words, to whom, and under which circumstances. The language of one context is "unfit" (*tidak cocok*) for the other and vice versa. This precise practical knowledge would be impossible if the various discourses were not intimately related to one another. The term "corruption" is synonymous with the terms "sin" or "evil" in one discourse, with the term "social disease" in another, and the term "mutual help" in a third. One expression goes along with a certain type of example and a certain type of explanation, and they all find their counterparts in the other discourses. In this dynamic intertextuality, the different discourses refer to each other and compete with each other. Roland Barthes's (1957, 1967) structural analysis of everyday myths formed an important starting point for such an uncovering of intertextual relationships among

---

5 The popular semiology of corruption is a rich but as yet little researched topic, which lends itself—like the study of corruption in general—to comparative research (see, for example, Blundo and Olivier de Sardan 2001).

discourses. Scientific discourses about corruption are part of the intertextual field, for above all sociological, historical, and social anthropological statements about corruption—especially if they explain corruption by social and cultural constraints—may be incorporated into the legitimizing discourses.

Following Michel Foucault who looks at discourses as constitutive of official truths that serve those in power, one would perhaps expect those in power to engage only in the official, critical state discourse about corruption, whereas subversive discourses about corruption that question the official truth would be employed by marginalized people. Yet, the legitimizing discourses about corruption that subvert the authority of the state, with all their obliqueness, their metaphorical code, their parody and populism, are also widely employed by those in power.

This shows that the discursive field of corruption is thus too complex to simply oppose official (critical) and subversive (legitimizing) ways of talking and writing about corruption. Indonesian officials use both critical and legitimizing discourses in strategic ways. As I will show in the next section, the Indonesian power elites—in the armed forces, for instance—use legitimizing discourses to mobilize and discipline their following, while in their public statements they denounce corruption.

Bourdieu (1982, 1984) focuses on sociologically significant distinctions of speaking and explains them through economic and cultural competition among social groups. The "fine distinctions" our interview partners made between legitimate and illegitimate forms of corruption and forms of "taking one's part," can be used to identify the social group to which they feel they belong. They use critical discourses to identify with one of the main ideological currents, and they invoke legitimizing ones to identify with a class or a strategic group (Hänni 2006). They legitimize the prevalent forms of corruption in their own social field, but readily criticize those forms current in other social fields—and even more so those in other classes. For this reason, "distinguished" ways of talking about corruption—and the "distinguished" corrupt practices themselves—function as codes of belonging to a certain social field. For officials in a certain department such distinguished codes serve simultaneously as legitimation of their own enrichment and as coercion to participate in order not to be treated as an obnoxious or even dangerous outsider.

The expression "half-*haram*" excuses embezzlement specifically for the group of religious officials, as does the use of the Arabic *fulus* (money) when alluding to informal payments. The same expressions would be out of place among members of the armed forces. An army unit at the north coast of Java, in contrast, uses the term "scooping" and calls its territory the "scooping pond" (*seseran*).[6] The extortion of protection money from the many shrimp farms of the area—about €4,000 per month[7] per farm—has given rise to this expression, which has become an exclusive code for extortion within this unit. Taking turns, corporals would

---

[6] The information related to this territorial unit of the armed forces has been provided by the project collaborator Budi (alias).
[7] Or IDR 35 million in 2001.

be sent on a "scooping" tour by their superiors. The use of euphemisms by the superiors integrates the corrupt practices into the command structure of the armed forces, since the use of such colloquial expressions excludes the possibility of criticizing the practice or even using the term "corruption" within the unit. The euphemisms and the practices they refer to thus help to reproduce the strong group cohesion of the military unit.

While legitimizing discourses about corruption are a reaction to public criticism, they are not addressed to the public but to in-groups engaging in corrupt practices and to "friends" invited to understand them. The legitimizing discourses primarily contribute to solidarity and cohesion within the in-group. They constitute an understanding among members of in-groups of how corruption should be properly carried out, about the hierarchies that have to be respected while doing so, and about the prestige to be gained by successful organizers of such practices. Their justification thus reveals crucial aspects of the social organization of systemic corruption.

The euphemistic, humorous metaphors of the legitimizing discourses seduce, reassure, and discipline officials in a community. Their vocabulary expresses clear expectations as to the roles to be played by officials in various positions. Inferiors and newcomers should not play "Mr Clean" by refusing their part. But neither should they surpass their peers and superiors in corrupt income, let alone in the display of the resulting wealth: this would make them less "likable" (*kurang disukai*). Superiors should not be "bitter" (*pahit*) by keeping the proceeds of corruption for themselves, but "sweet" (*manis*) and let their subordinates, their "followers" (*anak buah*), benefit. A stingy boss may be mobbed by his subordinates. Successful and generous providers of such additional income, in contrast, are admired for their personal power, bravado, and manliness. Female officials in turn should not show too much initiative in corruption—this is deemed "unfeminine." Their proper place is rather as a cashier and bookkeeper of informal office income.[8]

The Discursive Dynamic: Tabooing and Exposing Corruption

While critical and legitimizing discourses are represented as opposites, they are nevertheless connected to each other in a dynamic way. Four of the critical discourses about corruption share the preference for an abstract, normative code: corruption is called by an acronym, KKN, and described—depending on the ideological register in which the criticism is offered—as a social disease, an individual sin, an administrative dysfunction, or a market distortion. With the exception of the popular discourse, the critical discourses avoid everyday language, in which corruption is referred to in graphic, drastic, and morally ambivalent terms. To illustrate the tension between official statements and everyday language I present a short analysis of a section of President Megawati

---

8 Gender aspects of corruption remain largely understudied. Laila Khalid's research on the department of religious affairs in Yoyakarta is a rare exception.

Sukarnoputri's presentation of her government's program in August 2001 at the national assembly.

Her speech contained an example of the rigidly tabooing critique of corruption. She described it as a serious and grave problem and made the fight against it one of the five priorities of her administration. Like every other high-ranking politician she consistently avoided any reference to concrete corrupt practices and to the humorous everyday jargon connected to them. In the grave and stately speech she would have hopelessly undermined the credibility of her intention to fight corruption had any reference to "wet" ministries, "sweet" heads of department, or "knocking money" slipped in. While pledging her full commitment to fight corruption in the most general terms, she refused to address the everyday experience of corruption.

The special occasion of Megawati's speech seemed to demand a rhetoric that would distinguish her own determination to fight against corruption from that of countless previous speeches by other politicians, bureaucrats, and intellectuals. She chose to do so by evoking the only moment in Indonesian history when the state's power in the hands of a president had achieved totalitarian measures. This had been the months immediately after Suharto's rise to power when he ordered the mass killing of alleged communists in his measures to "eradicate communism down to its deepest roots." In analogy to the anti-communist rhetoric of the Suharto era, Megawati promised to use all her authority as the new president to "eradicate" corruption down to its "deepest roots." Thus assimilating her vocabulary and metaphors to Suharto's, Megawati paralleled her intended fight against corruption with Suharto's successful fight against communism. But contrary to Suharto's campaign, which had spread terror all over Indonesia and ruined the lives of millions, the rhetoric overkill in Megawati Soekarnoputri's programmatic speech hardly troubled the peace of heart of the bureaucrats in her administration. It was so exaggerated and so completely unlikely to be followed up by the corresponding Suharto-like cleansing of the bureaucracy from "corrupt elements" that it simply lacked credibility.

Her speech exemplifies the way the rigid official critique of corruption is tied to its tacit endorsement in practice. The fact that Megawati carefully avoided any reference to concrete corrupt practices means that she stayed within the established limits of public criticism of corruption. This was a most reassuring message between the lines for Indonesian officials—and a great disappointment for those who had believed in her will to reform the administration. Her extreme and unrealistic rhetoric merely compensated the vagueness of her actual plans to fight corruption.[9]

The contradiction between the official commitment to fight it and its condoning in practice on all levels of the administration makes the discursive control in talking about corruption a crucial element in the self-representation of the bureaucrats and the political class. It is highly significant that, with very few exceptions, bureaucrats and politicians continue to publicly denounce corruption

---

9 This analysis is based on the observations of the project collaborator Suwawan (an alias).

in a ritualized and abstract fashion, painstakingly avoiding straightforward and concrete expressions. The control of the discursive field of corruption by the administration thus involves the firm establishment of a taboo on speaking publicly about it in the language of its everyday experience. The strength of this taboo is well illustrated by the fact that also ordinary people, who have nothing to gain from it, tend to respect this taboo when talking publicly about corruption—thus unwittingly displaying their complicity with those who have an interest in keeping corruption in place.

Interestingly, just as the repressed truth about corrupt practices breaks through in many everyday discussions about it, and may then be accompanied by laughter, the official, normative criticism of corruption in the press is regularly subverted by jokes, satirical columns, and cartoons. They "translate" public statements of politicians and bureaucrats against corruption into a plain everyday language that reveals their hollowness. In cartoons, for instance, bureaucrats are often depicted publicly denouncing corruption while receiving a bribe behind their backs. These satirical textual and pictorial genres unveil the hypocrisy of the "serious" critique of corruption, which nevertheless all newspapers also engage in. Only under the guise of "un-seriousness" and light humor is it possible to publicly subvert the discursive regime about corruption.

The fact that the critique of corruption is tied to a taboo on publicly talking about it as an everyday experience is arguably a major obstacle to more efficient forms of critique. It namely prevents the practical knowledge of virtually all Indonesians about corruption from entering the public debate about it. Exposing the taboo on plain language about corrupt practices in public as well as the hidden continuities between public denouncements of corruption and systemic corruption might help to bring about an acknowledgment of the problem that is closer to the everyday experience of those involved in it. But discourses would not be those powerful ordering principles of speech, thought, and practice, which Foucault (1971) showed them to be, if this were so easily possible. Open debate about these issues will become possible only with the weakening of the power base of the current political system.

The Institutional Framework of Systemic Corruption in Indonesia

The intertextual relationship among discourses either condoning or condemning corruption reveals the actual operation of corruption in Indonesia. The first part of this chapter showed that the legitimizing discourses about corruption reveal a prestige system linked to its practice that fully supports the formal hierarchy of the administration, including the gender hierarchy that is incorporated in it. One's status in the administrative hierarchy determines the degree to which one can exert one's power as an individual official for the purpose of private enrichment. Systemic corrupt practices thus do not contradict the formal organization of the bureaucracy. They rather serve to stabilize it, since they are a means to discipline and reward the bureaucracy. Contrary to what seems to be taken for granted in the current debate about corruption, systemic corruption in the administration does not undermine the state as a whole—it may leave the administration more or less intact and make it even more powerful.

The organs of the Indonesian state—and above all the armed forces, as I will show in this part—thus fall into a category that seems to defy Max Weber's ([1922] 1976) ideal type of a rational administration: they are disciplined but at the same time deeply corrupt, they are capable of functioning efficiently even if they keep bending the rules that should govern their procedures, and they partly act in the public interest, although their more immediate aims are self-serving.

This part offers an admittedly tentative analysis of the institutional framework of systemic corruption from which the everyday forms of corruption and, ultimately, the discursive order about corruption derive. I call this framework "deep corruption," to connote the unsolved structural contradictions that have shaped Indonesia's history since its beginning as an independent state. But the choice of expression is of course also an allusion to Clifford Geertz's (1972) "Deep Play." In this famous essay he showed that in cockfights, Balinese distinguish between a superficial and a deep kind of betting. Bystanders would bet "superficially" on the cock they think will win, in order to make a personal gain. Those who bet in the inner circle around the cockpit, though, will always bet "deeply" on the cock of the owner they are obliged to or with whom they are supposed to identify in relation to the owner of the opposing cock. Co-villagers bet on "their" cock if it opposes a cock from another village, even if it is likely to loose. To the outsider, betting on cocks in Bali at first seems a straightforwardly individual enterprise, in which each bettor tries to maximize his personal gain. In fact, though, "deep" betting on cocks additionally reflects meanings, identities, and solidarities in a complexly factionalized social world. One may win or lose prestige in betting. To bet well and win money, in Bali, one has to invest one's money into group identities as much as into winning chances. In a similar way, corruption in Indonesia may seem to the outsider to be a straightforwardly profit-maximizing individual or group enterprise. But in fact, corruption also has a "deep dimension," in which the participants build group identities and solidarities—and even institutions—and in which prestige, obligation, and power are at stake.

"Non-budgetary" Government Finance

Critical discourses about corruption in Indonesia tend to represent corruption as individual acts committed in office in pursuit of private interests, rather than as also including institutionalized practices by which officials pursue a complex mixture of private, in-group, and public interests. This is the reason why the practice of what is euphemistically called "non-budgetary" government finance (*dana non bujeter*) is surprisingly little discussed in the context of corrupt practices, even though it is crucial in the production of systemic corruption.

A few commentators, however, have turned their attention to the widespread existence, enormous extent, and negative political consequences of "non-budgetary" financing of government institutions. Certain powerful government agencies—apart from the armed forces most famously the national strategic food agency *Bulog*—rely on huge "non-budgetary" finance in activities they do not wish to be held accountable for (Aditjondro 2000; Ascher 1997; Goodpaster 2002). The main purposes of this parallel financial infrastructure, also referred to as "war chests," is to avoid the control of parliament and the ministry of finance and to enhance the power of competing government institutions as well as help their leaders in pursuing their political aims.

In their everyday practice, government departments use their "war chests" to exercise influence in their interaction with other departments—just like ordinary citizens do in their interactions with the administration. One young former student activist, who was employed as a junior official in the state secretariat stated in an interview[10] how on his very first mission he had been surprised and ashamed to be handed envelopes containing a month's wages in each of the three offices he stepped into. The state secretariat was at that time in the process of rewriting the law regulating the special economic zones throughout the country, and the provincial governments tried to reclaim some of the competences they had lost when Suharto introduced special economic zones under the direct control of the central government. Both the provincial governments and the central authority tried to influence the bureaucrats drafting the law on their field trip—and the stakes were high.

Generally, officials everywhere in Indonesia have their "value" according to their status in the administration and the role their institution plays in important decisions. They receive smaller or larger amounts of money according to their "value" during their visit in a "host" office. At different occasions, they have to provide envelopes to be handed over to important guests from other ministries. These envelopes contain money from what in one case was called "account seventeen"—a code referring to the "war chest" of the institution. This mutual "generosity" with inter-institutional bribes in the higher levels of the Indonesian administration appears to be routinized and compulsory. Envelopes have to be given and in turn have to be accepted. When the above-mentioned junior official tried to refuse what he considered his first bribe, his counterpart implored him to accept it—for he was sure to lose his own lucrative position if his failure to bribe the junior official became known to his superiors. The superior and mentor of the young official later reprimanded him to accept such envelopes without further ado: "We take what is offered to us—but we don't ask for anything." There was never any further word about these bribes.

The Charitable Foundations of the Armed Forces

The most striking example of "non-budgetary" finance in Indonesia are the "charitable foundations" of the armed forces. The Indonesian armed forces entertain countless of these "non-profit" foundations, which administer the extra-budgetary income from military-owned enterprises, ranging from large-scale extortion of private enterprises, the illicit sale of the country's mineral resources (especially oil), the diversion of finances from the official budget, and the sale of study places at the military academy, to intra-governmental bribery and,

---

10 The interview was conducted by the author in Yogyakarta, in August 2001.

during the Cold War, secret payments by Western governments. The military's share of the official budget amounts to less than 2 per cent of the state's yearly expenses—a small sum compared to most other countries' defense budget. But its "non-budgetary" finance has been estimated to amount to a multiple of its official finance (Crouch 1988; Bertrand 1999a; Goodpaster 2002: 98). In this way the military escapes public accountability for the funding of some of its operations (Aditjondro 2000). The same strategy can also be found in the civil administration where individual agencies shore up "war chests," of which they dispose in their corporate interest.

The accumulation of non-budgetary finance in "charitable foundations" has helped the Indonesian armed forces to establish themselves as an increasingly powerful "state-in-the-state" from the beginning of the Indonesian Republic. The various units of the armed forces have entertained such "non-profit-foundations" since the 1950s, officially serving as welfare and pension funds for the soldiers of specific units and their families. The generals have always refused to account publicly for their finances, even when in 2000 the IMF tied its debt re-scheduling program to a full audit of these foundations (Bur 2000). The then minister of defense, the former general Juwono Sudarsono, was willing to comply with the IMF but was immediately forced to step down by the generals in charge of the foundations. The former president Suharto apparently used several charitable foundations of the famous Diponegoro army division, which were under his control since the mid-1950s, to finance his rise to power around 1965. Commanding over financial means that they refused to be held publicly accountable for, the generals could act with much more independence from central government than would have been the case if all their money had come from the state's treasury. The officers who removed Soekarno from power in 1965 and thereafter ruled the country for more than three decades were wealthy and well-connected political entrepreneurs.

Civil government institutions also value the raising and investment of "non-budgetary" finance as an informal but more or less legitimate practice. It is widely perceived to supplement public finances and make institutions less dependent on the arduous process of budget planning and implementation by an inert financial bureaucracy. Not having to apply for budgetary means in order to acquire trifle items and services is acknowledged to enhance the efficiency of the institution. This is why even critical press reports distinguish forms of "non-budgetary" finance from what might be called "ordinary corruption." "War chests" are considered to be part of a fiscal grey zone in which the public interest is being served, albeit by dubious means. Although these "war chests" may in the long run enhance the personal power and wealth of those who control them, they, at the surface at least, seem to not only strengthen the particular institution but the state as a whole, which is held to be too poor to pay for all the necessary expenses of the administration. Not their existence *per se*, but rather their often illicit origin, and the fact that the public is never allowed to know their true extent, is cause for concern.

"Non-budgetary" government finance thus accrues from informal state-entrepreneurship, which, in the eyes of its managers, the public should welcome rather than criticize, since it lessens the demands on the official budget. The public should therefore not discourage the practice by insisting on public accountability. The non-accountability of these foundations is morally legitimized by their charitable purpose as pension funds or as funds from which quick "un-bureaucratic donations" to the victims of natural disasters such as floods and earthquakes can be made. To demand public accountability for such generous ventures would amount to stinginess.

Such well-publicized and morally laudable uses of "non-budgetary" government finance are of course not their only—and certainly not their most important—purpose. "Non-budgetary" finance has become a necessity for senior officials because they, just like private citizens and firms, need money to bribe their counterparts in other departments or ministries that they need to interact with. I argue that the establishment of intra-institutional bribery—and of off-budget "war chests" to finance it—has been a major factor contributing to the proliferation of systemic corruption throughout the Indonesian administration. A historical account of the development of "non-budgetary" finance in Indonesia, therefore, contributes to a better understanding of corruption.

Historical Development of the Institutional Framework of Corruption in Indonesia

The analysis of the historical development of corruption offered here draws on a comparative historical approach that looks at the early post-colonial period as the formative years of the type of governance that can be observed today in many former colonies and that often involves systemic corruption (Eisenstadt 1973; Médard 2002; Leonard and Straus 2003). This approach has largely replaced the view, inspired by modernization theory, that it would be the pre-colonial social structures that are responsible for the existence of corruption (Huntington 1989). It is, moreover, equally skeptical toward putting the blame on the structures of the colonial states.

In Indonesia, independence fighters fought Dutch and British forces between 1945 and 1949. They had inherited weapons and command structures from the Japanese occupation army after its defeat in August 1945. The Indonesian fighters operated with little control by civil independence movements and supported themselves with a war-economy for which they could not be held publicly accountable. These independence fighters became the backbone of the armed forces of the young republic. But even as members of a formal army during peacetime they never completely renounced the enterprises that had subsidized their war-economy. The former resistance fighters refused to put them under the fiscal control of the central government. In the beginning, their enterprises tended to be lucrative ventures in those remote areas in which neither the allied fighters nor the central government had been able to establish firm control. In Southwestern Sumatra, for instance, the independence fighters had in the late 1940s taken control over the rich Lebong gold mines. From the proceeds they paid for the first warplane of the Indonesian Air Force. The local commander of the mines, Ibnu Sutowo, who later rose through the ranks of the civil administration, continued to "protect" the goldmines and other businesses, and in the 1970s became the famously corrupt director of the state-owned oil company Pertamina (Galizia 1995; Robison 1986).

Indonesia's civil government had been financially instable from the beginning—and as instable was its authority over its various institutions. One important reason was Soekarno's ominous pledge to the Dutch and the British in the cease-fire agreement of 1949 that in exchange for independence Indonesia would assume the complete costs of the four years long war of independence. Burdened with this huge debt, the state itself started out as a liability for the nation's economic and military elite. Especially the military found the pledge humiliating, and this may well have been a reason for it to perpetuate part of its war economy and thus to undermine the government's fiscal authority. To appease the military, Soekarno's government had to co-opt hundreds of thousands of former independence fighters by offering them jobs in the new civil administration.

During the 1950s the political climate became polarized and the economy remained weak and eventually collapsed under hyperinflation. Soekarno steered an anti-Western course that culminated when, in 1958, he put foreign-owned plantations and mining and oil companies under state control in order to bring money into the depleted government coffers. In this moment, the military, which had "protected" the foreign-owned plantations, dealt the government's fiscal authority a final blow by seizing part of these enterprises and thereby securing an income for itself that the central government was in desperate need of (Stoler 1985). The Western powers endorsed the Indonesian military in its oppositional stance against a regime that seemed to drift into the communist camp of the Cold War. The rift between the armed forces and the central government at that time led to the military's open establishment of a parallel financial infrastructure, their "war chests."

The resulting growing economic independence of the armed forces from the central government went in pair with their growing political influence. With the income from the plantations, the army actively supported secessionist movements in several of the "outer provinces" in Sumatra, Kalimantan, and Sulawesi. This situation would perhaps have been less fatal for Indonesia's democracy, if the central government had had a strong income base from taxes. But as it were, the nation's main income came from the sale of raw commodities such as oil and plantation products. The central government therefore directly competed with the armed forces for its income-base and the army's economic enterprises directly impoverished and weakened the central state. This antagonism only eased with General Suharto's dictatorship, which brought the country a quarter of a century of sustained economic growth. But the basic principle that the state's institutions and agents partly financed themselves by "non-budgetary" means became only further institutionalized during this period—and with it, generalized and systemic corruption established itself throughout the whole administration.

Richard Robison (1986) has shown how the armed forces and the inner circle of the Suharto government used part of the proceeds from Pertamina's oil and gas exports to literally fill their war chests for their military campaigns in East

Timor, Aceh, and throughout the country wherever any form of resistance against their firm grip on politics and the economy arose. During the 1970s, Suharto's "new order" government started to put former generals in command of all central institutions of the civil administration, establishing the so-called *dwifungsi* ("dual function")—the military-civil double function of the army. The generals in civil positions took with them the strategy to use "non-budgetary" finance to run their institutions by command.

In this way, the open competition and civil war between the government and the army under Soekarno, turned into an internal contradiction between the army's leadership of the state and its financial practices that undermined the state. One of the lasting legacies of the military dictatorship is the firm entrenchment of unaccountability of the administration for part of its activities. The overall effects of the widespread existence of "non-budgetary" government finance are a fragmentation of the state's institutional framework and its co-optation by those who sponsor and control the illicit war chests of the state's various institutions. As the state's institutions thus managed to escape democratic control and the leadership of the central government, they moreover became interesting partners for national and international entrepreneurs. The Indonesian army was again at the origin of this pattern. From the Cold War through the era of globalization, it derived its powerful stance vis-à-vis the civil institutions of the Indonesian state from the fact that it was an accepted partner of the Western powers and a protector of Western oil and mining companies and private Indonesian entrepreneurs against legal constraints and fiscal demands of the civil administration. For instance, bypassing Soekarno's derelict administration, Suharto immediately after his coup in 1965 brokered contracts directly between the army and Mobile Oil in Aceh and Freeport in West Irian (Bertrand 1999a). The establishment of such powerful economic and military neo-colonial interests that are beyond democratic control has ultimately been a triggering event for the establishment of systemic corruption.

From a historical perspective, it seems striking that both the colonial regime of the Netherlands Indies and the post-colonial regime as it took shape under direct and indirect military rule refused to be held accountable to the Indonesian public. In this perspective, it is probably justifiable to look at systemic corruption in Indonesia in part as a colonial heritage. At the same time, it can be seen as a neo-colonial construction, since the same economic agents that used the colonial state to exploit Indonesia's natural and human resources against the vested interests of the population as a whole, now use the venality of the administration to the same ends.

Conclusions

In conclusion I argue that to understand the persistence of systemic corruption in Indonesia even in the face of consistent criticism in the public and of strong pressure by the IMF and the World Bank it is necessary to understand the history of its establishment, the dynamic of the discursive field of corruption, and the function of corruption as a self-perpetuating prestige system within the administration. I have tried to make it plausible in the last part of this chapter that the parallel financial infrastructure of the state's institutions is the informal institutional basis on which the edifice of systemic corruption is built in Indonesia. In the first part, I have shown that the discursive regime on corruption is characterized by a deeply entrenched dynamic, which allows the criticism of corruption in general and abstract ways but makes it almost impossible to criticize it in the plain language that is closer to its everyday experience.

Both phenomena are linked to the powerful and often violent grip of the armed forces on politics in Indonesia. Indeed, the establishment of the parallel, unaccounted-for financing of state-institutions occurred during periods of intense power struggles between the central government and the armed forces. Public criticism of the army's role as an uncontrolled "state-in-the-state" was stifled in a climate of fear, which the military instilled in the Indonesian population with the massacres of 1965 and the subsequent dictatorship. I see the dynamic of the discursive regime about corruption in Indonesia as a product of the control of all public discourse about governance by the army's dictatorial rule.

The persistence of both "non-budgetary government finance" and the discursive dynamic about corruption after the end of the military dictatorship suggest that the system of only partially accountable governance has not been fundamentally changed by the democratically-elected governments of the reformation era since 1998. Indeed, even if the military may have renounced its formal political power, it still remains in charge of its many businesses and continues to partially finance itself through its "charitable foundations." The military is still a sufficiently strong and financially independent institution to be able to dictate the limits of democratic control in Indonesia.

The most important heritage of the military dictatorship is, however, that it helped to establish the strategy of parallel financing of state-institutions throughout the civil administration. The military and the civil administration are in this sense now a single strategic group, that is, a group that achieves its power and income through the same strategy, exploiting the same kind of resources and protecting their strategy of achieving power and income against the strategy pushed forward by other strategic groups (Evers and Schiel 1988).

The widespread criticism of corruption since the 1990s has put the Indonesian administration in a defensive position. To retain its legitimacy toward the public and toward the international creditor organizations, its leaders have to join in the criticism and to vow to fight for an accountable government. To retain its informal power-base, though, it has to continue and defend its strategy of "non-budgetary" finance and to assure its members of the legitimacy of "taking one's share" according to established informal norms.

Critical and legitimizing discourses may seem more contradictory to the outsider than to the insider of the administration as the formal and the informal normative systems that guide these practices contradict each other mainly in respect to public accountability and overall consistency of government. In terms of internal organization and the everyday functioning within administrative units—career patterns, prestige to be gained, hierarchy, institutional stability, and administrative competences—the formal and informal normative systems are complementary. However, competition for extra-budgetary income among various administrative units introduces striking inconsistencies in Indonesian government, in the long run drying out its fiscal base and weakening the ability of the state's leadership to coordinate and control the activities of its vast and fragmented bureaucratic apparatus.

The analysis of systemic corruption in Indonesia presented here thus confirms Evers' (1987) view that under the publicly endorsed self-representation of a Weberian rational administration, there is, in Indonesia, a powerful system of governance that strives for autonomy, rather than consistency and legitimacy.

References

Aditjondro, G.J. (2000) *Financing Human Rights Abuses in Indonesia*. International Action for West Papua (IAWP) (http://www.westpapua.net/docs/submissions).
Alatas, S.H. (1999) *Corruption and the Destiny of Asia*. 1st ed. 1968 under the title *The Sociology of Corruption*; 2nd ed. 1986 under the title *The Problem of Corruption*. Petaling Jaya: Simon and Schuster (Asia).
Ascher, W. (1997) From Oil to Timber: The Political Economy of Off-Budget Development Financing in Indonesia. Conference of the American Asianist Society, Chicago.
Assegaf, I. (2002) Legends of the Fall: An Institutional Analysis of Indonesian Law Enforcement Agencies Combatting Corruption. In: T. Lindsey and H. Dick (eds) *Corruption in Asia: Rethinking the Governance Paradigm*. Annandale, NSW: The Federation Press: 127–46.
Barthes, R. (1957) *Mythologies. Collection "Pierres vives."* Paris: Editions du Seuil.
—— (1967) *Elements of Semiology*. New York: Hill and Wang.
Bertrand, R. (1999a) L'armée indonésienne, une firme privée. *Le Monde diplomatique* October: 23.
—— (1999b) Tant qu'il Plaît à Monsieur. Le gouvernement pastoral comme matrice et alibi de la privatisation de l'Etat en Indonésie. In: B. Hibou *La privatisation des Etats*. Paris: Karthala: 285–319.
Blundo, G., and J.-P. Olivier de Sardan. (2001) Sémiologie populaire de la corruption. *Politique Africaine* 83: 98–114.
Bourdieu, P. (1982) *Ce que parler veut dire: l'économie des échanges linguistiques*. Paris: Fayard.
—— (1984) *Distinction: A social critique of the judgment of task*. Cambridge, MA: Harvard University Press.
—— (1987) *Choses Dites*. Paris: Editions de Minuit.
Bur, H. (2000) Melongok Bagaimana Tentara Mengelola Uang [A Glance at How the Army Manages Money]. *Kompas* November: Jakarta.
Crouch, H. (1988) *The Army and Politics in Indonesia*. Ithaca, NY: Cornell University Press.
Eisenstadt, S.N. (1973) *Traditional Patrimonialism and Modern Neo-Patrimonialism*. London: Sage.
Evers, H.-D. (1987) The Bureaucratisation of Southeast Asia. *Comparative Studies in Society and History* 29: 666–85.
—— and Schiel, T. (1988) *Strategische Gruppen—Vergleichende Studien zur Staatsbürokratie und Klassenbildung in der Dritten Welt*. Berlin: Dietrich Reimer.
Foucault, M. (1971) *L'Ordre du discours*. Paris: Gallimard.

Galizia, M. (1995) *Aufstieg und Fall der Pasirah. Soziale und kulturelle Veränderungen im Spannungsfeld zwischen zentralstaatlicher Vereinnahmung und lokalen Machtstrategien.* Berlin: Reimer.

Geertz, C. (1972) Deep Play: Notes on the Balinese Cockfight. *Daedalus* 101: 1–37.

Goodpaster, G. (2002) Reflections on Corruption in Indonesia. In: T. Lindsey and H. Dick (eds) *Corruption in Asia: Rethinking the Governance Paradigm.* Annandale, NSW: The Federation Press: 87–108.

Hamzah, A. (1984) *Korupsi di Indonesia. Masalah dan Pemecahannya* [*Corruption in Indonesia. The Problem and its Solution*]. Jakarta: Gramedia.

Hänni, S. (2006) *Korruption in Indonesien. Strategische Gruppen, koloniales Erbe und kulturelle Legitimationsmuster*, vol. 32. Arbeitsblätter. Bern: Institut für Sozialanthropologie, Universität Bern (http://www.anthro.unibe.ch/arbeitsblaetter/ab32-haenny.pdf).

Huntington, S.P. (1989) Modernization and Corruption. In: A.J. Heidenheimer, M. Johnston, and V.T. LeVine (eds) *Political Corruption: A Handbook.* New Brunswick, NJ: Transaction Publishers: 377–88.

Jomo, K.S. (2003) *Southeast Asian Paper Tigers?: From Miracle to Debacle and Beyond.* RoutledgeCurzon Studies in the Growth Economies of Asia 46. London: RoutledgeCurzon.

Leonard, D.K. and S. Straus (2003) *Africa's Stalled Development. International Causes and Cures.* Boulder, CO: Lynne Rienner Publishers.

Lopa, B. (2001) *Kejahatan Korupsi dan Penegakan Hukum* [*The Crime of Corruption and the Maintenance of Law*]. Jakarta: Penerbit Buku Kopmas.

Lubis, M. and J.C. Scott (eds) (1985) *Bunga Rampai Korupsi* [*An Anthology of Corruption*]. Jakarta: LP3ES.

Médard, J.-F. (2002) Corruption in the Neo-Patrimonial States of Sub-Saharan Africa. In: A.J. Heidenheimer, M. Johnston, and V.T. LeVine (eds) *Political Corruption: A Handbook.* New Brunswick, NJ: Transaction Publishers: 379–402.

Oester, K. (1996) *Unheimliche Idylle. Zur politischen Rhetorik heimatlicher Bilder.* Bonn: Böhlau.

Onghokam (1983) Corruption: The Old Name was Tribute. *The Jakarta Post.*

Rais, A. (1999) *Amien Rais menjawab. Isu-isu politis seputar kiprah kontroversalnya.* Bandung: Mizan Pustaka.

Robison, R. (1986) *Indonesia: The Rise of Capital.* Sydney: Allen and Unwin.

Schwab-Trapp, M. (2001) Diskurs als soziologisches Konzept. Bausteine für eine soziologisch orientierte Diskursanalyse. In R. Keller, A. Hirselande, W. Schneider and W. Viehöver (eds) *Handbuch Sozialwissenschaftliche Diskursanalyse*, vol. 1. Opladen: Leske und Budrich: 261–84.

Stefes, C.H. (2005) Understanding Systemic Corruption. Some Methodological Questions. Paper presented at the Central Eurasian Studies Society 6th Annual Conference, Boston, MA (http://www.umsl.edu/~mk6c3/panels/Systemic_Corruption_Chris_Stefes_CESS_05.pdf).

Stoler, A.L. (1985) *Capitalism and Confrontation in Sumatra's Plantation Belt, 1870–1979.* New Haven, CN: Yale University Press.

Toer, P.A. ([1954] 2002) *Korupsi.* Jakarta: Hasta Mitra.

Transparency International (2006) *Corruption Perceptions Ondex 2006* (http://www.transparency.org/policy_research/surveys_indices/cpi/2006: accessed February 27, 2007).

Weber, M. ([1922]1976) *Wirtschaft und Gesellschaft. Grundriss der verstehenden Soziologie.* Tübingen: Mohr.

The Indeterminacy of the Law and the Legal Profession

Chapter 4

Corruption Judgments in Pre-war Japan: Locating the Influence of Tradition, Morality, and Trust on Criminal Justice

Andrew MacNaughton and Kam Bill Wong

The chapters collected in this volume attest to the difficulty field researchers face when trying to locate corruption in practice. The nature of corruption often precludes a direct search; it regularly exists in the indeterminacies of everyday life where its definition becomes confounded in its ambiguity. *References* to corruption, as distinct from the actual *practices* of corruption, can nevertheless help us get a clearer view of certain closely related concepts and institutions. The references to corruption we deal with here are those found in the highest criminal appeals court of pre-Second World War Japan.[1] Judges ruling on corruption in the civil service at the time constructed their arguments in an atmosphere of strong state morality campaigns, which often appeared to contradict Japanese traditions of gift giving. We argue that references to corruption in the discourses of appellants and judges can help to locate "public trust" and "law"—just as Gupta (1995) for example uses corruption discourse to map out people's interactions with "the state" as a translocal entity.

As an historical, document-based study we began this research with no physical "field" in which to observe the praxis of judges or appellants. Had we set out to study the specific *nature* of corruption in Japan through these court documents this shortcoming would certainly have posed problems. Yet, our aim is to focus on the *judgment* of corruption and *defenses against the charge* rather than on the practice of corruption itself. What this research tells us of the interdependent relationship between law (as statute), corruption (as sullied trust), and moral rectitude (as public trust) makes it clear that there is more than one way to search out, analyze, and—possibly—confront corruption.

Public mistrust in Japan's power-centers of government, bureaucracy, and business has been represented as a trend largely fueled by the highly publicized

---

1 Kam Bill Wong's PhD research in sociology and criminology at the University of Hong Kong has produced original English translations of a large number of pre-Second World War Japanese Supreme Court rulings that had previously been unavailable to a wider audience.

political and bureaucratic bribery scandals of the postwar period (Pharr 2002). The "Recruit scandal" of 1988, named after the parent company that organized an opportunity for politicians to profit on insider trading of its subsidiary's initial stock offering, brought the forced resignations of Prime Minister Takeshita and Finance Minister Miyazawa as well as charges of bribery against company executives (Iwai 2002). The earlier Lockheed scandal (1976) that brought down Prime Minister Tanaka and exposed his acceptance of roughly two million dollars in kickbacks from the Lockheed Corporation (see Johnson 1986) is more appropriately seen as the beginning of this long-lived concern in postwar Japan with corruption scandals (Pharr 2002). Widespread frustrations with the "structural corruption" (kōzō oshoku) of politics in Japan continued with more reports of *amakudari* ("descent from heaven")—the bureaucratic retirement phenomenon whereby highly placed government officials get a position in the board of a private company upon retirement and thereafter mislead the public tendering process through their still active connections to relevant government offices.[2]

Practices such as *amakudari*, which engender public distrust in government bodies and officials as well as in corporations, have been specifically criminalized and prosecutions do take place. However, continued social/electoral distrust toward politics in Japan may indicate that the public perception of "structural corruption," engendered by the close relationship between government, bureaucracy, and big business, runs deeper than these specific practices. The public perception of corruption does not stop at the criminalized act, nor is it merely an episodic response to that act. Pharr (2002) offers a quantified exploration of this public perception and finds it to be rooted in dissatisfaction with the character of political leaders and corrosive of the bonds between citizens and their democratic institutions.

The Japanese judicial system has enjoyed a less distrustful public appraisal[3] by being outside of the government/bureaucracy/business "corruption triangle." It is, however, placed in the unenviable position of passing judgment where public distrust has already blackened the accused on a level of character. The nature of corruption charges against civil servants therefore often requires judges to intervene against institutionally widely accepted and practiced behaviors in an attempt to restore or protect the public trust (Goda 2000). Dealing with these cases, these judges operate within a rather grey intersection of legal statute, public morality, and cultural notions on gift giving in different institutional settings.

---

2   Despite a 2003 amendment criminalizing specific placements of retired bureaucrats, charges of *amakudari* continue to appear and are widely discussed in the domestic media (see Suzuki 2004). The criminal charge can, however, only be applied within two years after a bureaucrat's retirement and can be entirely subverted if a special investigative panel gives consent to the new employment in advance of retirement.

3   Pharr (2002: 846) quotes a Gallop-Yomiuri poll result from 1995 as showing the most trustworthy reactions going to police and prosecutors, hospitals, and courts, at 42, 35 and 29 per cent respectively, while the local government, national legislature, and prime minister take only 9, 6, and 3 per cent.

In order to better understand the influence of moral principles in Japanese adjudication we present a study of court proceedings from the beginning of the twentieth century. Looking at the judiciary's role in this period in building legal convictions on corruption-charges in the civil service and thereby appreciating the importance of extra-statutory influences on legal practitioners helps us rethink "law." We will show that Japanese judges of the prewar Supreme Court negotiated the intersection of legal statute, morality, and culture by expanding the legal process to accommodate more ambiguity while at the same time applying exceedingly high moralistic standards.

The Daishinin, or Great Court of Cassation, as the Supreme Court was then known, ruled in a period of intensified political interest in nurturing a unique Japanese spirit to counteract an onrush of Western-derived modernization efforts. Japan has a long history of gift-giving traditions in which offerings are seen as a cultural obligation and an expression of gratitude and emotional indebtedness. Labeling these gifts as bribes and criminal acts of corruption was thus seen by many Japanese as a form of misrepresentation brought about by the perceived ills of Westernization. However, the early reign of the Shōwa Emperor (beginning in 1926) saw a particular urgency to shore up a national policy centered on the Imperial House[4] in which the civil service was urged to set an example in the national family and rid itself of corruption. For this reason, Daishinin rulings from the prewar period provide an especially clear example of a judiciary pressed to legally and morally rationalize convictions (specifically those for bribery) that quite often flew against culturally condoned behaviors (defined here as customary conventions of gift giving).

It is important to realize that to have a teacher, mentor, or patron who has given guidance or support, places the recipient in a celebrated position of indebtedness in Japan (Johnson 1974). The student, in such a case, would be emotionally indebted and compelled by all the force of that which is culturally apropos and ideal, to venerate the teacher through gifting—at specified times—in perpetuity. The sort of gift varies in the cases we will examine, but even where the giver opts for cash currency there is no confusing the gift for anything as blatantly utilitarian as cash might suggest. Crisp, new bills would be inserted into any number of special, festive envelopes commonly available at all stationers for the explicit purpose of gifting.[5] On such gifting occasions the festive envelopes and fresh bills would act to plainly differentiate a "gift" from a "bribe." However, the circumstances of a student's relationship with the teacher may include additional reciprocal obligations such as expectations of preferential treatment beyond the continued understood sponsorship. It would then be firmly in an appellant's interest to show theirs as an obligation born of the virtuous and idealized Japanese "public" as opposed to a more contractual (read "foreign") obligation of quid pro quo. Emotional indebtedness to one's teacher is an often-expressed theme in Japanese

---

4 Bix (2000) provides an excellent historical analysis of the role played by the Japanese Imperial House in prewar national policies and identity.

5 Ordinary circulated money has a tendency to be associated with "dirt", quite possibly because it is usually covered in it.

life, particularly so in the policies of the early Shōwa Emperor's rule. Teachers, as members of the civil service were to be held accountable for any actions that might bring public shame or distrust to the "Japanese family," but at the same time they were to incur the debt of Japanese society.

We begin this chapter with a brief explanation of the historical forces that shaped the institutions of the Japanese judiciary. This is followed by a consideration of the theoretical and institutional relationship between Daishinin judges and the law. Then, using several original translations of Daishinin rulings on bribery as illustration, we draw out the culturally-informed reasoning process used by judges to rule on corruption. Culturally sanctioned gift-giving and respect-showing manners figure prominently in the reasoning and defenses given by appellants in these cases and will be examined in detail. We conclude with the implications of this reasoning process to our understanding of this legal system and argue that these corruption cases show that statute alone was not effective against corruption and that extra-legal, moral principles applied by judges were ultimately the means of conviction.

The Daishinin, Japan's Prewar Supreme Court

A spirit of institutional modernization moved through Japan in the late nineteenth century, ending the Tokugawa Shogunate and leading to the foundation of a new legislative government under a restored emperor in 1868 (the Meiji Restoration). Seven years later, further institutional changes were brought in under the Meiji Emperor to separate judicial, administrative, and legislative powers that had remained indistinguishable under the *dajōkan* system of the early restoration government. This led to the establishment of the Daishinin in 1875, prior to the promulgation of Japan's first modern constitution of 1889, known as the Meiji Constitution. Translated also as the Great Court of Cassation, the Daishinin was in fact closely modeled at the time on the structure of the French *Cour de Cassation* as the Meiji Government had a preference for institutions of civil law to bring Japan in line with Western powers. From its establishment through to its replacement by a new Supreme Court at the end of the Second World War, the Daishinin operated, with slight variations in the number of chambers and judges, as the highest appellate court for criminal and civil cases. The new constitution of 1946 followed shortly after the Daishinin's replacement.

The Daishinin's independence from the executive powers of government was limited only by its official supervision and administration by the Justice Ministry. Judges were, and continue to be, selected by the Ministry although changes to the structure of government following the war allow the new Supreme Court to manage administrative staffing and spending where this was impossible for the prewar Daishinin. Despite this close supervisory relationship to the Justice Ministry there is no evidence to suggest that judiciary independence was compromised at any time in the 71-year history of the Daishinin. A famous case from the Daishinin's early rulings is often cited as proof of that independence: in 1891, a Japanese policeman assigned to guard a visiting Russian Prince was charged with attempted murder when he slashed the prince with a sword in the city of Otsu (hence, this case is known as the Otsu-case). In brief, the government pressed the Daishinin President to have the policeman sentenced to death, but the court refused to be led by political or administrative will and instead followed the penal code to apply the maximum sentence of life imprisonment.

The Daishinin court documents referred to throughout this chapter do not record the names of judges, the numbers of judges present for cases, or any mention of dissenting judges' opinions. We know that cases had to be heard by at least five Daishinin judges and that during the 1930s the maximum number of judges on staff to hear cases in the nine chambers was 45, but this does not mean that only five judges were present for each case nor that their decision was without internal dissent.[6] The fact that rulings appear to be unanimous and of a single voice—that of the Daishinin rather than that of five judges—does not prove that the Daishinin judges actually thought of themselves in this way. We believe, however, that the rulings can, in the nature of Ben-Ari (1997), provide both an instrument and an object of analysis to illustrate the conceptual framework used by judges and the cultural themes dominant in the assertion of and defense against bribery and corruption charges in the Japanese civil service.

A Judge's Role in the Law

Whereas the present-day Supreme Court in addition to being the highest court of appeal also serves to actively uphold the constitution of Japan, the Daishinin was strictly concerned with the hearing of appeal cases from the lower courts (High Court, Circuit Court, and Prefectural Courts). The Daishinin worked closely within the available statutes of law, including the Meiji Constitution, but its work, as that of the modern courts, was always stated as the application—rather than interpretation—of these statutes. This draws attention to the fact that the Daishinin, as well as the wider modern judiciary, was held subject to the legal codes promulgated by Japanese lawmakers via the bureaucrats of the Cabinet's Legal Systems Bureau. These codes were, moreover, most often adapted or recommended on the advice of legal scholars of the time. Before ever reaching their intended application in a court of law, these legal codes were ostensibly made standard and broadly legible to essentially head-off the necessity of any interpretation at the judiciary level. Henderson (1980) gives an illustrative description of this structure of the Japanese legal system and shows that its statutes thus have a preeminent importance vis-à-vis the judiciary. He contrasts this with the generalized case of the American legal system in which the statutes' effective importance is formally lower than the courts' interpretations (established by precedents) of those statutes. Japanese legal theorists such as Eiichi Hoshino (2003) and Takeyoshi Kawashima (1975, 1979) have long written on characteristics

---

6   For instance, the opinions of dissenting judges have appeared in court rulings since the end of the Second World War as a result of legislative changes to the court system and documentation styles.

of Japanese law, including the view of judges adhering to a set of dominant rules. A corollary of the Japanese statutes' relative higher significance is the technically non-binding nature of Japanese court precedents.

Seigo (2000) describes this statutory preeminence through the eyes of Japanese legal theorists writing in the immediate postwar period. Traditional legal theorists writing at that time held that judges stuck with statute most faithfully and only reached beyond statutes, to apply their own interpretations, wherever these did not suit the immediate case circumstances. This is contrasted with the views of more contemporary theorists who claim judges rule based on their own intuition and merely use statute as the tools to rationalize the ruling (ibid.: 166). In both views there is room for a judge's interpretation though it is weighted with greater or lesser significance. In both views, moreover, the source of the reasoning involved in this interpretation appears to be a broader institution beyond the written law of statute although there is ambiguity in the debate on how to define this institution.

Binding precedents in judicial experience entail the unification of a judge's interpretive tools with a concept of written law, according to Dworkin (1985). For illustration purposes Dworkin relies on the phenomenon in common law of judges' binding interpretations becoming part of the law in a piecemeal process of law-generation where law can be said to resemble an evolving work of literature. Under a common law system each judge may well be "like a novelist in the chain" (ibid.: 159). Japanese civil law cannot, however, be assumed to accommodate judges in this way. Henderson (1980) contrasts the judgment-centered common law of the US with the statute-centered civil law of Japan to illustrate the difficulty of translating law to or from Japanese, but his findings also form a good example of the significantly different relationship Japanese judges have to their law as compared to US judges and their law. In the Japanese case, the unique legal terminology and what Henderson (1980: 127) calls the "comprehensiveness of code coverage and structural symmetry" within the legal system make it abundantly clear that this is a *system*, unlike the piecemeal chain of binding precedents authored by US judges.

The theoretical relationship between a judge and the law has been extensively addressed in the Japanese legal literature and shows evidence of a progression toward a model that increasingly values judges' interpretive ability. Indeed, the historical unimportance of the Japanese judiciary's interpretation of statute should not be taken to mean that Japanese judges have historically lacked interpretive license. As we will see in the Daishinin rulings on corruption, even these judges, while not "novelists" of "legal literature," were adept at an art of some interpretive kind as they applied statute to malfeasance through a judicio-cultural process of reasoning. While their role did not officially include the interpretation of statute, the application of case specifics to statute necessitated an interpretive approach in each case. Articles 197 and 198 of the Criminal Code (relating to the offence of bribery) were designed around generalized terms such as *houeki* ("legal interest" or "legislative intent") and "official civil service duty," which left nearly unlimited room for the Daishinin judges' judicial interpretation. The Japanese legislature endeavored to give reasonably clear and concise terms to these articles, but under the doctrine of *nullum crimen sine lege* (no crime without law) they had to avoid the elaboration of specific terms—as this could lead to the miscarriage of criminal justice—and shun redundant verbiage—as this could result in legal loopholes in the two said articles.

The principle reasoning tool that surfaces repeatedly in the Daishinin rulings analyzed here involves a process of building a convincing connection between the official duty of a civil servant and the illegal interest of the alleged briber. This process, known as *taikasei* in the Japanese criminal law community, is as much a term for the corresponding relationship between unsavory interest and one's duty (also known as *taika kankei*) as it is an expression of the method followed in constructing the relationship. In our analysis of the corruption cases to follow, it is a formula for successful conviction that first describes the two constituent elements of illegal interest and official duty and then ensures that they are brought together to *suggest* corruptibility in the civil service. Support for the application of *taikasei* in Daishinin rulings can partly be found in four specific pieces of legislation[7] but what gave *taikasei* its overwhelming power in the Daishinin was the political and moral urgency in the pre-Second World War period to strengthen a unique concept of the public domain in the Emperor's name, with civil servants as its exemplars.

We will now set out the origins of this urgency. From the beginning of the Meiji period (1868) to the prewar Showa period (1926), the slogan *messhi hōkō* (selfless devotion) had been a popular tool of governance used to promote a hierarchical vision of society where the sense of public (*ōyake* or ~*kō*) could extend vertically as well as horizontally. The same selfless devotion expected of commoners to the Emperor was also to be expected by commoners of each other—and of the Emperor leading the idealized national family on behalf of the commoner.[8] In the meaning of its original Chinese character, *ōyake* denotes government and ruling authority, as well as a populace or "public" in the English sense of the word. Many Japanese social researchers (see Katō 1992; Maruyama 1986; Mito 1976; Watanabe 1997) have given it a special place as a term for ruling power in the consciousness of Japanese that predates the more recent horizontal term of *shakai* (society, public).

With the Emperor restored to a place at the top of the social hierarchy during the Meiji Restoration, the Meiji government set out to quicken modernization efforts by establishing many government-sponsored public institutions modeled

---

7 Both of the primary elements needed to construct *taikasei* are found within statute, specifically Articles 197 and 198 of the prewar Japanese Criminal Code. But *taikasei* itself is not explicitly set out in criminal law. Instead, it can be understood as a consequence of Articles 57 and 23 of the Meiji-era Constitution and an extra-legal sense of the public realm. Article 57 stipulated that the courts had to exercise judicial power according to law in the name of the Emperor while Article 23 stated that no Japanese subject would be arrested, detained, tried or punished unless according to law (the source of the *nullum crimen sine lege, nulla poena sine lege* doctrine in Japanese law).

8 The "Imperial Rescript on Education" of 1890 is a familiar example promoting this sort of national ideology which had the effect of deepening public veneration for the Meiji Emperor (Bix 2000: 30f.).

on those found in Europe and the US at the time.[9] These new institutions were adopted in the broader meaning of a public (*ōyake*) that was closely bound to the conservative national ideology of Japan with the Emperor as the filial head. Because of this conceptual distinction, where *ōyake* included both the public and the legitimacy of government simultaneously, we can see that the adoption of another nation's public institutions to this environment would automatically make the new institutions Japanese. The politicization of this "public" ideology could then act as a sort of check on the fears of "Westernization" evoked by the transferal of institutions and the process of modernization. Seen in this light, the imposition of strict liability on civil servants through *taikasei* was thus not only a warranty for the protection of "public" interest but also of all that *ōyake* represented (government legitimacy and the Emperor's filial position) in a period in which fears of an increasing adoption of Western values were widespread. Daishinin judges were ruling in an era of "purifying politics" (Mitchell 1996: ch. 4) following the weakening of political parties in the 1930s and were determined "not only to maintain fairness in the performance of official duties by civil servants, but also to maintain social confidence in the fairness of official duties" (Saito 1996: 254). This had the effect of giving the Daishinin a strong imperative to shape elements of a case so that they would fit the law and to rationalize the link through reference to the larger "public" realm where their contributions to "maintain[ing] social confidence" (ibid.) in the civil service fit into a strong national ideology.

The idealized "public" hierarchy of a national family including judges and civil servants alike was a defense measure against a perceived rush toward embracing Western institutions. We will show that the arguments in defense of bribery charges in the prewar years appeal to this public ideal *because* it stands as a bulwark to supposed Westernization. "Public" in the broadest sense of *ōyake* provided a less apparent location for things corrupt than the imported or foreign "other" in the eyes of accused and accusers. Where a gift in Japan is popularly seen to acknowledge a pre-existing social or emotional debt (*giri* or *on*) then payment of that gift can be seen as a restoration of social or emotional harmony between those involved. Foreign residents often find themselves not fully included in these situations of indebtedness, precisely because, as they feel, they are not expected to fully participate in the interdependent "favor bank" and "sticky" repayment

---

9   This included the Daishinin and other legal institutions. In the formative years of the Meiji Restoration, Japanese legal scholars studying abroad brought back legal codes and administrative methods predominantly from France and Germany. The result was a Roman Civil Law system with institutions such as the Daishinin patterned on the French Court of Cassation. Japanese legal theorists such as Oda (1993) have asserted that this foreign origin amounts to a distinctly foreign nature of and distaste for law in Japan. Hoshino (1986) argues that statutory laws in Japan cannot function in the way that domestic forms of law such as *ikeru-ho* and *shizen-ho* ("laws of life" and "laws of nature") can, because of their origin in the West. Seigo (2000) counters this argument and presents Yoshio Hirai (1989, 1991) to shift the debate away from "legal nationalism" and toward a consideration of extra-legal influences on judges and the law.

(Antepara 1995: 180, 178).[10] This is a shared experience in the idealistic ōyake "public" of the time.

Culture and Corruption in Five Illustrative Daishinin Cases

Case 1: Indebtedness to a Teacher

This, like all of the cases to be examined here, is the case of an appellant who had already been charged with a specific crime and then brought his case to the Daishinin in order to seek exoneration from the criminal charges and allow some reclamation of his former life.[11] Dr Satoru Takanaka had been charged in a lower court with accepting bribes from the families of several of his students. From March 1931 to February 1935, seven families were alleged to have given him bribes in the form of cash and gift coupons in order to secure his private tutoring for better examination results and help their children to gain acceptance at his public college. Dr Takanaka was a mathematics teacher at a public college in Osaka with a doctoral degree from the prestigious Tohoku Imperial University. His duties at the college had included preparing examination questions and marking those examination papers. At the same time he provided private tutoring to students after school.

Dr Takanaka described the nature of his alleged offence as the perfectly innocent giving and accepting of *gifts* in accordance with socially accepted convention. The value of the gifts varied from 5 to 20 yen (roughly equivalent to US$40 to US$170 today). Dr Takanaka claimed that these gifts were given out of "emotional indebtedness" (*on*) to his educational efforts. He stressed that emotional indebtedness to the Emperor, one's parents, and teachers was a traditional observance with a long history of importance to the Japanese people. He then lamented those Westernized Japanese who had trouble understanding how social harmony was the result of this indebtedness. The government of the time also called for the observance of a harmonious relationship between teacher and student. In Dr Takanaka's view, the imported values of the West were weakening customary Japanese social practices, such as the recognition of emotional indebtedness, and carried the misguided potential for him and other teachers to be regarded as money-making machines. The agencies of criminal justice might now mistakenly re-evaluate the teacher-student relationship and thereby destroy a Japanese tradition. To emphasize the customary nature of the gifts in this relationship, the mother of one of Dr Takanaka's students was called as a witness in this case. She testified that she gave gifts to Dr Takanaka on all

---

10 Antepara (1995) explains this as "an *interdependent* lifestyle that most modern Westerners can hardly imagine, let alone experience in their atomized lives" (178f., original emphasis). He likens the social cohesion to that of Japanese rice: "sticking together like Japanese sticky rice" (178).

11 This case can be found in the Japanese Criminal Law Collection (*Keishū*) Vol. 17, p. 110, dated February 25, 1938.

festive occasions in order to show him due respect as her son's teacher. Even after her son's graduation from Dr Takanaka's tutelage her gifts continued to be given in the same spirit of preserving a relationship of emotional indebtedness—making this a virtuous gifting with no element of *taikasei* whatsoever.

At the beginning of their judgment, the Daishinin agreed with the appellant that Japanese should pay due respect to teachers and make efforts to recognize this as a virtue. The bottom line was that gifts must be confined to customary convention. The judges admitted that it was often difficult to distinguish a gift from a bribe, but in this case the social role and scope of official duty of the teacher were seen to make the possibility of criminal corruption more apparent. Although it was a matter for school regulations to prevent him from doing so, there was a possibility that examination questions might be leaked to students in the course of tutoring. If this possibility existed then the acceptance of gifts could constitute *taikasei* and the money given would be considered a bribe. Citing the likelihood of bribes under these circumstances, the Daishinin declared that after the students' enrollment, the offers and acceptances of gifts for Dr Takanaka's provision of private tutoring were not of the nature of customary convention. Considering human weakness, a teacher's acceptance of valuables from students worried the Daishinin's judges. The 16 "gifts" with a total value of 165 yen (roughly US$1,400 today) were declared bribes and not gifts of customary convention.

The Daishinin judges' reasoning process was focused on the possibility of a civil servant's loss of integrity under the temptation of excessive gifts. They held that the possible leakage of examination questions and the acceptance of valuables (presumably) in return constituted *taikasei* and thereby led to an offense of bribery. The judges rationalized their ruling by insisting that the corruptibility was formed as a result of the public's loss of trust in the integrity of public servants. The virtue and moral value of teachers and civil servants at large were subject to public concern. This case indicates the Daishinin's strong emphasis on the maintenance of public confidence in the civil service and the importance of morality in its reasoning process.

The witness called to testify in Dr Takanaka's case alluded to the gifts she gave him on "all festive occasions" as a way to overcome the *taikasei* by providing an alternate, morally virtuous explanation for the gifts given. The judges acknowledged the gift-giving tradition but questioned the specifics of its timing, quantity, and relationship to Dr Takanaka's duties, thus establishing *taikasei* and leading to a conviction. It is impossible to say if Dr Takanaka could have avoided this outcome with stronger support for his cultural defense. Festive gift-giving occasions in Japan extend to the relationship between companies as well as between individuals, and in these corporate cases there was an acknowledgment that gift giving was a part of business and could even be recorded as such.

Case 2: Gift Giving vs Bribery

In the next case we see an example of gift-giving obligations officially recorded by a company with well-documented records of gifts given and received as a part of their business practice.[12] This example was the seventh judgment delivered in the prewar Showa period on the issue of bureaucratic corruption and represents one of the clearest examples of a cultural defense to a criminal charge. Three appellants, a briber and two bribe-takers, moved through lower courts to challenge the grounds of their earlier convictions but found little sympathy from the Daishinin.

The briber and principal appellant in this case, Shinji Kumejima, was the sales manager of a large electric lamp bulb company in Osaka known as Osaka Denkyu Kabushiki Kaisha. The company produced a bulb suitable for municipal street lamp standards and relied on sales to municipalities in the area of Osaka. The city of Kobe was a valued client and Kumejima would have been remiss as a sales manager if he had not made his appreciation and indebtedness known to the customer as a means of ensuring future business relations. On the two gift-giving occasions (*o-seibo* at year-end, and *o-chūgen* in mid-summer) in each year between 1923 and 1925, he gave monetary gifts to the director, purchasing officer, field supervisor, and warehouse keeper of the Kobe Metropolitan Government.

The two bribe-takers who filed appeal that day were fulltime civil servants with the Kobe Metropolitan Government. Their positions in the Kobe government are not given in the court record but we are told that they were not direct recipients of Kumejima's alleged bribe. Instead, they were alleged to have taken gifts from a second company, Suzuki Company, which supplied their departments. Details of Suzuki Company are not provided so we cannot be sure of the goods involved except to say that the company and these two civil servants would have been in a relationship analogous to that given for Mr Kumejima and the bureaucrats from the Kobe city purchasing office. These gifts had been given on the same occasions and during the same period and the two bureaucrats would have represented a patron to the indebted supplier just as in the case of Kumejima's dealings with the city.

Mr Kumejima condemned the verdicts of the lower courts on cultural grounds that held that the gifts were expressions of gratitude to the company's customers and important institutions for the maintenance of the company-customer relationship. He gave these gifts on behalf of the company in accordance with *o-seibo* and *o-chugen* traditions and the customary business practice of the company. The amounts given as gifts were insignificant in comparison with the company's annual turnover. Their accounting ledgers even contained a full record of these expenses for each occasion of each year of the company's operations.

Bribe takers and briber alike first sought to eliminate the elements of their circumstances that established *taikasei* in the eyes of the court. Mr Kumejima's approach was to present himself as an agent of the company acting on its will and in its interest. The bribe-takers attempted to show they had no duties which could be "bought" to benefit the briber since they held junior or internally-oriented positions. In addition, one of the purchased gifts[13] given by Suzuki Company

---

12 *Keishū* 8: 609.

13 The nature of this gift was unspecified in court records but it may be helpful to imagine a large bottle of rice wine or a case of fruits. Consumables of this kind are popular at gifting times of year and department stores and supermarkets always stock special items for these purposes.

was suggested to have actually cost less was reported in the records of Suzuki Company. The bribe-taker was eager to point out that this meant that either Suzuki Company or the merchant who had provided the gift to Suzuki Company had over-quoted the price and had therefore been dishonest. This may have been a tactic to sow doubt in the minds of the Daishinin judges. All three argued that the very fact that these gifts were given during *o-seibo* and *o-chūgen*, culturally obligated and universally recognized occasions for the exchange of gifts for continued patronage, made the prospect of bribery ridiculous and unlikely.

The court record shows that two questions were particularly relevant to the Daishinin's ruling: was the culturally recognized tradition of gift giving on *o-seibo* and *o-chūgen* distinguishable from the act of giving a bribe, and did the company have vicarious liability for the criminal actions of its staff?

The Daishinin ultimately refused the appeal and supported the corruption verdict against Kumejima and the two civil servants. Notwithstanding the traditional Japanese practice of gift giving on the occasions of *o-seibo* and *o-chūgen*, the offer and acceptance of gifts in any way related to a civil servant's official duty belonged to the purview of *taikasei*. In establishing the existence of *taikasei* the two articles of the Criminal Code that dealt explicitly with bribery, articles 197 and 198, were addressed. Article 197 required the Daishinin to make clear the official duties of those charged, while article 198 concerned clarifying the objective of the act of gift giving and the interest of the recipient. The reasoning process behind the ruling appears to be very straightforward. For *taikasei* to be confirmed, the value of the gift, the social/employment status of the briber and bribe-taker, and the duration or frequency of gift giving are all irrelevant and thus unacceptable as appeal grounds for a charge of corruption. The Daishinin's conceptual framework to distinguish a bribe from a gift simply depended on demonstrating the link between a civil servant's duties and the interests of the second party; that is, it depended on demonstrating *taikasei*.

The issue of the second question facing the Daishinin, the idea of an individual claiming that their employer has vicarious liability when it places them in a criminal situation, was determined to be inapplicable to a Japanese bureaucratic corruption case. The judges declared that it was a matter of course for company employees to be directly liable in a bribery offence even if the employee accepted the bribe for the benefit of the employer. The Daishinin followed an old Japanese judicial value, stipulated in Law number 52 in the Meiji Criminal Code which stated that every Japanese should take responsibility for his own behavior unless special statute gave him the ability to do otherwise. The company-employee relationship was no shield against convictions for bribery.

Even with uncontested company records in evidence to support the culturally condoned practice of gift giving, the first concern of the Daishinin judges—establishing *taikasei*—still managed to cast doubt on the legality of gift-giving practices. It could be argued that the underlying question concerning the distinction of a gift from a bribe went unanswered. The threat of immorality involved in a link of *taikasei* effectively overshadowed a cultural defense. Under the Daishinin judges' expanded interpretation of case elements, the immorality of an abuse of the civil service for private gain could easily amount to criminality. To the Daishinin, *taikasei* was immoral because it implied poor integrity of the civil service and an attempt to purchase the civil service at the expense of the public interest. The civil service was not supposed to be purchasable. The integrity of the Japanese civil service ought not to be contaminated.

In the final three cases discussed here the attention turns to the two components of a *taikasei* link—the possibility of illegal interest in the minds of the briber and bribe-taker, and the desired role or duty of the bribe-taker—as the best hope of appellants and the chief concern of Daishinin judges.

Case 3: No Guilty State of Mind

Is a bribe not a bribe if one of the parties does not realize it is so? Bribe takers in the two previous cases implied that they were not aware of the bribe when they claimed that what they did was culturally condoned gift giving. The claim of gift giving does not address the charge of purchasing the civil service since even a gift of indebtedness to a teacher or a customer-relation gift is recognizable as part of some kind of an exchange—though for a more indeterminate time period and for an unspecified return. To overturn a claim of *taikasei*, an appellant must eliminate the appearance of specific expectations and direct returns from the gifting.

The appellant in this case attempted this defense in his role as the arresting police constable in an act of intimidation against an illegal establishment.[14] The constable is not named in court documents but we know that he was not a particularly high ranking police officer and was assigned to the police service in a municipality in Fukushima Prefecture.[15] In June 1924 he conspired with the staff of a transportation firm to intimidate gamblers in a local illegal gambling hall. His friends from the transportation firm were to pose as gamblers on a pre-arranged evening at this illegal gambling hall. On that evening, the off-duty constable would put on his full police uniform, go to the gambling hall and pretend to arrest these gamblers in an attempt to embarrass the operator of the hall. All went as planned and the hall operator paid the constable to have the supposed customers released on the spot rather than be dragged into greater public scrutiny.

Lower courts inflicted double punishments on the appellant by convicting him of the offense of criminal intimidation for acquisition of property and the offense of accepting a bribe. The constable argued that *taikasei* only existed in the mind of the illegal gambling hall operator. The constable himself had no intent of a *taikasei* nature. The cause of the hall operator's reaction was portrayed to be the unconscious effect of his criminal intimidation rather than the result of any expectations of bribery. The appeal to the Daishinin came as a result of this

---

14 *Keishū* 6: 512, dated 8 December 1927.

15 Police in Japan are national civil servants in a hierarchy of local, prefecture, and national offices. The police at the time of this case were charged under the Peace Preservation Law of 1925 to combat the appearance of communism and held arrest powers in the case of certain behavior that ran counter to the national essence, or *kokutai*. For more on this see Parker (2001).

reasoning; it was a criminal injustice to inflict double punishments for the one crime of criminal intimidation.

The Daishinin refused this proposition and justified double punishments by ruling that the hall operator's act established the *taikasei* for both. The police uniform scared the hall operator and made him believe he had to pay a bribe. In view of the resulting payment to the constable, the Daishinin judges insisted that *taikasei* need not exist in the minds of both parties in the criminal case. The mere presence of *taikasei* in the interpretation of the case was enough to allow for conviction on corruption charges.

Throughout the judgment, the Daishinin had not indicated whether it considered the appellant to be a police constable on duty. Ostensibly, this is a case of paying a bribe by mistake while under criminal intimidation. The delivery of judgment in this case confirms that it was not necessary for both the briber and the bribe-taker to share a corrupt intent. The case conveyed the immutable message that a civil servant was expected to have integrity whether on or off duty. Though the constable had the intention to commit an offense of criminal intimidation only, his criminal act was subject to strict criminal liability for the offense of accepting a bribe. Bribery concerns the influence of those who exercise a public function rather than a private function. The Daishinin's judicial decision apparently belonged to a social defense.

If the police constable had carried out his act of criminal intimidation as a civilian instead of a civil servant, he may have been able to evade prosecution. The high moral zeal of the justice system was most intense where applied to the civil service. Clearly, being an off-duty police constable, as opposed to an on-duty police constable, made no difference to the Daishinin judges' deliberations. The ambiguity of a police constable's identity became a danger in itself. Ambiguity appears in many of these cases as an invitation to corruption. Where it exists in the relationship between alleged briber and bribe-taker, it forces a moral, expansionist reasoning process that leads to *taikasei*. Where it exists in the role of a civil servant's duty it becomes a fiercely contested element of identity and culpability.

Case 4: Definition of Organizational Role

This next ruling bears some resemblance to the second case above, in that it explores the relationship between the appellant and his organization, but differs significantly in that the organization in this case is the civil service, whose vertical structure was well-known to the Daishinin.[16] The appellant was a junior administrative officer in the Hyogo Prefectural Government, dealing with forestry issues. Residents of a small village in the prefecture wanted to secure a special permit from the prefectural government for the sale of their land. Between mid October and December 1925, they gave the administrative officer a total of 450 yen in cash and 20 yen in lavish food. As a result of the officer's assistance in the permit application, the Hyogo Prefectural Government granted a permit to that

---

16 *Keishū* 9: 599, dated July 29, 1930.

village on 18 December 1925. In a social gathering to celebrate the granting of the permit, the head of the village presented a 3,000-yen gift to the officer in an open presentation ceremony.

In an attempt to escape charges by eliminating the possibility of *taikasei*, the officer argued on appeal that he was ordered by his superior to handle the permit application. This duty essentially fell outside of the scope of his normal work authority and it was only because he was *ordered* to do it that he was put in this situation.[17] The officer argued that the openness of the act of presenting the gift could confirm the official intent of the 3,000-yen gift. How could he be responsible for the villagers' act when he had been made to exceed his authority by processing this application?

The Daishinin judges agreed with the brief facts stated by the appellant but rebutted his appeals with an expansionist assessment of the administrative hierarchy of the Hyogo Prefectural Government. They declared that all administrative officers of the prefecture were under the management of its governor. It was a fact that the appellant originally had no statutory power to deal with such permit applications. Nevertheless, his internal posting to the Fourth Division of the government hierarchy newly gave him that power. With regard to the 3,000-yen gift, the Daishinin agreed that it was an open ceremonial occasion but stated that a government official should not accept any gift without the permission of his superior. Social standard was a judicial yardstick to gauge the legal acceptability of events such as this, which should then fall within the visible scope of that social gathering (the Daishinin did not elaborate on how this "visible scope" might be determined). His superior's approval was a precondition but the Daishinin further added that the corruptibility of a bribe would invalidate the superior's permission to accept it.

For the first time in the prewar Showa period, the Daishinin delivered its judgment with reference to the organizational chart of a prefectural government. On the surface, this chart showed that the appellant had no statutory power under the law to handle a land sale permit application. This was factual and could be seen to limit his deviant behavior to mere immoral wrongdoing. In order to plug this loophole and to rationalize its verdict to put the moral blameworthiness on a par with criminality and thus confirm *taikasei*, the Daishinin judges adopted an expansionist interpretation. They interpreted the governor of Hyogo Prefecture as a parental figure in the vertical structure of the prefectural government to show that all of the prefecture's civil servants were under his supervision and instruction. The Daishinin treated the internal posting order issued in the mayor's name as a source of legal power of statutory status though it was not set out in any of the prefecture's legislative instruments. In this way, the fact that an officer had been ordered to exceed his legal authority could not be used in defense by the appellant to invalidate the appearance of *taikasei*.

This case reflects a reasoning process that places a great deal of stress and recognition on the parental power of a vertical organizational structure. The

---

17 Curiously, neither the public prosecutor nor the appellant gave evidence to show allowances or restrictions in the officer's power in this regard.

Daishinin judges perceived this one administrative officer of the prefecture to be acting out of his own immoral greed as a "black sheep" in an otherwise virtuous family structure. The ruling was rationalized with reference to the vertical structure of the Hyogo Prefectural Government's organizational chart instead of with reference to the statutes which might have defined his actual working position. The gift's open presentation ceremony would not exonerate the appellant of the criminality inherent in the bribe.

The means of defense chosen by this appellant appears in court rulings throughout the period included in K.B. Wong's study as well as in more recent cases of the modern Supreme Court. Former Prime Minister Kakuei Tanaka was found guilty of accepting bribes in the Lockheed verdict of 1983 when it was held that he had the power as Prime Minister to tell All Nippon Airways to buy Lockheed's L-1011 aircraft. Tanaka had asserted that this was in fact beyond his authority and was reported to be "shocked" that the High Court judges found otherwise (see Johnson 1986: 16). Tanaka's style of politics is legendary as a prime example of the "structural corruption" in the machinery of Japanese governments (Johnson 1986; Mitchell 1996). Despite this, he died professing his innocence and awaiting his chance to prove in a Supreme Court appeal that Leftist detractors were to blame. For him, the knowledge of just how much money it took to mobilize bureaucrats and get something done in government was an essential and appreciated political attribute.[18] As a bureaucrat himself, the appellant in the Hyogo case above may not have seen money as a catalyst for administrative efficiency in the way that the future Prime Minister Tanaka would, but it is clear that he saw little need to hide the "gift" as an illicit thing (given his defense of the villagers' open ceremony).

Case 5: Expanding the Role of the Bribe Taker

We have seen in the preceding cases how the Daishinin judges expanded their interpretation of specific elements of appellants' cases in order to create a link of *taikasei*, or at least stir the prospect of a link through ambiguity. In the first two cases this was done by questioning the acceptability of traditional Japanese gift-giving practices to the moral value of a civil servant's position. In the last three cases, including this next one, the elements of greatest interest to the judges have been the organizational role and occupational duties of the appellants. Roles are of course not fixed and anyone familiar with the work of Dorinne Kondo (1990) or Takie Sugiyama Lebra (1992) on the multiplicity of "Japanese selves" may be excused for wondering just how the Daishinin judges could rule with such confidence on this element. The Daishinin held civil servants accountable with the strictest liability where the appellant's role as a civil servant appears even to have eclipsed their role as a person (the only names appearing in these rulings are

---

18 For example, Chalmers Johnson (1986) reports that former Prime Minister Tanaka gave between 3 to 5 million yen to every member of the Diet as an *o-chūgen* gift in 1974. For a more recent estimate of the unseen costs of operating in Japanese government, see Iwai (2002).

those of non-civil servants); liability this strictly applied would also have utility when, as in this case, the added complexity of changing roles over time appears as an element of the appellant's case.

In this ruling the Daishinin reinforced its strict liability approach to define an offender's organizational role in order to suggest *taikasei*.[19] The appellant worked as a secretary for the Japanese Railway Authority. Upon his new posting to be the officer-in-charge of Kurasiki Railway Station on September 28, 1933, the owner of a food stall inside Okayama City Railway Station gave him a 150-yen government bond as a farewell gift in appreciation of the "convenience" given by the appellant during his service there. The appellant appealed his lower court bribery conviction on the grounds that the gift was given in connection with his old post at the Okayama City Railway Station after completing his duties there and could in no way apply to his current work at the Kurasiki Railway Station. On the public prosecutor's charge sheet, no details were provided to explain the expectations of the alleged briber nor what past "conveniences" were rewarded with the gift in this case.

The circumstantial evidence showed that 150 yen constituted an excessive gift for a civil servant but the element of *taikasei* relating to a civil servant's past post was uncertain. The Daishinin judges would have to expand the scope of *taikasei* to ensure their decision this time. They ruled that the specificity of a civil servant's official duties was not a necessary consideration. Linking undue remunerations with the most general duties of any civil servant was sufficient for their purposes. The duties of the appellant's new and old posts were of the same general nature. Being the secretary of a railway station, he accepted 150 yen relating to the "convenience" he had provided the briber in his past post. This could be considered the offense of accepting a bribe.

Without prior corrupt conspiracy made implicit or explicit, giving a gift with a link to the general past duties of a civil servant constituted a bribe. The public prosecutor's inability to define the term "convenience" reflected an unclear concept of the appellant's corrupt interest in this case. Consequently, the substantive evidence needed to prove the corrupt ingredient of *taikasei* was unavailable. But to the Daishinin, the appellant's deviant behavior was inexorable. In order to fit the *taikasei* model, the judges delicately interpreted the appellant's old and new posts as sharing a common, general nature. The continuity of his official duty was thus established and *taikasei* made apparent. To what extent these two posts shared a "general commonality" beyond relating to "secretarial work," the Daishinin did not elaborate in court documents.

The full definition of every crime contains an expressed or implied proposition as to a certain criminal state of mind. The Daishinin judges in this case had not explored or explained the criminality of "convenience" or the briber's criminal intentions of presenting an excessive farewell souvenir. The judgment merely implied an unproven assumption of corrupt intent. The expansionist interpretation used by the judges simply adjusted the role of the accused and the meaning of his actions to fit the *taikasei* formula with strict liability. The act of a

---

19 *Keishū* 15: 282, dated March 16, 1936.

civil servant's acceptance of 150 yen was undoubtedly blameworthy, but whether this moralistic blameworthiness could amount to criminality was open to the Daishinin's interpretation and they decided it was a criminal act.

Implications and Conclusion

The Daishinin rulings examined here all show a very strict, morally justified liability at work against corruption in the civil service. Taro Yayama (1990) has looked at the strict prosecution in the "Recruit scandal" and compared it with a case from 1937 known as the "Teijin affair" to argue the potentially chronic existence of "procuratorial fascism" in the Japanese justice system. Certainly the period of the 1930s marked a particularly moralistic turning point in Japanese politics with the decline of party politics coming as a result of increased anti-corruption measures brought in by revisionist bureaucrats and military figures (Mitchell 1996). Prosecutors achieved a prewar record of 4,471 arrests[20] for corruption in the civil service in 1936, and it is a reasonably safe bet that most of these were convicted given the Daishinin's rigid application of *taikasei*. In more recent times, calls continue for the lessening of heavy-handedness in the Japanese prosecutor's office. Plea-bargaining and other investigative tools have been suggested to bring a more transparent and efficient approach to justice (Tachi 2001). Certainly *taikasei* remains a tool in the same system of law at use in the modern Supreme Court, but any suggestion that current serving judges apply it with the same strict morality-based zeal of the Daishinin judges should be greeted with suspicion. The historical period of the Daishinin was one, as we have seen, in which judges and civil servants alike experienced "purifying politics" with pronounced attention to ideals of incorruptibility.

In constructing a link of *taikasei*, the Daishinin judges frequently expanded the illegal interest of the briber and the applicable duties or role of the bribe-taker until these elements could be made to form a relationship or until such a relationship could be seen as suspicious. Once *taikasei* had been established to incriminate the appellant, it effectively side-tracked any defense. The cultural ambiguity surrounding the gift-bribe divide and the specific-general role disagreement were ostensibly ruled upon but only by first applying *taikasei* to sow the seeds of public mistrust. This made it possible for "purifying justice" to convict the betrayer of the public trust, rather than the practitioner of a time-honored Japanese custom such as *o-seibo* or *o-chūgen*.

The Daishinin judges themselves did not necessarily see their rulings as purposely sparing Japanese customs like *o-seibo* and *o-chūgen*. The continued assertions of innocence by many bribery convicts, including those of former Prime Minister Tanaka, were sustained by a perception that these "bribes" were in fact "gifts" and their function was popularly condoned and even necessary. The judges

---

20 See Mitchell (1996: 91). Mitchell cautions that the actual number of arrests within the civil service was most likely higher than reported due to the anti-communist campaigns of the time.

passing these rulings were aware of the critical importance of the relationships and institutions that these "gifts" sustained and in Dr Takanaka's case above they actually stated as much in the ruling. The significance of *taikasei* to every conviction shows that the operational meaning of corruption was the squander of public trust by members of what was supposed to be an example of virtuosity in a public organization at the Emperor's service. This meant that the priority in ruling against corruption was actually the establishment of who squandered the public trust and not who accepted or gave a "gift." An application of *taikasei* actually rendered any "gift" instantly a "bribe" by association without altering any ambiguities in or around the gift itself.

We also saw how an official definition of civil service duty could be expanded in the case of the minor functionary in the Hyogo Prefectural Government office. Daishinin judges invoked an idealized version of the appellant's entire office as a representative stratum of the larger, vertical public hierarchy. Corruption rulings then become a lens through which we see the influence on the judiciary of political culture in a reformist era of Japanese nation building. The Daishinin's political independence from the executive powers of government is not in question here. Technically, the judges were as free to operate in the lead up to the Second World War as they had been at the time of the Otsu-case (1891). However, it was precisely the same moralistic, anti-corruption sentiment that militarists used to discredit and dissolve party politics in the years leading to war that also colored the Daishinin judges' particular use of *taikasei*. This was the hidden realm we often expect corruption to represent. Where corruption is seen as an attack on trust in a public ideal, *taikasei* gave judges the means to fix this "hidden," extra-legal ideal to articles of criminal law to ensure legal convictions on a par with the true offense (that is, a non-statutory offence). Daishinin judges worked within a rich system of legal statute including many laws brought in to criminalize specific acts of corruption. But, ironically, corruption in the civil service was only assailable through moral conviction in the expansive judicial application of *taikasei*.

Taikasei, and the public ideal animating it, had the power to reinforce or protect legal authority and ideological institutions of national infrastructure such as the Japanese national family ideology. Daishinin judges, as judges in a system of civil law, were not in the practice of adjusting the law to address a case. Their expansion of case elements to fit the law initially shifts the emphasis of their judgments to non-statutory aspects. Finding and demonstrating the lack of adherence to a popular ideal of public trust relied on a flexible reading of case elements that could later be tied to legal representations of a civil servant's "duty" and their legal or illegal "interest" (defined by articles 197 and 198). It is unlikely that Daishinin judges saw this construction of *taikasei* as something outside of the legal system given the completeness of their accounts and the comprehensiveness of their linking to written statute. This should therefore serve to shake any assumptions about the uniformity of law in the hands of a judge or even any neat divisibility of graded legal "layers" in the hands of theorists. The study of corruption cases in the prewar Japanese civil service shows that more effective measures against corruption need something other than merely a more comprehensive statute. The study moreover shows that extra-statutory influences and adjudicative processes are accommodated even by practitioners of an extremely positivistic view of law.

References

Antepara, R.B. (1995) A Bad Case of *Giri*: The Small Town Life of Tokyo. In: Minoru Wada and Anthony Cominos (eds) *Japanese Schools: Reflections and Insights*. Kyoto: Kyoto Shugakusha.
Ben-Ari, E. (1997) *Japanese Childcare: An Interpretive Study of Culture and Organization*. London and New York: Kegan Paul International.
Bix, H.P. (2000) *Hirohito and the Making of Modern Japan*. New York: HarperCollins.
Dworkin, R. (1985) *A Matter of Principle*. Cambridge, MA: Harvard University Press.
Goda, H. (2000) Preparation and Implementation of Japan's National Public Service Law. In *Progress in the Fight against Corruption in Asia and the Pacific*. Papers Presented at the Joint ADB-OECD Conference on Combating Corruption in the Asia-Pacific Region. Seoul: Asian Development Bank and Organisation for Economic Co-operation and Development, December 11–13.
Gupta, A. (1995) Blurred Boundaries: the Discourse of Corruption, the Culture of Politics, and the Imagined State. *American Ethnologist* 22(2): 375–402.
Henderson, D.F. (1980) Japanese Law in English: Reflections on Translation. *Journal of Japanese Studies* 6(1): 117–54.
Hirai, Y. (1989) *Hōritsugaku kisoron oboeki* [*Notes on the Fundamental Theory of Law*]. Tokyo: Yūhikaku.
—— (1991) *Zoku hōritsugaku kisoron oboeki* [*Notes on the Fundamental Theory of Law, Continued*]. Tokyo: Yūhikaku.
Hoshino, E. (2003) *Minpō ronshū* [*Collected Papers on the Civil Code*]. Vol. 5. Tokyo: Yūhikaku.
Iwai, T. (2002) Clearing up the Murk in Political Finaces. *Japan Echo* 29(5): 29–32.
Johnson, C.L. (1974) Gift Giving and Reciprocity among the Japanese Americans in Honolulu. *American Ethnologist* 1(2): 295–308.
Johnson, C. (1986) Tanaka Kakuei, Structural Corruption and the Advent of Machine Politics in Japan. *Journal of Japanese Studies* 12(1): 1–28.
Katō, T. (1992) *Shakai to kokka* [*Society and the State*]. Tokyo: Iwanami Shoten.
Kawashima, T. (1979) Japanese Way of Legal Thinking. *International Journal of Law Libraries* 7(2): 127–31.
—— (1975) The Individual in Law and Social Order. In: C.A. Moore (ed.) *The Japanese Mind*. Honolulu: University of Hawaii Press.
Kondo, D.K. (1990) *Crafting Selves: Power, Gender and Discourses of Identity in a Japanese Workplace*. Chicago, IL: University of Chicago Press.
Lebra, T.S. (1992) Self in Japanese Culture. In: N. Rosenberger (ed.) *Japanese Sense of Self*. Cambridge: Cambridge University Press.
Maruyama, M. (1986) *"Bunmeiron no gairyaku" wo yomu jo* [*Reading Fukuzawa Yuichi's "An Outline of Civilization"*], vol. 1. Tokyo: Iwanami Shoten.
Mitchell, R.H. (1996) *Political Bribery in Japan*. Honolulu: University of Hawaii Press.
Mito, T. (1976) *Kō to shi* [*Public and Private*]. Tokyo: Miraisha.
Oda, H. (1993) *Japanese Law*. London: Butterworths.
Parker, L.C. (2001) *The Japanese Police System Today: A Comparative Study*. Armonk, NY: M.E. Sharpe.

Pharr, S.J. (2002) Public Trust and Corruption in Japan. In: A.J. Heidenheimer and M. Johnston (eds) *Political Corruption: Concepts and contexts*. New Brunswick, NJ: Transaction Publishers.

Saito, O. (1996) Structure of Corruption in Japan. In: Academic Office of the Seventh IACC Secretariat (ed.) *Anti-Corruption for Social Stability and Development*, Collected Works of the Seventh International Anti-Corruption Conference. Beijing: Hong Qi Publishing House.

Seigo, H. (2000) Postwar Japan and the Law: Mapping Discourses of Legalization and Modernization. *Social Science Japan Journal* 3(2): 155–69.

Suzuki, K. (2004) Changing Pattern of *Amakudari* Appointment: The Case of Regional Banks. The European Institute of Japanese Studies, Working Paper 198 (September).

Tachi, Y. (2001) Role of Public Prosecutors in Japan. In: *Taking Action against Corruption in Asia and the Pacific*, Papers Presented at the Third ADB/OECD Conference on Combating Corruption in the Asia-Pacific Region. Tokyo: Asian Development Bank and Organisation for Economic Co-operation and Development, November 28–30.

Watanabe, H. (1997) *Higashi ajia no ouken to shisō* [*Royal Power and Political Concepts in East Asia*]. Tokyo: Tokyo Daigaku Shuppankai.

Yayama, T. (1990) The Recruit Scandal: Learning from the Causes of Corruption. *Journal of Japanese Studies* 12(1): 93–114.

Chapter 5

Corrupted Files: Cross-fading Defense Strategies of a Vesuvian Lawyer

Livia Holden and Giovanni Tortora

Naples' ring road, which sometimes runs all too closely beside or over a heterogeneous sequence of buildings, offers a fascinating panorama stretching, almost uninterrupted by the Vesuvian suburbs, from the deadly foot of the volcano down to the once-remote beaches and cliffs. From the road, it is almost impossible to see the ground because of the thick tangle of houses of various heights and styles—some of them stunningly carved out from the volcanic tufa rock, others boldly competing with the modern architecture of major European cities. Such an "every-kind-of-regulation-defying" landscape, by offering unusual beauties on closer inspection, embodies the peculiar flavor of this area where defiance of the legal authorities is so entrenched that it even forms part of the region's tourist appeal.

One would not be surprised to find a correspondingly relaxed attitude toward the law among Neapolitan legal professionals, who are said to outnumber their Parisian and New York colleagues. In fact, the frequent attacks by the national and international press on Neapolitan lawyers accused of supporting organized crime merely enhance the image of the local lawyer managing corruption conspiracies and achieving their legal or illegal concealment. Such an image, as well as perpetuating the constructed determinism between the malfunctioning of the legal machinery and the illegal activities of its parts, overlooks the elements that constitute the concrete boundaries between the legal and illegal in the everyday practice of a lawyer. It thereby ignores the multifaceted grounds of praxis that lie beneath the tangled landscape of justice and injustice.

As co-authors of this article, Giovanni and I are both sources of the present study but in different ways. Giovanni's authorship addresses the necessary acknowledgment not only of his extraordinary role as a consultant in the delicate domain of organized crime but also of his active involvement in the analysis.[1]

---

1   Since my very first fieldwork in South Asia I have been struggling with the notion of "informant." The term seemed a rather derogatory way of referring to the people who shared sometimes very intimate details of their lives with me and were ready to overcome the gap between our different local frames of reference. To me, they have been and still are above all friends; but this fact, even if central to my fieldwork, would not adequately describe their various roles as active collaborators in the research. Hence, the use of different terms throughout my other works, including: "native" for its literal meaning of

This experience even went beyond the framework of reciprocal anthropology in which consultants take an active part in the whole process of the construction of academic knowledge including the collection, analysis, and dissemination of findings.[2] Our collaboration sometimes generated a polyphony of voices in which our individual contributions merged. As an academic I am the one who should be held responsible for sometimes disregarding the conventional narrative rules of wiping out any ambiguity about the actual authorship through the use of "I" and "s/he." I should also be considered responsible if the result of this choice could, against my intentions, be interpreted as yet another subtle way of imposing the academic voice. My effort here is to reconstruct the modalities of our experiences, in which my complete and unconditional adherence was sometimes necessary to apprehend some of the trajectories of Giovanni's professional life. For this reason, I request the reader to speculate about the actual authorship of the various parts of the chapter. Such an ambiguity gives an idea of the reciprocal transformations required during the fieldwork and reproduces the process of trying to grasp what I was seeing with the new interpretive tools offered by Giovanni's collaboration.

This chapter[3] offers a detailed analysis of three criminal cases undertaken by Giovanni, a defense lawyer practicing in a small Vesuvian town—one of Naples's suburbs. It concentrates on the terms of the communication between the defense lawyer and his clients within both the legal environment and the milieu of organized crime. Thereby it highlights the pragmatic grounds underlying the major turning points in the defense strategy. We avoid the realm of blatantly corrupt actions and instead focus on the micro-events where the categories of legal and illegal are pragmatically re-shaped in relation to contextual interests. By

---

local inhabitant in order to emphasize the local perspectives of local knowledge (Lynch 1993); "consultant" as a specialist/well informed person (Basso 1979; Lassiter 2005); and sometimes "informant" for its common yet unfortunate use in the anthropological literature. In the present chapter, the term "consultant" seemed most appropriate to the role of Giovanni Tortora.

2   Since my first experiences as an anthropologist I have often carried out fieldwork in collaboration with my husband, Marius Holden, anthropologist and film-maker. In spite of not co-authoring this chapter he substantially collaborated to the various phases of its production and I am deeply grateful to him for his consistent support and dialectical contribution. We have experimented so far various kind of collaborative ethnography both as pluridisciplinary team and with consultants. Among our collaborative works see Holden and Holden 2000; Holden and Sharma 2002; Holden, Holden, and Manfredonia 2004; Holden, Holden, and Manfredonia 2005; Holden et al. 2006. For my personal trajectory toward collaborative ethnography see Holden, *Hindu Divorce* (forthcoming). On collaborative ethnography as team research see Buford, Reuben, and Patillo-McCoy 2000. For a recent methodological overview of collaborative ethnography with consultants see Lassiter 2005. For more details on *Doing Nothing Successfully* as visual experiment see Holden et al. 2006.

3   The final version of this chapter was written during Livia Holden's stay as visiting scholar at the Socio-Legal Research Centre at Griffith University in 2007. We are very grateful to all the staff and especially to Prof. Giddings, Prof. Johnstone, and Prof. McDonald for the excellent environment and valuable advice.

analyzing the legal discourse in the everyday praxis of files opened and archived in the lawyer's office, we explore the spatio-temporal evolution of corruption as (im)perceptible sequences sneaking into the defense strategy. In order to clarify the terms and the stakes of the dialectical collaboration that form the basis of this chapter, a presentation of epistemological sources will precede the account of the sequences witnessed, re-visited, and re-enacted while following the ordinary praxis of Giovanni's case-load. Our collaboration progressively re-shaped the terms of the research. During this process some of my initial parameters of analysis were modified. Our relationship was transformed and at times interrupted by the writing of this text because of the complex stakes involved in my entry into his world. A feeling of mutual respect, which allows reciprocal criticism, has however been laid as the basis for future intellectual enterprises.

Scaffolding

The material offered hereafter was collected during extensive fieldwork carried out since the summer of 2003 in Naples and its suburbs. I have elsewhere described the initial conditions and terms of this field research.[4] It is, however, necessary to elaborate some of the elements characterizing my entry into the field here in relation to the development of a methodology, which I see as the scaffolding of the building site discovered "there" and reconstructed "here." Within the framework of reciprocal ethnography some spatio-temporal adjustments had to be made both to my consultant's everyday praxis and to my own academic references (Bourdieu 1980: 36f.). Thus, the epistemological premises that I present here are those of building a communication network for the development of analytical tools that would be useful for the presentation of data in an academic setting.[5]

As a Neapolitan born into a family of lawyers, having a background in law myself, and having carried out fieldwork on lawyers and legal institutions in South Asia[6], I inevitably had certain expectations regarding the site of my research. I was returning to the place that I left at the age of three but with which I had links that had been constantly fed by my family's network. I felt immediately overwhelmed by the richness and density of the site in which I was engaging. Unlike my previous field experiences, my position of native enabled me to immediately catch, or at least guess, the countless nuances of meaning in the events I was witnessing or

---

4   The data in this chapter stem from fieldwork research carried out within the international project "Comparative Micro-sociology of Criminal Procedures" directed by Dr. Thomas Scheffer and hosted by the Freie University in Berlin. For an account of my initial steps in the field see: "On One's Own Ground: Consultant and Social Scientists in and beyond Academia" (forthcoming).

5   See the use of notions such as actants, code-switching, meta-pragmatics attacks, and legal meta-pragmatic unities later in this chapter.

6   Among my papers on legal institutions and lawyers in India see Holden (2003, 2005).

being told, and I often regretted the constraints of subject and time that obliged me to make a selection.

The constant and frequent allusions to corruption and illegality did not come as a surprise. Notwithstanding my limited experience of Southern Italy, I felt as if I was actually re-entering the world of clientele so well described by Dorothy Zinn (2001), in which the "*raccomandazione*"[7] not only structurally shapes social relationships but also contributes to the Southern Italian identity.[8] What primarily caught my attention were the specific silences and mimics and the general tacit consensus around this theme. It was rarely absent from everyday discourses, yet never explicitly uttered.

The fee to be paid to some local boss to avoid unwanted losses, the bribe to be given to the law court's usher to put a case in the "right place," and even the transfer of the Public Prosecutor for "ambient incompatibilities"[9]—all of those facts, along with innumerable others, were told with the specific mix of urgency and modesty in those who have intimate knowledge yet dare not be direct. Their speech was punctuated by sudden silences and meaningful looks upward, almost alluding to a superior entity, if not divine then at least equally mighty.[10]

My feeling of ease and amazed contemplation soon ran up against the limits posed by the progressive distancing of my lawyer relatives. Despite their initial promises of complete support for my research, they soon realized that my full access to their legal practices could affect our relationships and preferred to avoid such potential danger. Giovanni was presented to me as a way out of the dilemma of taking the risk of allowing me full access to their professional lives.[11] This led to the re-specification of my role of researcher by restoring a degree of useful "extraneousness" (Srinivas 1996: 232f.) and formed the beginning of a fruitful collaboration.

Giovanni, a young lawyer in the suburbs of Naples', appeared to me as the epitome of a Southern Italian lawyer. He admitted very openly that, in spite of not himself having any affiliation to organized crime, many of his clients came from that background. Thanks to my introduction through the family network, a certain degree of trust was already established and the access to his practice was

---

7 "Recommendation," often with criminal implications: pressure for eluding the law is made on the basis of social relationships.

8 On clientship in Southern Italy see Eisenstadt and Lemarchand (1982) and Graziano (1973).

9 In 1999 the journalist Giorgio Bocca was accused of libel by the Neapolitan lawyers' society, because he published an article in the national newspaper *La Republica* entitled "The Capital of Illegality," in which he related how thousands of Neapolitan lawyers requested the transfer of the Public Prosecutor Cordova. He argued as well that those lawyers were supporting organized crime and were directly linked to some of the political class defined as "the robbers of Italy" because they used to open bank accounts to receive bribes and kickbacks. See Cassazione penale, sez. Quinta, 14.1.2002, n. 1188.

10 On the peculiar tension between occultation and mimicry in corruption see Blundo's argument (this volume) on the descriptivity of corruption.

11 I am grateful to my cousin Silvia Maltese for her assistance with negotiating my role as a researcher in our family entourage.

not an issue. Instead, the analysis of data very soon became a matter of discussion. I realized that Giovanni's files shared certain features with everyday discourse in the way things were left unspoken and allusions were made to local references. His files unequivocally presented "gaps" and "silences" which from time to time rendered the document "corrupted" and suddenly hindered my understanding. These files embodied the linguistic opposition between transparency and opacity. At some crucial places they no longer pointed to an object beyond; instead, they interrupted any possibility of a transparent semiosis. I could not understand the reason for such sudden opacity. Was this simply my ignorance of the subtleties of legal procedures or was it something else?

Giovanni himself turned out to be the most efficient remedy for the impasse created by my initial concentration on files. I was very soon involved in enlightening sessions with Giovanni who, as the author of the corrupted files, enjoyed listening to himself while reviving some forgotten stages of the cases. These discussions were recorded on film by Marius, my husband, who also collaborated in the research project (cf. n. 3). Giovanni took an half-hearted pleasure in listening to himself when we watched the footage together. Although he did not always like the performance of his accounts, he began to esthetically appreciate the construction of his hypothesis.

The more Giovanni engaged in the urgency to explain, the more the corrupted files became transparent in meaning and thereby began to reveal riveting paths of analysis. Yet, almost simultaneously, criticism from a deontological, ethical, and legal level began to grow in me and to become a source of embarrassment. I was suffering the dilemma so well described by Flood (1983: 145f.) who, after sharing the drinking habits of the subjects of his study, started wondering about the reliability of his own fieldnotes. In fact, I dreaded reconstructing these significant corruptions in an academic context. The nature of these corruptions could not be understood without some sort of even minimal involvement on my part and I began to wonder not only about my ethical and legal responsibility, but also about my ability to take sufficient distance to relate my experience.

As an anthropologist, I had already engaged in collaborative projects not only in the classical configuration of wife and husband, both anthropologists, but also together with consultants. However, the peculiarity of this situation pushed me further in the dialectical constructions previously experienced. I had to give up—at least temporarily—part of my singularity in order to adhere convincingly to a world in which "belonging" would be an unacceptable option, yet "openly disagreeing" would signify the complete failure of my effort to understand.[12]

The collaboration between Giovanni, Marius, and myself took different forms during our two longer stays in the field in 2003 and 2004. A gradual evolution occurred from a transfer-type of relationship in which trust operated as an occasion to let off steam for Giovanni, to Giovanni becoming more actively engaged and taking on the position of guide and finally even of critical interlocutor

---

12 For a report on the recent history of belonging in relation to organized crime see Jacquemet (1996: 19–58).

in our collaborative project.[13] Similarly to other long-term relationships developed in the field, our fieldwork continued even from home.[14] This chapter was planned in Naples but was written and re-written in Berlin and at the Gold Coast campus in Australia through several conversations during reciprocal visits, phone calls, shared materials, shared field footage, and eventually shared drafts.

Unlike more conventional approaches this work does not intend to answer contingent problems of formal justice.[15] Its aim is not to find new or more efficient ways of fighting corruption. Nor is it to argue about its immorality. Rather, by drawing on the modalities of corruption, we want to reveal its essentially multi-layered nature, often not perceptible to foreign eyes. For this purpose, concerns about the absolute truth in relation to the facts recounted by the informants are irrelevant: what is considered of primary importance is the construction or rather co-construction of those facts by social actors. The rejection of the rigid dichotomy between the supposed objectivity of the researcher and the supposed subjectivity of the informant was initiated by Geertz (1973; 1983: 55–70) and is now almost taken for granted in current scholarship. Yet the difficulties of dialogue in and beyond academia must have discouraged the application of such theoretical achievements, since collaborative and reciprocal ethnography is still rare.[16] By blurring the boundary between the voice of the anthropologist and that of the informant, this work also sets out provocatively to overcome the claim for the superiority of scientific knowledge on social actors' perspectives.

This chapter agrees with Cain's suggestion that "those wishing to understand lawyers should read what they say about themselves, no matter how pompous, tedious or self-adulatory the text may be" (Cain and Harrington 1994: 20). Through our collaboration as anthropologist and lawyer, we furthermore try to develop dialectically Cain's subsequent reflection: "Lawyers are not wrong about themselves. The problem is rather that they do not understand the implications of their being so right" (ibid.). The above statement is an interesting portrayal of the often conflicting relationship between lawyers and social scientists and of the different roles and legitimacy of both disciplines in society. For that reason we reconstruct the polyphony of voices informing the choices by Giovanni in

---

13 For detailed examples of how relationships in the field shape the fieldwork itself see Georges and Jones (1980).

14 As during our previous fieldwork in South Asia, some of the relationships established in the field seem to be destined to last forever, and to evolve, for better or worse, with time. On our experience of fieldwork from home see Holden and Holden (2002).

15 For a non-exhaustive list of works on corruption and organized crime in Italy from a more conventional perspective see Baglivo (1983), Barbagallo (1988), Barbagallo, Marmo, and Calise (1988), Behan (2002), de Blasio (1897, 1973), Rossi (1983), Sabetti (2002), and Sales (1988). For a socio-legal approach framing a macro and micro analysis of corruption within the Italian political context of the 1990s see Nelken and Levi (1996). For a recent anthropological study see Schneider and Schneider (2003)—see also its review by Sabetti (2003). Among the sociological analyses of formal misconduct among lawyers see Arnold and Hagan (1992).

16 For an outstanding collaborative work developing a dialectical perspective see Worth and Aidar (1972).

the defense strategy (Ducrot 1984: ch. 8). Different, sometimes overlapping and contrasting, voices—often belonging to the same speaker—together construct the narrative.[17] For the sake of the story's relevance, anthropologist and consultant, as co-authors of the narrative, at times merge and become indistinct, whereas at other points one moves to the background.

The model created by the Russian philologist and structuralist Propp (1968) for the analysis of the narrative elements of folktales seems particularly appropriate to Giovanni's favorite metaphor of lawyering as a fight between good and evil. Similar to Propp's scheme, Giovanni often views himself as the hero who, thanks to some external intervention (the donor, in Propp's model), can potentially achieve the success of an almost impossible enterprise. The challenge for Giovanni is to foresee the right sequence of steps to reach success. His dramatic narrative style together with his incessant quest for the next logical step also perfectly matches the model for the analysis of the narrative structure developed by Propp's disciple Greimas. Greimas's semiotic scheme focuses on the distinction between, on the one hand, an abstract and logical level characterized by oppositional and negational terms and, on the other hand, the more concrete narrative level where such relations are actualized (Greimas 1970: 157ff.). In Greimas's scheme of narratology the story is seen in the terms of a quest proceeding along binary oppositions. The hero accepts a contract on the basis of which he must fight for the attainment of an object. He must pass different tests before eventually defeating a villain, often a traitor, and thereby obtaining victory.

Greimas's scheme is somewhat imaginatively applied hereafter by using the notions of "hero," "traitor," "fight," "victory," and "performativity." The notion of actant (Greimas 1974, 1976) as later developed by Latour with the Actor Network Theory (1987, 1988) is used in the form of actantial direction: a directional concretion of forces in a given text. The actant can be both an abstraction or a collective character or even different characters playing similar roles (Greimas 1970, 1976, 1983; Greimas and Courtes 1983). Human and non-human instances are both considered as actants for their relevance in determining a specific action within the observed network (Callon 1986; Latour 1988). Finally this chapter also draws from the application of Propp's models by Jacquemet in his linguistic study on the mega-trials concerning organized crime in the 1990s (Jacquemet 1991, 1992a, 1992b, 1993, 1994, 1996, and 2001). However, in order to privilege the nuances of praxis the above-mentioned concepts and semiotic categories will not be applied with theoretical rigor and will function primarily as inspirational reference.

Forecasting (Lack of) Success

In 1998 Giovanni was nominated by Mr Buonomo, from jail, as his defense lawyer in a case in which he was accused of participating in a multiple homicide. It was a case of little importance at the national level, yet it was the first time that the

---

17 On the notion of narrative as data, see also Czarniawska (1997).

Piovra clan had entrusted Giovanni with the defense of one of their affiliates. Giovanni had previously been the legal counselor to Buonomo's cellmate, a man convicted to 29 years imprisonment, in his efforts to obtain a permit to attend a burial. Although Giovanni did not obtain the permit, rumor had it that he was the lawyer who could get things done.

Buonomo's relatives went to Giovanni's office for a first meeting and Giovanni's attitude was thoroughly examined. It was a crucial moment. Apparently my professionalism was not enough as Buonomo's relatives did not want to find just an expert. I had to show my belief in Buonomo's innocence. "*Avvoca' sinun ce credete vvoi ...*" ("My lawyer, if you do not trust [your client] yourself ..."). I was to be there not only for technical assistance but also for moral support in what was their tragedy. Most of the time, I can understand if a client is guilty or not. Yet when I took up this case, I built in myself the inner conviction of my client's innocence. "*Ma è chiaro che il vostro parente è innocente. Dobbiamo fare luce sui motivi di questa soffiata*" ("It is evident that your relative is innocent. We have to point out the motives for this tip-off.")

The first step was already taken: not only was Giovanni empathetic with Buonomo's relatives, but after a quick estimation of the case, he decided to take the risk to go to trial and plead innocent. This was the much-awaited opportunity to make himself known within the world of the organized crime. "The family just trusts me, and trusting my client is nothing but the lawyer's duty. I do not have to do any specific legal research, and this case will just be my publicity campaign."

The situation was unequivocally presented by Giovanni as a good opportunity to make a career. But what about Giovanni's actual freedom to take or refuse this case? Was Giovanni's involvement in organized crime at that precise moment not a taken-for-granted fact by his clients? Could his involvement have been already traced in other seemingly insignificant events, such as his participation in a boss's burial, or the meeting with a runaway convict? In spite of Giovanni's denial, it seemed that the odds of Giovanni's refusing to defend Buonomo in court were very low. Notwithstanding the possibility of many (un)predictable outcomes, this story was obeying the rhetoric of persuasion from its very beginning. Giovanni's visitors, appropriating and manipulating the legal language of lawyers, were incorporating Giovanni in a legitimate mission leading to a possible illegal involvement. "*Avvoca' sinun ce credete vvoi ....*" The exact words and the vernacular prosody of that unfinished sentence echoed in Giovanni's head almost as if to remind him of its pragmatic coded implications. Those five suspended words sanctioned both the common goal of lawyer and clients and their binding relationship, which stemmed from the lawyer's duty of acting in the interest of his client but merged with the necessity to obtain an outcome in conformity with his unquestionable innocence. Those five words were self-explanatory. Adopting a metalinguistic device significant to both the world of law and the world of organized crime, Giovanni's clients were displaying their ability to manage different repertoires.[18] Giovanni, like the hero of Russian tales, went to trial following the order of his

---

18 On the management of different styles of language and code-switching in a courtroom see Jacquemet (1996: 118–22, 133).

commissioners for obtaining the acquittal of his client, in exchange for fame and riches. "*Avvoca' sinun ce credete vvoi ...*" played the role of an actant in the story since it formed the semantic unity capable of directing powerful forces toward a specific outcome. In its role of actant that sentence sent Giovanni out to walk the line where the boundaries of legality and illegality are blurred.

In fact, according to Giovanni's favorite image of the legal process as a fight, he stood as one soldier against an army, with the daunting task of securing the victory of both the hero and his mission. Even if it was not explicit, it was evident that Giovanni had to obtain the acquittal of a guilty client. He had the mission to save his client but similar to the hero of Greimas's folktales (1970, 1983) he also had to protect himself from the danger of saving a guilty client at all costs. Hence both the mission and the hero were at stake: needing and obstructing each other at the same time, both were nonetheless necessary to the flow of the story. The paradoxical character of his mission clearly laid in the kind of involvement demanded of Giovanni for obtaining the acquittal: how could he imply that he believed in his client's innocence while knowing he was guilty?

If Giovanni acted primarily for the success of the mission it could mean his own failure by being faced with legal responsibility or with physical danger to his own person as the result of the adversarial clan's revenge. Giovanni wanted to avoid both and gradually manipulated the content of his mission to avoid these dangers. The chances for him to refuse this case and face the implications were probably at this stage already very limited. Eventually the hero would have to work hard to find a way out of the paradox.

The Promising Beginning of a Vendetta Strategy

The multiple homicide for which Buonomo had to go to trial and for which Giovanni was appointed as defense lawyer in 1998 dated back 11 years. For a long time the police had no clue about its perpetrators, until during another trial a *pentito*, the equivalent of the American mafia's turncoats,[19] accused Mr Buonomo and seven other people of having taken part in the crime.

"Unfortunately, the testimony of the *pentiti*, if considered reliable, is by law conclusive for punishment. Consequently, in spite of the efforts of the Public Prosecutor and of the defense-lawyer to clarify the facts and the stories, the conclusive elements will be given during the trial by the collaborators of Justice." The above was Giovanni's recurrent anticipation of the uncertainty of the outcome. Such a degree of uncertainty was difficult to bear for Giovanni, who remained pessimistic in spite of reminding himself that after such a gap of time the Public Prosecutor could not have found any evidence other than the *pentito*'s declaration.

Considering the overall lack of historiographic details, Giovanni began to mobilize a notion which had only been alluded to at the time of the first meeting

---

19 Since the 1990s the Italian government has adopted a series of statutes protecting those affiliated to organized crime who accepted to collaborate with justice.

with his client's relatives: the vendetta.[20] It could be argued that the *pentito*'s sudden memory did nothing but confirm his vendetta motive. Thanks to his contacts, Giovanni was in a good position to inquire further into the motives for a vendetta and consequently provide the judge with objective elements undermining the *pentito*'s testimony. In this way Giovanni could hopefully obtain an acquittal, or at least a reduction of punishment for his client. Even in the case of a sentence hope would not be completely lost, as potentially the appeal judgment would reverse the judgment of the inferior law court. The hero was cleverly introducing at least the possibility of a victory for himself.

At this point the story had acquired the following actors as Giovanni's opponents: the *pentito*, or traitor; the Public Prosecutor, probably trusting the *pentito*; and the law, which provided the tools for the declaration of the *pentiti* to be productive. The alignment was changing and Giovanni was again to face a powerful set of opposing forces with a sole ally, his client's family. As a defense tactic the vendetta indeed had the greatest potential because, in the context of Southern Italy, it did not immediately require a specific reason. "Everybody knows that mafia stories are at some point linked to vendetta." This also explained why the police at the time of the commissioning of the facts did not bother to inquire further once it was ascertained that the murder took place within the milieu of the organized crime.

As a worst-case scenario, Giovanni imagined he would not manage to convince the judge of the *pentito*'s motives for vendetta and Buonomo's extraneousness to the crime, and would thus have to anticipate a life sentence for his client. The best outcome would be that the *pentito*'s declaration would be seen as fitting a vendetta design against Buonomo, in this way undermining the credibility of the accusation. However, even if it would not be possible to completely convince the judge of the supposed vendetta, its powerful role would not be entirely lost. Giovanni would use the motive of vendetta to obtain a second-most-beneficial outcome: a reduced sentence or otherwise an appeal.

All the above options ensured Giovanni of the much-awaited fame coming from being trusted as a counselor for an important case irrespective of the outcome for his client: Giovanni was confident he would be able to manipulate the content of the mission as long as he was given the chance to engage in a full-length trial.

Cheating to Win

Some time later, however, some of Buonomo's co-defendants, who were on trial together with him for the multiple homicide, decided to ask for the *patteggiamento*, a special settlement procedure that would allow them to avoid trial and receive

---

20 For a collection of works including anthropological, historical, and philosophical perspectives on the vendetta see Verdier, Poly, and Courtois (1980).

a reduced punishment.[21] This was annoying for Giovanni for two reasons. First, Buonomo could allow himself to be persuaded to follow this step, which would deprive Giovanni of both financial income and professional triumph. Second, a previous sentence in the same case could affect the conviction, if not of the judge, then surely of the jurors having to decide Buonomo's destiny. In spite of still being at a loss for details of what happened, Giovanni persuaded his client of going for the vendetta strategy by capitalizing on his claim of innocence and convincing him that going to trial would be his only chance to stand up against the *pentito*.

Given the already low chances of success, Giovanni's choice appears reckless: instead of welcoming a safe way out, he reinvested in his strategy knowing that it would potentially lead to a life sentence for his client. With the excuse of not contradicting the assumption of innocence of his client, he was betraying Buonomo in order to secure success for himself. "I was closing a door for my client by opening one for myself, but by doing so, I would possibly display the strength of my pleading and gain the favor of my audience, and obtain a beneficial outcome for my client after all!"

Buonomo, who because of a pervious sentence had to serve several years of jail anyway, decided to follow Giovanni's advice and to go to trial for participating in the multiple homicide, thus refusing the *patteggiamento*. In April 1998, the *pattegiamento* process for Buonomo's co-defendants concluded with a 21-year prison sentence, reduced to 14 years thanks to both the alternative method and their collaboration in becoming themselves *pentiti*. It was the first of the many forecasted (un)successful strategies for Giovanni and his client. Not only did the judge recognize the credibility of the *pentito* but one of Buonomo's co-defendants was called as a witness and collaborator of justice against Buonomo. Giovanni requested and obtained the documents of the *patteggiamento* judgment and the police protocol dating back to 1987. He hoped to find new hints in order to better defend his client at the trial and in this way transform the forecasted (non) success into a success.

Against the Power of Words

Possibly my client's judge would follow the same logic as the judge who recognized the credibility of the *pentito*. I could only deconstruct the Public Prosecutor's discourse. To avoid a complete defeat, I had to try to understand the judge's reasoning on the basis of his judgment, and consequently develop an alternative discourse, a discourse of criticism.

The odds again seemed against Giovanni but he did not exclude the possibility of a change in luck and set out to resist the defeat embodied in the judgment. The text of the judgment, despite not containing any legal consequences for Giovanni's

---

21 For more details on the *patteggiamento* or *applicazione della pena a richiesta delle parti* (application of the penalty by request of the parties) see Delmas-Marty and Spencer (2002: 372f).

client, was much more than a semantic representation of the judge's discourse. It was a voice against which Giovanni tried to produce a counter-narrative, or at least a resistance tactic. Giovanni seemed aware of such a peculiar network of communication between the text of the judgment and himself. "Hence my defense work focused on detecting the modalities of evaluation of the witness's credibility to try to undermine the testimony with the help of the same text that had previously supported it." Giovanni spotted the weak points in the *pentito*'s credibility and, almost theatrically recreating the scenario, started to read out some extracts of the hearing by alternatively personifying the judge and the *pentito*:

> Judge: Do you remember whether the defendant was present at the meeting in which the elimination of such person was decided?
>
> *Pentito* (Giovanni is speaking with a strong accent): Your Honor, I would not deny, I would not deny at all because we were used to seeing each other so much and so much ... that practically we used to meet every day. We were at his place all the time. So, I will not deny that he was there.

Here, code-switching from standard Italian to Italian with a strong accent marks Giovanni's breakthrough into full performance. By personifying both the judge and the *pentito* his performance on the one hand displays the extent of his knowledge and on the other hand distances himself from the audience (Hymes 2004: 90f; Jacquemet 1994).

"The above passages are not conclusive of the presence of that person at the place and hour of the commission of the crime. We have to be very clear because if a person is not present at the moment of the decision, that person cannot be considered as an instigator. In such organizations some people have the power to decide, and some other people don't have such power. However, those persons can very well be the material perpetrators of crimes. To have a career as a criminal lawyer, it is essential to know criminal life."

> Judge (Giovanni is speaking with his usual accent): You should tell us clearly whether the defendant was present at the meeting or not!
>
> *Pentito* (Giovanni is again speaking with a strong accent): Your Honor, I don't remember, because if I remembered I shall remember a lot of people, and a lot of facts ... Because to tell the truth it was a continuous coming and going, Your Honor.

At this point, Giovanni had prepared two kinds of meta-discursive attacks.[22] The first one was based on the confrontation of the *pentito* with the hard facts, meaningful not only to the public "out there," the so-called "good people," but especially meaningful to the *pentito*, and consequently to the judge, who put his trust in the *pentito*'s knowledge of the world of organized crime. Giovanni showed that he knew the rules of criminal life by explaining the difference between the

---

22 For a detailed analysis of similar meta-discursive strategies in Neapolitan law courts see Jacquemet (1996: 163).

perpetrators of a crime—those who committed the killing but who were not necessarily physically present at the meeting where the killing was decided—and the instigators—the ones who decided on the multiple homicide, in other words the ones who "had to be there" at the meeting. The second meta-discursive attack was more generally based on trying to attract the attention of the judge to the *pentito*'s vagueness and to the looseness of his narrative. Both attacks had the purpose of creating a breach in the alliance between the judge, the Public Prosecutor, and the witness.

Notwithstanding his elaborate defense preparation, Giovanni was pessimistic about the outcome as he sensed the alignment between the Public Prosecutor, the judge, and the *pentito* as too strong. Besides, the vendetta argument seemed to be heading for failure, as he could not find any corroborative element. Some kind of actantial direction was its only support: hostility would come from the *pentito* and act toward his client. Such hostility was, however, still too vague and could not be effectively mobilized as confirmation of a proper vendetta because the action of a previous offence was missing (Greimas 1983a: 225–46). Giovanni was aware that his meta-discursive tactics would not be strong enough against the powerful alignment of actors and actants. As a soldier left alone at the front, he was gathering his last munitions, conscious of a certain defeat, yet at the same time anticipating the taste of the fame that the approaching battle would bring.

Deus Ex Machina

In 2003, shortly after the committal to trial, a *deus ex machina* materialized in the form of a procedural error, which could lead to the acquittal of Giovanni's client: the Public Prosecutor forgot to include the second *pentito*, Buonomo's ex-co-defendant, in the witness list. This was the miracle that could secure the victory of both the hero and its mission. Since it is necessary to have two reliable witnesses for a conviction, Giovanni's client would be acquitted if the Public Prosecutor could call only one witness. Suddenly, Giovanni's interest in the case was reawakened, but he decided to keep quiet in order to take full advantage of his adversary's error. Almost forgetting his luck, he worried about the details that could come from the testimony, and once again he summarized the facts for me, making me realize to what extent they had until then been pushed into the background by the many steps of the legal procedure.

The facts were the following. Two rival societies belonging to the Piovra clan and to the Macchia clan were fighting for control over territory in the Vesuvian area. Both clans wanted to agree to a truce, and Mr Calogero, from the Macchia clan, offered his office as a neutral meeting place. Mr Calogero, however, did not show up at the meeting. Nor did Mr Forti, the Piovra clan's affiliate and the designated victim of the ambush. Mr Ricci and Mr Porretta, affiliates to the Macchia clan, arrived only later and were immediately gunned down. A few years later, Mr Calogero, suspected of betrayal, was killed too.

Giovanni went through the file again and seemed to discover the police protocol for the first time: "Look! There is nothing conclusive about the responsibility of my client ...," I said: "It sounds promising, then." Giovanni looked at me rapidly and said: "But he ...." Unwillingly surprised, he tried to change the subject. Anyway, irrespective of the historical facts, whether his client had killed the victim or not, the charge was homicide, and, as such, Giovanni risked his client's "life" (life's sentence). "Another element in my favor is that these people wanted, in fact, to kill another person. This case is merely grounded on hypothesis. There is no certitude."

Giovanni still seemed to be afraid, in spite of his excellent secret about the prosecutor's error to include the second *pentito*, which felt like a time-bomb in his pocket. He would possibly free himself of the uncomfortable role of traitor by eventually appearing in the clothes of the hero. Yet the organized sequences of time that had earlier allowed him to conceive his defense tactics one after another had now been replaced by the uncertainty of events at the trial. For the first time, the alignment in the fight was in Giovanni's favor, but he somewhat feared the outcome. More lawyers would be present in the courtroom of the hearing. "They are experienced senior-lawyers. It is more difficult for me than for them because I am the defense-lawyer of the killer. They are defending the instigators. It is a much easier task because they are not linked to the materiality of facts—all the more so as the reason of the murder is not clear."

Witnessing the Invisible

The testimony, from a high security prison, was done via video-conferencing. The *pentito*'s back appeared on the screen and all sorts of technical problems made understanding what he was saying difficult. Sometimes there was video but no audio and vice-versa. The defense lawyer of one of the co-defendants asked to interrupt the hearing to reconnect the communication and try for a better audio. Nobody seemed to hear properly. Only the judge claimed to hear perfectly and repeated to the lawyers what was said. He kept suggesting that the witness should move away from the microphone. The echo indeed then ceased but the voice, in spite of all sorts of technical re-arrangements, became even more indistinct.

My presence in the audience was not a source of disturbance any more. The initial surprise among the spectators at noticing somebody extraneous to both the legal scene and the kinship network had given way to a reassuring attitude of indifference. I could not understand a single word of the testimony, possibly because of my position among the crowd. However, there were enough speakers in the room. I was wondering what Giovanni could hear from his bench. He appeared confused. The Public Prosecutor asked the witness if he knew a series of people. The *pentito* missed a name and the judge asked him insistently if he knew that person. Suddenly there was an argument between a defense lawyer and the judge. The lawyer maintained that the judge was not acting according to the procedure: "I am very surprised at you, Your Honor. You are trying to put a name in the mouth of the witness!" The judge kept on asking but no longer insisted on that exact person. The hearing concluded with the judge dictating the testimony for the records.

Intermezzo

I met with Giovanni briefly, as he was in a rush. He appeared negative. Why—given the fact that apparently there again was no certitude about the facts and the persons involved? Giovanni hated the video-conferencing technology. "It interrupts the rhythm, it does not allow the participants to create any atmosphere, the feelings are blocked, the sequence of question/answer cannot be respected. This interferes too much with the immediacy of the criminal trial. The cross-examination is not effective anymore. The quality of the audio was too poor. The single words were not audible. How could the judge understand anything at all?" The matter was evolving and becoming complex. Indeed, I remembered having seen Giovanni and the other lawyers in discussion with the judge at the end of the hearing. We could not hear anything from the bench reserved to the public. I needed Giovanni to tell me something about that.

A Systemic Trap

Giovanni did not have the time or the willingness to explain what had happened during the animated discussion between the judge and the defense lawyers at the end of the first hearing. I was therefore left with merely a supposition about his apparent lack of interest at the very moment in which he had the possibility of achieving the most unexpected and best outcome. I was going to the second hearing hoping to detect in the official procedure at least a hint of the secret deal that had possibly discouraged Giovanni.

The lawyers were joking amongst themselves. Giovanni was consulting his files, worried as usual. Somewhat theatrically, the Public Prosecutor was opening his gown to show off his new jeans-suit to his colleagues. The people involved in the trial, including the policemen, the defendants, the witnesses, and the relatives, all seemed to be part of the same community. After some cheerful exchanges, the hearing started. The screen switched on and a new *pentito*'s back appeared. He wanted to be heard first, but the judge wanted to be sure about the presence of his lawyer. The lawyer was not there as he had not been informed. The chancellor started to call around, and in the meanwhile another person's back appeared on the screen. It was Coppola, Buonomo's ex co-defendant.

The Public Prosecutor slowly repeated the facts but suddenly interrupted himself to ask Coppola about his participation in the multiple homicide. "I have already been sentenced," Coppola said. Thus the Public Prosecutor asked after the reason for the meeting before the homicide. The audio was again very bad, and I could not hear anything. Nobody seemed to be bothered and the Public Prosecutor moved on with his sequence of questions very fast, barely waiting for the answer, but pausing significantly from time to time: "Who decided the homicide?" The technician pointed out the audio problem again and the judge instructed Coppola almost irritatedly to move away from the microphone. "The meeting was attended by eight people …," Coppola repeated. The examination proceeded without interruption for a little while.

> *Public Prosecutor*: Did you ever take part in similar meetings?
> *Coppola*: No.
> *Public Prosecutor*: Can you tell exactly where the meeting was held?
> *Coppola*: Via Barbaglia n. 26.
> *Public Prosecutor*: When did you hear about the meeting?
> *Coppola*: That same day.
> *Public Prosecutor*: How many people were with you the day of the homicide? What kind of arms did you have?
> *Coppola*: We were just two. We had four guns and one rifle. After the murder, we set the car on fire and got rid of the weapons.
> *Public Prosecutor*: Four guns and one rifle for only two people?
> Coppola: I already said that!

The Public Prosecutor was finished. The examination did not bring any new elements, but that was not its aim. The Public Prosecutor did nothing but reproduce the police protocol from his file. It was now the turn of the defense lawyers. A co-defendant's lawyer insisted on checking details, the exact date, the hour, the season, how many days after he had left prison, how he had reached the place, and whether the police protocol had been signed by the witness. The same questions were asked over and over again in different phrases, almost without waiting for answers. More on contextual details followed: was it sunny that day, at what time did it grow dark? Time seemed to stretch indefinitely. What was the defense lawyer looking for? I could not recognize the alignments in the contest that was going on in front of my eyes. I perceived some kind of resignation pervading the courtroom at the most anticipated moment. After about 20 years from the facts, when finally the law was to decide the destiny of the defendants, the defense lawyers seemed to do nothing but waste time.[23]

Suddenly the judge scolded the defense lawyer for his irrelevant questions. "The witness does not remember and we must go on with the trial." Angrily the lawyer accused the judge of preventing the witness from explaining the facts in general terms. Evidently there was a difference between the truth researched by the judge and the truth researched by the lawyer in that specific context. The judge was only interested in some details and not in others. The lawyer wanted the witness to speak, maybe in a desperate attempt to find a hint to undermine his credibility. It was now Giovanni's turn to proceed with the cross-examination:

> *Giovanni*: Did you have some decision-making power at the time of the homicide?
> *Coppola*: No.
> *Giovanni*: Do you remember how long that fateful meeting in which the homicide was decided lasted?
> *Coppola*: It was a matter of seconds ... in words ... of minutes.
> *Giovanni*: Are you able to tell whether Mr. Buonomo was present at that meeting?
> *Coppola*: No, he wasn't there.
> *Giovanni*: Since when have you been an affiliate of the Piovra clan?

---

23 On taking time and delaying legal procedure as defense strategy see Holden, Holden, Manfredonia, and Serrao d'Aquino (2006).

Coppola: How can I tell since when ... I used to live 300 m. from that person and at 100 m. from that other person? We are all together.
Giovanni: Did you know Mr Buonomo's family before the homicide?
Coppola: No.

Giovanni did not appear satisfied. He seemed to be on the point of asking another question, but the judge was in a hurry and decided to carry on with the examination himself. He repeated the question asked by the defense lawyers: "What was your role during the meetings?" The witness had a marginal role and remembered how Mr Buonomo was usually present at the meetings. "He was among the ones who gave a substantial and straightforward support to the *onorata famiglia*."[24] Giovanni asked how he knew of the presence of his client if he was not sure about his own presence at the meetings. But time was up. The judge cut the interrogation short saying that the witness knew from hearsay. The hearing was finished. The screen was switched off and the courtroom was suddenly silent. The chancellor was writing.

The judge was rushing to collect his files and his suitcases to get away but the defense lawyers stopped him. As if the lights had been switched on on a different stage set, the animated exchange only alluded to by Giovanni started while the public was leaving the room. I wanted to stay and Giovanni told the policeman that I was with him. The judge suddenly seemed to realize my presence and expected me to leave. Then I thought that the judge himself wanted to leave! But the lawyers spoke loudly almost all at the same time. Eventually the judge promised that their clients would be allowed the last word. Giovanni finally deployed his secret weapon by saying that because of the Public Prosecutor's procedural fault the trial could be annulled. As a prey looking for an escape, the judge restated that if the lawyers would ask for annulment he himself would call the forgotten witness at the end of the hearing. "Art. 507 [Criminal Procedure Code]!," he said in a warning tone. Art. 507 of the Criminal Procedure Code provides the judge with the possibility of calling the forgotten witness at the end of the hearing after the examination of the defendants. This is a dreadful event for the defense because it overturns the rule according to which the last word is granted to the defense. As Italian lawyers still use to invest in the final pleading, this was a very bad turn of events. The judge left the room and everybody disappeared.

I left the courtroom with Giovanni. For once he appeared happy. After this defeat I was wondering whether he was hoping for a victory for next time, or whether it was just the wonderful weather outside. He told me that there was no hope for his client. But, he said: "I was contacted by a robber. He is being investigated in connection to a well-known hold-up in a local bank. He is probably guilty. It even made headlines because of the ordinary citizens queuing at the local branch. It's a big case."

---

24 Seemingly coming from the context of the Sicilian mafia the term "onorata famiglia" (lit. honored family) stands for organized crime. It refers to the complex relationships that grounding on honor and kinship constitute the network of rights and obligations of its members.

Marketing (Il)legal Logic

"What is the difference between defending a robber who killed a policeman and a killer who killed a criminal? Guilty defendants have the right to legal counseling anyway," said Giovanni, avoiding my questions concerning his position in Buonomo's case. The puzzling element of this story was that apparently at the very moment that our hero was given the chance for an honest and unquestionable victory for both himself and his mission, he withdrew from the fight and even confessed that he thought that his client might be guilty, almost more to justify his betrayal than because of a sudden moral or legal concern.

Buonomo's trial was not coming to an end yet, but it was as if it had already been decided. The alignments were destroyed and the time sequence distorted. Art. 507 was all that was left standing. The judge's deal was that he would call the forgotten witness anyway but in exchange he would allow a last word to the accused. By using this ultimate weapon, the judge did not have to fight to obtain the consent of the lawyers, who could only retreat. Giovanni was not proud of his role as traitor, yet he repeated to himself that he was no longer convinced of his client's innocence.

Furthermore Giovanni was himself busy figuring out the defense of the robber whose business card had been found on the scene of the robbery. During the hold-up a policeman had been killed. The robber's participation had also been inadvertently tipped off by his own son, who, worried about his father, openly went to look for him at the site of the crime. "Once again the police did not gather enough evidence against my client. Even the analysis done on the bullets used for killing the policeman did not bring any conclusive element against him." The greatest concern for Giovanni was about whether to go for a full-length trial or not. What would be the most successful approach?

Time was now flying by. Giovanni was called in the middle of the night by a killer. For €3,000 he had just murdered a crucial witness of a racket involving the prostitution of minors. He consented to meet him in a secluded place and listened to his story: who sent him, how he killed the victim, and who saw him while he was running away from the scene of the crime with the gun under his arm. In no time they went to the police and the man was put in jail.

This time Giovanni was not balancing between the role of hero and the role of traitor. He was both of them. By walking again on the thin line between legal and illegal, he would secure success for himself and possibly a beneficial outcome for his client. Giovanni had a perfect plan: the witness to this murder had suffered from sexual assault during his childhood. Giovanni had already contacted a well-known criminologist who would testify about the witness's unreliability to relate the facts logically because of his horrible past. Would the family of his client pay all the money demanded by the criminologist?

My impression was that he had changed tracks. Giovanni no longer hesitated to pursue his own personal success regardless of the implications. In the meanwhile, in spite of my disconcerted feeling about the recent transformation of Giovanni's practice, I continued to follow Buonomo's trial. Everything proceeded slowly. The same questions were repeated. The lawyers rephrased previous questions and changed their sequence. Giovanni insisted on the role of the witness in the clan. He inquired into his contacts in jail. Then suddenly came the key question: the one concerning the affiliation to the *onorata famiglia*. Thanks to his contacts, Giovanni knew that at a certain point Coppola had ceased to receive money from them any more. This could have been the reason for his revenge! But there was no evidence linking the Coppola family to Buonomo. After many highs and lows, the vendetta tactic ended here, because it failed the minimal requisite of a link between the opposing parties. Everything led to the conclusion that the dice had already been cast and that in spite of the actors' inner motivations and the powerful alignments of the actants, the fight would officially conclude with the triumph of law over organized crime.

Giovanni kept asking. By drawing on his local knowledge, he cleverly reinterpreted the notion of the materiality of facts. From a strictly legal point of view the instigators were not materially involved in the crime; in the context of organized crime, however, the instigators were the people "materially" involved in the crime as they were the ones physically present at the moment of the decision-making about the murder. In contrast, in strictly legal terms the material perpetrators of the homicide were "dematerialized" by the series of ritual procedures always preceding a mortal mission: getting rid of any identity cards, mixing all the guns together, and wearing gloves. In this way no direct link could ever be established between one individual and the killing. Giovanni would keep this new weapon behind his back until the very last session of the trial.

Giovanni had also changed his mind about organized crime. Whereas he previously did not hide his spontaneous admiration for the ability of bosses of organized crime to deal with the complex mechanisms of legal procedure, he was now declaring that they were simply stupid. His final pleading was nevertheless carefully organized: a third option appeared in Giovanni's pleading as if by magic. While everybody's efforts were focused on establishing the degree to which the defendants were affiliated to the Piovra clan, Giovanni had adjusted his target by admitting his client's possible involvement, but only in a secondary role. At the same time he provided the technical explanation concerning the "dematerialization" of the perpetrators. His discourse did not bring forth any further evidence but it did convince the jurors. Buonomo was sentenced to a longer time than his co-defendants who chose the *patteggiamento* but he escaped a life sentence.

After having been dragged into an unwanted deal by his peers, Giovanni won an unexpected victory. He had achieved the paradoxical aim of the victory of both the hero and its mission. The impossible coexistence of hero and traitor in the same actor had been overrun by the implicit connotation of traitor in relation to his peers. What his peers, in spite of their status and experience, had failed to achieve for their clients, Giovanni, the hero, had accomplished: he had saved Buonomo from a life sentence. The metaphor of the trial as a battle, however, was no longer convincing. Lawyering was becoming a sort of routine, where the outcomes were predictable and one's efforts became dedicated merely to the small space that existed for negotiation.

Concluding Comments: No Need for a Choice

This was the story of a young lawyer struggling for his career in the difficult context of Naples's suburbia and I have been lucky enough to share with him part of his progressive disenchantment with the legal profession. Is it possible to pinpoint corruption in this story? Could it lie perhaps in Giovanni's affiliation to organized crime or in the bribe to be given to the expert for undermining the witnessing? From a formal legal perspective, it was surely not in the manipulation of Buonomo's defense strategy. The more we enquire into the context of corruption, as it happened with Giovanni's corrupted files, corruption itself dematerializes: from opaque it becomes intelligible and thereby legitimates its own system of references. We do not want to establish the facts of corruption in a framework of legal responsibility, nor are we interested in pursuing a theorization of corruption irrespectively of praxis. Giovanni was never charged with corruption and the facts and the hints of Giovanni's progressive involvement with organized crime are not dealt with here in order to establish his legal responsibility. They show instead that corruption does not always necessitate a precise legal misconduct.

At specific times Giovanni's disenchantment, while being a continuum—possibly still in progression—featured a peculiar convergence of human and non-human instances. There are at least three examples of non-human actants in our stories: the sentence uttered by Giovanni's clients at their first meeting; the *patteggiamento* judgment, which in spite of not bearing any legal consequences for Giovanni's client, played a tangible role in the materialization of the specific defense tactic of meta-pragmatic attacks; and art. 507 CrPC, whose unexpected use by the judge led the lawyers to accept an awkward deal.

Since they belong to the realm of law but follow modalities that can only be understood with reference to praxis, I suggest defining the specific junctions of legal process in which the actants display or disclose their performativity as legal meta-pragmatic unities. Examples of legal meta-pragmatic unities in our story are Giovanni's first meeting with his client for the multiple homicide case, the choice of an alternative judgment by the co-defendants of Giovanni's client, and the deal between the judge and the lawyer.

The legal meta-pragmatic unities, in specific concretized form, allow the story to proceed beyond the abstract logic of the legal system by highlighting the career of legal reasons manufactured by actors and actants in view of a beneficial outcome (Scheffer 2003, 2004). The moments mentioned before are characterized by the fundamental uncertainty described by Flood as the essence of lawyering. "The fundamental uncertainty is that the deal might collapse, which for the lawyer might possibly mean losing the client and the fee" (Flood 1991: 67). Giovanni, like most lawyers, is driven by the necessity to attract clients with "big" cases in an effort to increase his reputation. He learned to manipulate and direct his clients' interests for the benefit of his professional career (Kritzer and Krishnan 1999).

However, Giovanni did not have to choose between the reasons for supporting the defense of Mr Buonomo and his own personal success. His choices did not present themselves as black-and-white options between honestly constructing a defense strategy or pursuing personal success through corruption and open manipulation of the law. The inner logic of organized crime allowed him to both respond to his client's need to claim innocence and shift freely from the role of hero to the role of traitor, walking on the thin edge of a grey area and duplicating himself to avoid the theoretically paradoxical confusion between the role of the traitor and the role of the hero (cf. Greimas 1974, 1976; Tarasti 1994).

Giovanni concluded that the process as a fight between "good" and "evil" is after all very much a systemic abstraction. His interest progressively shifted to the tiny procedural interstices that in a specific context allow an immediate benefit (cf. Bourdieu 1980). The positivist discourse about the certitude of law was accordingly re-specified in the light of local dynamics, whose networks act undetected by the official system. The predictable outcome, susceptible to being reproduced, therefore became the one following the local logic. Thus, corruption developed beside the exact event in which the illegal fact was materialized thanks to a network in which individuals act within the boundaries of local legality.

For a long time Giovanni has been critical of my analysis because of its potential consequences from the perspective of formal law. Our different professional affiliations may have played an important role in our conflict. The way in which corruption is highlighted in this chapter appeared to Giovanni as a sort of accusation of materializing corruption in the shadow of the law. I am not concerned, however, with the formal definition of corruption. Rather I want to attract attention to the paths that legal discourse takes when it pursues outcomes unnoticed by formal law. Lawyers are a specialized, skilled group accounting for the legal system to lay people (Sacks 1997) and this implies much more than simple routine (Giddings and Robertson 2002). Local legal praxis shows that relationships concur with discourse to shape the law in a broad sense (Cain and Harrington 1994). By responding to local logic, everyday legal praxis is the virtual reference both of lay people and of professionals, outside of the mapped routes of state law, and draws on much wider horizons than written texts (Twining 2000: ch. 5; Woodman 2002). Corruption thrives in and beyond formalism and by understanding its modalities it is also possible to grasp why corruption works so well when it responds to the need of praxis. And because when corruption responds to the needs of praxis it does so very efficiently, the boundaries of legal and illegal cannot but remain blurred. While the uncertainty of the local becomes intelligible with the help of local references, formal legal definitions help to the perpetuation of uncertainty.

Hence the interest of grasping local dynamics. As an anthropologist I am fascinated by the stories told in this chapter not because of designating the wrongdoers but because they make evident the complementarity of corruption and law. By looking at the modalities of corruption it appears that, unlike other crimes such as murder or theft, it is difficult to pinpoint the corrupted action beyond his formal definition. Corruption is illegal merely because it was designated as such by positive law and this definition loses its meaning beyond legal formalism. Ultimately corruption thrives along the shadowy paths of formal legality because law is needed for its very existence. By taking on himself the risk of balancing between legal and illegal Giovanni feels like a surgeon who saves people's life and can thereby transform the illegal into legal. "When I am asked how I can do what I do, I always say that the ones asking me those questions have a wrong perspective. Would you ask a surgeon the same thing? When I do the impossible for my clients, I feel very close to the surgeon who operates to save people's lives. Indeed I operate in a very similar manner to rescue people from jail."

References

Arnold, B.L. and Hagan, J. (1992) Careers of Misconduct: The Structure of Prosecuted Professional Deviance among Lawyers. *American Sociological Review* 57: 771–80.
Baglivo, A. (1983) *Camorra S.P.A.* Milano: Rizzoli.
Barbagallo, F. (1988) *Camorra e criminalità organizzata in Campania*. Napoli: Liguori.
Barbagallo, F., M. Bruno and M. Calise (1988) *Camorra e criminalità organizzata in Campania*. Napoli: Liguori.
Basso, K. (1979) *Portraits of "The Whiteman:" Linguistic Play and Cultural Symbols among the Western Apache*. Cambridge: Cambridge University Press.
Behan, T. (2002) *See Naples and Die*. New York: Palgrave Macmillan.
Blasio, A. de (1897) *Usi e costumi dei camorristi*. Napoli: Pierro.
—— (1973) *Nel Paese della Camorra: L'imbrecciata*. Napoli: Edizioni del Delfino.
Bourdieu, P. (1980) *Le sens pratique*. Paris: Les Editions de Minuit.
Buford, M., A. Reuben and M. Patillo-McCoy (2000) Do You See What I See? Examining a Collaborative Ethnography. *Qualitative Inquiry* 6: 65–87.
Callon, M. (1986) Some Elements of a Sociology of Translation: Domestication of the Scallops and the Fishermen of St Brieuc Bay. In: J. Law (ed.) *Power, Action and Belief: A New Sociology of Knowledge*. London: Routledge and Kegan Paul: 196–233.
Cain, M. and C.B. Harrington (1994) *Lawyers in a Postmodern World: Translation and Transgression*. New York: New York University Press.
Ceglowski, D. (2000) Research as Relationship. *Qualitative Inquiry* 6: 88–103.
Czarniawska, B. (1997) *Narrating the Organization: Dramas of Institutional Identity*. Chicago, IL: University of Chicago Press.
Danby, S. (1997) *The Observer Observed, the Researcher Researched: The Reflexive Nature of the Phenomena*. Proceedings Australian Association for Research in Education Annual Conference, Brisbane.
Delmas-Marty, M. and J.R. Spencer (eds) (2002) *European Criminal Procedures*. Cambridge: Cambridge University Press.
Ducrot, O. (1984) *Le dire et le dit*. Paris: Les Edition de Minuit.
Eisenstadt, S.N. and R. Lemarchand (eds) (1982) *Political Clientelism, Patronage and Development*. London: Sage.
Flood, J. (1983) *Barristers' Clerks: The Law's Middlemen*. Manchester: Manchester University Press.
—— (1991) Doing Business: The Management of Uncertainty in Lawyers' Work. *Law and Society Review* 25: 41–72.
Georges, R.A. and M.O. Jones (1980) *People Studying People: The Human Element in Fieldwork*. Berkeley, CA: University of California Press.
Geertz, C. (1973) *The Interpretation of Cultures*. New York: Basic Books.
—— (1983) *Local Knowledge: Further Essays in Interpretive Anthropology*. New York: Basic Books.

Giddings, J. and M. Robertson (2002) Lay People, for God's Sake! Surely I Should be Dealing with Lawyers? *Griffith Law Review* 11: 436–64.

Graziano, L. (1973) Patron-Client Relationships in Southern Italy. *European Journal of Political Research* 1: 3–34.

Greimas, A.J. (1970) *Du sens I*. Paris: Seuil.

—— (1974) Les actants, les acteurs et les figures In: C. Chabrol (ed.) *Sémiotique narrative et textuelle*. Paris: Larousse.

—— (1976) *Entretien sur les structures élémentaires de signification*. Ed. Frédéric Nef. Bruxelles: Editions Complexes.

—— (1983) *Du sens II*. Paris: Seuils.

Greimas, A.J. and A. Courtes (1983) *Semiotics and Language: Analytical Dictionary*. Bloomington: Indiana University Press.

Holden, L. (2005) Official Policies for (Un)official Customs: The Hegemonic Treatment of Hindu Divorce Customs by Dominant Legal Discourses. *Journal of Legal Pluralism* 49: 47–74.

—— (2003) Custom and Law Practices in Central India: Some Case Studies. *South Asia Research* 23: 115–33.

—— (forthcoming) *Hindu Divorce*. Aldershot: Ashgate.

—— (forthcoming) Comparison in Action. In: D. Nelken and F. Bruinsma (eds) *Comparative Legal Culture*.

—— (forthcoming) "On One's Own Ground: Consultants and Social Scientists in and beyond Academia".

Holden, M. and L. Holden (2000) *Runaway Wives. Customary Divorce and Remarriage in Shivpuri District (Madhya Pradesh-India)*. Documentary in Hindi with English subtitles, 40 mn. Melbourne: Access Studio.

—— (2002) Distant Voices for a Home-fieldworker, Anthropology from Within (http://www.anthropologyfromwithin.net).

Holden, L. and S. Sharma (2002) Nyay aur yug: Piparsod ke Brahman ke vicar, A Oriente!, Milano: La Babele del Levante. Paper in Hindi and Italian (Giustizia e tempo. Riflessioni di un Brahmano di Piparsod), 22–9.

Holden, M., L. Holden, and L. Manfredonia (2004) *The Paper's Monster*. Documentary film in Italian with English subtitles, 10 mn.

—— (2005) Experimenting *Collaborative Visual Anthropology*. Documentary film, 15 mn.

Holden, M., L. Holden, L. Manfredonia, and P. Serrao d'Aquino (2006) *Doing Nothing Successfully* (http://www.insightsproduction.net/doing_nothing_successfully2.html).

Hymes, D. (2004 [1981]) *In Vain I Tried to Tell You*. Lincoln: University of Nebraska Press.

Jacquemet, M. (1991) Men of Honour, Men of Truth: The Case against the NCO. PhD disseration, Berkley: University of California.

—— (1992a) "If He Speaks Italian It's Better:" Metapragmatics in Court. *Pragmatics* 2(2): 111–26.

—— (1992b) Namechasers. *American Ethnologist* 19(4): 733–48.

—— (1993) Effets de vérité: récits de la Nouvelle Camorre Napolitaine. *Traverses, Revue du Centre Georges Pompidou* 8, Paris: 68–77.

—— (1994) T-Offences and Metapragmatiques Attacks: Strategies of Interactional Dominance. *Discourse and Society* 5(3): 299–321.

—— (1996) *Credibility in Court*, Cambridge: Cambridge University Press.

—— (2001) The Making of a Witness. In: A. Di Luzio, S. Guenthner, and F. Orletti (eds) *Culture in Communication*. Amsterdam: John Benjamins Publishing Company.

Kritzer, H.M. and J.K. Krishnan (1999) Lawyers Seeking Clients, Clients Seeking Lawyers: Sources of Contingency Fee Cases and their Implications for Case Handling. *Law and Policy* 21: 347–75.
Lassiter, L.E. (2005) *The Chicago Guide to Comparative Ethnography*. Chicago, IL: Chicago University Press.
Latour, B. (1987) *Science in Action*. Cambridge, MA: Harward University Press.
—— (1988) *The Pasteurization of France*. Cambridge, MA: Harward University Press.
Lynch, M. (1993) *Scientific Practice and Ordinary Action*. Cambridge: Cambridge University Press.
Marrazzo, G. (1984) *Il camorrista*. Napoli: Pironti Editore.
Nelken, D. and M. Levi (eds) (1996) *The Corruption of Politics and the Politics of Corruption*. Oxford: Blackwell.
Propp, V.J. (1968) *Morphology of the Folktale*. Austin: University of Texas Press.
Rossi, L. (1983) *Camorra: Un mese ad Ottaviano*. Milano: Mondadori.
Sabetti, F. (2002) *Village Politics and the Mafia in Sicily*. San Francisco, CA: ICC Press.
—— (2003) Review of Jane C. Schneider and Peter T. Schneider, *Reversible Destiny. Mafia, Antimafia and the Struggle for Palermo*. *The American Historical Review* 108: 1552–53.
Sacks, H. (1997) The Lawyer's Work. In M. Travers and J.F. Manzo (eds) *Law in Action*. Aldershot: Dartmouth.
Sales, L. (1988) *La Camorra, le Camorre*. Roma: Editori Riuniti.
Scheffer, T. (2003) The Duality of Mobilization. Following the Rise and Fall of an Alibi-story on its Way to Court. *Journal for the Theory of Social Behaviour* 33: 313–47.
—— (2004) Materialities of Legal Proceedings. *International Journal for Semiotics of Law* 17: 2356–89.
Schneider, J.C. and P.T. Schneider (2003) *Reversible Destiny: Mafia, Antimafia, and the Struggle for Palermo*. Berkeley, CA: University of California Press.
Srinivas, M.N. (1996) *Village, Caste, Gender and Method*. Delhi: Oxford University Press.
Stocking, G.W. (ed.) (1983) *Observers Observed: Essays on Othnographic Fieldwork*. Madison, WI: University of Wisconsin Press.
Tarasti, E. (1994) *A Theory of Musical Semiotics*. Bloomington, IN: Indiana University Press.
Twining, W. (2000) *Globalisation and Legal Theory*. Cambridge: Butterworths.
Verdier, R., J.P. Poly, and G. Courtois (1980) *La vengeance: etudes d'ethnologie, d'histoire et e de philosophie*, 4 vols. Paris: Cujas.
Worth, S. and Adair, S. (1992) *Through Navajo Eyes*. Reprinted 1997. Albuquerque, NM: University of New Mexico Press.
Woodman, G. (2002) Why There Can Be No Map of Law. Paper presented at the XIIIth Conference of the Commission of Folk Law and Legal Pluralism. Thailand: Chiang Mai.
Zinn, D. (2001) *La raccomandazione: Clientelismo vecchio e nuovo*. Roma: Donzelli.

Corruption Accusations
and Political Imaginaries

Chapter 6

Corruption Narratives and the Power of Concealment: The Case of Burundi's Civil War

Simon Turner

In Burundi, years of undemocratic and ethnic rule, followed by genocidal violence, guerrilla warfare, and general insecurity have, in the past couple of years, given way to peace, reconciliation, ethnic and political power sharing, and democratic reforms. However, in spite of these political developments, many ordinary Burundians still fear that things can go dreadfully wrong. Although they hope that the country will remain on the narrow path to permanent peace, they fear that it could take the broad avenue back into violence and exclusion any day. And given the bloody history of this small country, these fears are not unfounded.

This chapter draws on fieldwork carried out between 1997 and 2005 among Burundians in Burundi itself, and in Tanzania, Kenya, Belgium, and Denmark, where they had moved in order to escape the civil war in their country. This has given me the opportunity to follow people's responses to the ups and downs of the conflict and the political process in Burundi and to discover that it was often through corruption narratives about political opponents and rivals that people attempted to grasp their own misfortunes. For instance, when comparing the apparent success of one rebel faction fighting against the government of Burundi with that of less successful others, people would confide in me that that faction's success was based on its leader being on the payroll of the president. Similarly, when opposition political movements split into factions, there would be many rumors that these movements had been bribed by the army or the president with weapons, money, or even combatants.

The first time I heard this kind of story was in Denmark in 1997, when the civil war in Burundi was at its hottest. The exiled leader of one Hutu movement was explaining to me his lack of success in the battlefield compared to another armed movement. He believed that the leader of the other movement—originating from the same region as the president—had actually been supplied by the government with arms and soldiers.

I argue in this chapter that these corruption narratives seek to unravel power by trying to unveil hidden connections and causalities. In this manner they attempt to explain the success of some politicians and the misfortune of others, relying on a perception of political power as depending heavily on hidden practices and on concealing true intentions.

The authors of this volume argue that what is legally defined as corruption may not always be perceived as illicit or illegitimate by those involved. And vice versa, that practices that might be formally legal can become condemned as morally illegitimate and corrupting. This reflects the double meaning of the word "corrupt," which on the one hand refers to unlawful activity and on the other hand refers to moral deterioration. The latter understanding is an important ingredient in Burundian corruption narratives. Narratives about corruption are highly moral as they judge the legitimacy of actions—bearing in mind that an illegitimate action is not necessarily equivalent to an illegal action. Corruption narratives are moral evaluations of the ways in which power is being administered in society. This chapter seeks to explore how ordinary Burundians express their discomfort with the political leadership and morally evaluate politics and politicians through stories about corruption and dirty, secret deals.

By "looking behind the scenes"—searching for dirty deals in the "underworld"—corruption narratives also express fears that things are not what they appear to be. Power based on illegal, corrupt connections is considered to be "false power," immoral and illegitimate power that will collapse once uncovered. This is especially worrying in the case of Burundi as people fear that the superficial harmony that is present nowadays might break down once the real workings of power surface. Hence, corruption narratives among Burundians also express anxieties and doubts about the future of their country and a general anxiety that things may still go wrong.

For example, at one level, the story about the rebel leader being paid off by the president functioned as an excuse for the leader telling the story to explain his own relative failure. At a deeper level, however, it warns of "false power." For as much as the rival movement might appear to have power, it is, according to this narrative, ultimately based on lies and deceit. "Money corrupts," as the old saying goes. So, while the rival rebel group might presently be doing well on the battlefield, its power is fake.

Although in these corruption narratives secrecy is linked to "false power," a central argument in this chapter is that all power relies on secrecy (see also Turner 2005b). Power relies on assumptions of a secret side to power—an assumption that there is more power backstage. Corruption narratives are about addressing this secrecy of power—false or legitimate—by probing into its dark underbelly.

In sum, this chapter explores how corruption narratives are used to morally evaluate politics, arguing that such narratives reveal an intimate relationship between power and secrecy. Before analyzing corruption narratives in Burundi it may first, however, be fruitful to explore the parallels with a closely related topic, namely witchcraft narratives.

Narratives of the Occult

As Blundo and de Vries so aptly argue in their contributions to this volume, corruption shares many features with witchcraft. First and foremost, they are both concerned with what is hidden—with what goes on behind the surface. Witchcraft and corruption narratives also both relate to power and wealth, explaining why some people suddenly become rich while others remain poor. Peter Geschiere (1997, 1999), amongst others, has convincingly argued that witchcraft stories have a leveling effect on societies. The Comaroffs, in turn, link witchcraft to what they call millennial capitalism, where wealth appears to materialize out of thin air—usually through obscure and intangible networks and flows (Comaroff and Comaroff 1999, 2000). In witchcraft narratives—as in urban legend (Turner 1993)—the "other" is assumed to become wealthy and powerful by means of something taken from "us." Hence the rumors about trafficking in human body parts (Bastian 2003; Campion-Vincent 2001; Scheper-Hughes 1996; White 1997) or people being transformed into zombies at night and forced to work in faraway plantations (Comaroff and Comaroff 1999, Geschiere 1999). In these cases, the body parts or the labor that is stolen, is used to make a "profit" elsewhere, almost in a classical Marxist analysis of exploitation and the production of surplus value.

This zero-sum logic also applies to the individuals accused of being involved in witchcraft. If indeed someone becomes powerful by using witchcraft, they are bound to become weak in other aspects of life, according to witchcraft rumors. Thus the material wealth accumulated through witchcraft might, for instance, be earned at the cost of loosing one's fertility, as a particular case described by the Comaroffs shows: "On a certain day when the accused arrived, [people] shouted from the street that she was a witch with a shrinked [sic] vagina. ... They also said that her son 'Zero' has no male seed and that he could not impregnate a woman" (Comaroff and Comaroff 1999: 289). According to the zero-sum logic of witchcraft rumors, this witch's supernatural and artificial wealth has its price: the natural, reproductive wealth of herself and her son. Her wealth is cannibalistic and unsustainable in the long run. In other words, she might seem wealthy and powerful, but in actual fact she is poorer than most people because she cannot reproduce.

The same logic applies to the corruption narratives that I explore. They attempt to explain why some people appear to be so powerful when there is no apparent reason, seeking elucidation in illicit and hidden connections. A central characteristic of corruption is that someone enriches him- or herself at the expense of others, creating a kind of parasitic wealth, similar to the power and wealth created through witchcraft. Furthermore, corruption narratives claim that those who try to take the shortcut to power pay a high price in the long run, because corrupt practices also lead to moral corruption, and the power that one achieves is false. Such power becomes worthless, once its underlying mechanisms are disclosed.

The rumors that I explore here are about political leaders—effectively evaluating the moral standards of these political figures and conveying how people in Burundi believe politics *ought* to be. For this reason, we might, with Ellis and Ter Haar (2004), claim that the rumors are inherently religious, as they evaluate politics in moral terms. However—still following Ellis and Ter Haar—the rumors about corruption are religious in other ways as well. Like religion, rumors attempt to make sense of the world in a cosmological manner and explain not only *how* but also *why* things occur. Ellis and Ter Haar point out that "religion refers to a belief in the existence of an invisible world, distinct but not separate from the visible one" (2004: 14). This obscure universe of spirits is believed to have impact on the visible, material world. The aim of rumors, then, is to unveil this concealed universe and reveal the secret forces that control our world. And if this is not possible, then at least they draw our attention to the existence of such occult powers.

Along similar lines Mbembé argues that in African cosmology everything has a hidden side. He observes: "[I]n this universe marked by the primacy of the spoken word ... societies developed a magical attitude towards words" (Mbembé 2001: 144). One cannot take anything at face value because inherent in everything that is said, is its opposite: the unsaid—the secret. The spirit world might be invisible, but it is not distinct as such; it is a part of everything. Everything has its double—and this secret, invisible, and unspeakable double is just as important in determining the fate of things. Corruption narratives are religious in the sense that they operate with concepts of secret powers controlling the material world. And they are political in the sense that they comment on and scrutinize politics, not only on the surface but also at the level that is assumed to lie underneath the surface. It seems therefore relevant to further explore the relation between secrecy and power.

Secrecy and Power

Elias Canetti argues that "[s]ecrecy lies at the very core of power" (Canetti 1984 (1962): 290). Secrecy and the capacity to disguise one's thoughts and intentions were essential abilities of "the despot of history." The despot is a man who has much to conceal and who "knows exactly what should be left unspoken" (ibid.: 294). Democracies on the other hand lack secrecy, Canetti claims, and without secrecy, democratic leaders lack the ability to make decisions and hence lack power. Does this mean, then, that secrecy becomes irrelevant in democratic, enlightened, and transparent politics? I would claim not. Even under democratic, allegedly transparent regimes people often assume that decisions are made elsewhere—hidden from the public eye—in secrecy. And this is where "real power" is expected to rest. The result is a paradoxical "double concealment," hiding the secret under the surface of transparency. From such a perspective only rumors, about for instance witchcraft or corruption, reveal what is hidden.

Hence, transparency does not necessarily mean the end of secrecy; or of rumors about secret conspiracies. West and Sanders (2003) argue that the promotion of transparency in democratic regimes appears to produce its opposite; conspiracy and conspiracy theories. Inherent in the concept of transparency is the idea that a transparent "surface" permits us to look inside and see the "real" workings of power. Paradoxically, this notion of a transparent surface strengthens, according to the contributions in West and Sanders (2003), the suspicion that power operates behind a "façade." By assuming that there is a surface, one also assumes something below the surface. This is similarly the case in witchcraft stories. Usually they are about localizing the occult powers beneath the visible surface. Likewise, corruption, both of the legal as well as of the moral type, is seen to take place underneath the surface. Corruption is about covering up and using official means for unofficial purposes. Through corruption narratives "common folk" attempt to peer beneath the surface and catch a glimpse of what they perceive to be the "real" powers that control their vulnerable lives. They interrogate the relationship between the surface and the "underside," between the official and the unofficial, between the spoken and the unspoken. As with witchcraft, rumors about corruption express the suspicion that power is not what it makes itself out to be and that real power acts behind the scenes, hiding its true intentions from the public eye. Corruption narratives are thus not the result of primitive, exotic political imaginations. Indeed, these kinds of conspiracy theories are manifest in mainstream culture around the world, and, as opposed to what modernist thinking might assume, they are not on the retreat. On the contrary, they seem—like witchcraft—to be on the rise.

So, if secrecy is so important to power, what is there behind the surface of appearance? Do we find the "hidden hand" of history? Or the "iron fist?" I would argue that we find neither. However, as opposed to the neo-Nietzschean perspective that is widespread in so-called post-structuralist science, I argue (with Copjec 1994, Dolar 1998, Žižek 1989, and Taussig 1999) that the "belief in the secret" is essential for the working of power. According to Taussig (1999) it is too easy to simply do away with the secret by claiming it does not exist. We must assume it to exist for power to function (Copjec 1994). We must assume that something is hidden behind the veil and underneath the surface. Conspiracy theories and corruption narratives try to lift the veil, thereby reinforcing the notion of a veil hiding the operation of power. They assume that behind it a big secret is hidden. And this is where the concept of the public secret helps us. "To put it bluntly, there is no such thing as a secret. It is an invention that comes out of the public secret, a limit-case, a supposition, a great 'as if,' without which the public secret would evaporate" (Taussig 1999: 7). The trick of the public secret is to remain on the verge of disclosure: the secret is not quite uncovered—thereby revealing that it does not exist—but enough glimpses are given to strengthen the assumption that something is going on behind the scenes.

Rumors and conspiracy theories do exactly this. Those peddling in conspiracy theories believe they are able to shed light on the occult connections that are assumed to exist beneath the surface. But as much as conspiracy theories try to unearth and shed light, they also are content with letting things remain obscure and opaque. They do not necessarily fully reveal what they assume to be the true link between various events. They simply hint that there might be such a connection. They do not shed light on the occult. They simply testify to its existence. As West and Sanders argue, conspiracy theories and occult cosmologies do not reduce the world's complexities, as some analysts might suggest. On the contrary, "they do the opposite, rendering the world more complex by calling attention to its hidden and contradictory logics" (West and Sanders 2003: 17). In this manner, they keep the secret alive, reinforcing it while making its existence known. The secret is that there is no secret (Taussig 1999).

In Žižek's argument (1997: 157f.), the father always relies on the threat of using more power than he does and probably more than he can actually muster. The paradox of power, he says, is that symbolic power is by definition virtual: power-in-reserve, the threat of its full use that never actually occurs. The immediate consequence is that this power is magnified in the imagination of his children/subjects. But it also leaves room for doubt. Is he bluffing? Is he a phony? It is this doubt that sustains his authority. But it also creates space for conspiracy theories that threaten with his downfall.

Rumors and corruption narratives in Burundi reflect this ambiguity in relation to power. On the one hand, the accusations of corruption—of real power being wielded in secrecy— contribute to an overwhelming sense of confronting an omnipotent political opponent. They conjure up the perception that whatever "we" do—whether we register and vote or we go out and fight—"they" will always be one step ahead of us because they play by other (dirty) rules. If one naively sticks to the books, one is effectively excluded from power. Here the rumors of corruption only reinforce the perception of power-in-reserve; that there is more where it comes from (wherever that may be). On the other hand, the rumors of corrupt politicians expose them as phony. They reveal the apparent power and position of certain politicians as mere appearance—a surface phenomenon—hiding their actual lack of power. The web of secrets and lies is necessary in order to cover up this lack. For if the secrets are revealed they loose their power. These illicit deals only do the trick as long as they are kept secret. Once they are unearthed and become visible to the public eye, they loose their magic, as they cannot stand the light of day. The goal of rumors on conspiracies and corruption is therefore not only to find explanations in an insecure world (see, for example, Feldman 1995, Turner 2002) but also to destroy this secret exercise of power by unearthing it and revealing it.

The Conflict in Burundi

Explanations for the conflict in Burundi are highly contentious both among scholars and among political actors.[1] Similarly, it is impossible to define once and for all what it means to be Hutu or Tutsi in Burundi. For the sake of this argument, however, it suffices to say that both Rwanda and Burundi are composed of a Hutu majority (*c.* 85 per cent) and a Tutsi minority (*c.* 14 per cent) while the remaining ethnic group, the Twa, play no role in political life. In pre-colonial times, the Tutsi tended to belong to the ruling elite while the Hutu were agriculturalists.

---

1   René Lemarchand (1996) has called this the "meta-conflict," that is, the conflict about what the conflict is about.

However, the system was rather fluid and was only hardened and reinforced during Belgian indirect rule that privileged the Tutsi (see Chrétien 1990; Gahama 1983; Lemarchand 1970, 1996). While a small Hutu elite from the north dominated the Rwandan state after independence from Belgium in 1962, the nomenclature in Burundi was mainly Tutsi from a certain region in the south. In 1972, a small Hutu uprising was brutally repressed by the Tutsi-dominated army, resulting in the systematic killing of some 150,000 Hutu. The 1972 massacres were followed by a period of tight one-party rule, firmly in the hands of a small Tutsi elite. Mention of ethnicity was banned and dismissed as a colonial invention. Meanwhile, Hutu in exile began mobilizing politically and rallying around their ethnic identity, particularly in the political party Palipehutu (Parti pour la Libération du Peuple Hutu). The pressure from Palipehutu and from international donors led the regime in the early nineties to introduce democratic reforms, leading to general elections in 1993 and a landslide victory for the moderate "Hutu" party, Frodebu (Front pour la Démocratie au Burundi).[2] The army was, however, never reformed and just three months after his election, the president was abducted and killed by Tutsi officers, pushing the country into massive killings of Tutsi civilians by the Hutu population and of Hutu civilians by the armed forces and Tutsi militias.[3] After this, the political situation deteriorated strongly and a number of Frodebu members started an armed rebel group, the CNDD (Conseil National pour la Défence de la Démocratie). For a variety of reasons, this group and the armed wing of Palipehutu have since split into numerous factions. Following negotiations between the Tutsi-dominated government and a number of Hutu opposition parties and rebel groups a peace accord was reached in August 2000. Since then, the majority of rebel groups have joined the accords, leaving out only one faction that does not trust the agreement and believes the Tutsi are still in control behind the scenes.

Buying Off the Opposition

In the introduction I mentioned the rumor that some rebel groups were being supported by the Tutsi government. The logic behind this rumor appears in numerous shapes among the Hutu. Either the rival party is directly bribed by the Tutsi, as in this case, or it is influenced in a more subtle and indirect way. Thus, for instance, Palipehutu supporters—known to be more uncompromising and radical than other Hutu movements—would explain that one big difference between them and their rival, the CNDD, was that their party did not allow Tutsi members. CNDD supporters saw this as evidence of the racist ideology of Palipehutu. Palipehutu members, however, claimed that the Tutsi could function as spies and hence destroy the party from within. In spite of what the Tutsi members of

---

2 The more radical Palipehutu had been banned in Burundi, leaving room for Frodebu, which was not officially a Hutu party (see also Turner 2001).

3 An estimated 30,000 Hutu and 30,000 Tutsi were killed in a few months. It is still strongly debated whether or not this could be characterized as genocide.

CNDD said, they were believed to harbor ulterior motives and hidden intentions. However much Tutsi members of so-called "Hutu" parties like the CNDD supported party ideology, risking their lives at times, they were still suspected by Palipehutu supporters of harboring other loyalties. Their secret loyalties made them ambiguous and untrustworthy figures and, more important, jeopardized the credibility of the whole party/movement in the eyes of Palipehutu members.[4]

It is not only Tutsi becoming members that would corrupt the party. I was also told in conversations with Hutu refugees in camps in Tanzania (1997–1998) that many CNDD members had married Tutsi women. This is a common narrative in relation to Hutu who do well in life and therefore "marry up," and it draws on a number of age-old ethnic stereotypes about the beauty and dangers of Tutsi women (see Malkki 1995; Taylor 1999). I have since, during fieldwork in Nairobi, Belgium, Bujumbura, and Denmark heard countless complicated stories about the perils of marrying a Tutsi woman. She will continue having children with Tutsi men and bring them up as Tutsi, they say. In this way the Hutu husband is in effect housing and feeding a whole family of Tutsi, which clearly illustrates the concept of the Tutsi as parasites, living off the labor of the Hutu. The Hutu husband on the other hand is too blinded by her beauty and too naïve to believe that she is exploiting him this way. Limited space does not allow me to go into all the ethnic stereotypes and the ideas of purity and impurity at play here. The point is that these principles are brought into the domain of politics when it is claimed that Hutu leaders in the CNDD often marry Tutsi women.

According to such rumors, these leaders obviously believe that they have so much power and status that they ought to marry a (prestigious) Tutsi woman. But as with the money that the president allegedly gives to certain opposition politicians, these wives only provide power and prestige on a superficial level. At the deeper, hidden level the Tutsi women undermine the power of their Hutu husbands.

While the CNDD was being accused of receiving bribes from the Tutsi, there were also rumors that the party used bribes to get its will.[5] Thus it was held in the camp in Tanzania that the CNDD paid the Tanzanian police not to arrest their members when they engaged in illegal activities—such as military training and cross-border attacks—and to arrest Palipehutu members without reason. If CNDD members were arrested, they would soon be set free, it was claimed (implying that freedom comes at a very concrete price in Tanzania). This is an example of the perception that power is the result of dirty deals behind the scenes. Not only can the CNDD be bought for money and made to look powerful, but the party can also buy power itself, by bribing others. In both cases the power is perceived to be artificial, destructive for others, and ultimately self-destructive.

---

4 For discussions of hidden intentions and ethnicity see Appadurai (1999) and Turner (2005b).

5 The more elaborate rumors claimed that the money that the CNDD used for bribing Tanzanian authorities had its origins in the Burundian government, thereby linking the two kinds of bribery.

These rumors are all about looking for the real center of power and trying to explain not only how, but also why, Burundi is in such a bad state. They try to pry beneath the surface and look for hidden connections that might explain and clarify. The rumors constitute attempts to map the sinister side of power. At the same time they are moral evaluations of power, because they distinguish good power from bad power. And although the latter tends to dominate, it is the former that must win in the end. Political power is believed to operate on two levels; one is visible—"open" as Burundians would say—and the other is hidden (or "closed"). The former kind of political power relies on the will of the people and is formulated in clear, open ideological statements. The latter relies on trickery and ruse, based on money. Even large-scale violence is often perceived to be "open" and hence more honest than other modes of exercising power. In the public imagination violent events represent times when hidden plans and schemes surface and when the Other shows his true intentions. In this manner, many Hutu almost cherish the massacres in 1972, 1988, and 1993 because the Tutsi then showed the outside world what they were really up to (Turner 2001). Similarly, many Tutsi see the killing of tens of thousands of Tutsi in 1993 as the culmination of a long plan by the Hutu to exterminate the Tutsi and keeping this event out in the open and making sure it is not hidden away in political manoeuvres is the primary objective of several Tutsi organizations today (such as Action Contre Génocide and Puissance Autodéfence Amesekanya—see Turner 2005b).

Central to these stories is the idea that hidden power is malign, but also that—in the sort term at least— such dirty power can be effective. However much Palipehutu, in the eyes of its supporters, might remain pure and untouched by corrupting power games, it is also loosing out on the battlefield as well as in the formal political field. There is a general sense that as long as "we" do not learn the game of *realpolitik*, we will lose out. We might remain pure but what good is that if our enemies and our rivals continue to play dirty tricks? So there is a sense that one has to play along on the same lines and learn how to work power in secret places, constantly balancing the dilemma between moral purity and *realpolitik*. Around the globe, a well-known excuse for taking part in corrupt activities is that everyone does it—especially the "big fish"—so why should I not? And this is not simply an excuse, disclaiming any moral responsibility. Rather, it builds on the perception that corruption is so endemic, so ingrained in society, that it is de facto the only way to make things work (see Blundo, Holden, Smart and Hsu, and Znoj, this volume).

Opportunists of War and Peace

In August 2000 the Burundian government and a number of opposition parties and movements signed a peace agreement in the Tanzanian town Arusha to end seven years of civil war and to set a power sharing agreement and democratic reforms into motion. It was agreed that during a three year transitional period, political power was to be shared between the parties involved—and hence between the ethnic groups, the Hutu and Tutsi. During this transitional period, many Hutu politicians who used to live in exile in neighboring countries and in Europe have chosen to join the peace process, returning home and entering the government. Others are more hesitant and remain in exile, often spreading conspiracy theories about the hidden agendas of the peace process, thereby reconfirming their own choice to remain in exile.

However, Burundians living in the country also interpreted the events and created conspiracy theories about the process. In this context two types of rumors circulated. One concerned the rebel leaders who were accused of simply joining the peace process in order to get a chunk of the peace dividend and a place in government. The other concerned the Hutu who now allegedly held public positions without knowing what hidden power games they were involved in. I will return to the latter in the next section.

The first type of rumor goes back to the fact that rebel movements in Burundi have a long history of splitting into factions. While this has sometimes been explained as the Tutsi dividing them, another explanation has recently arisen. Usually, one faction would decide to join the Arusha accords and sign a peace agreement with the transition government while the remaining faction would pledge to continue fighting. Since the faction that pledged to continue fighting seemed each time to continue with the same strength, people began speculating whether the other leader—the one who had signed a ceasefire agreement—actually had any combatants under his command in the first place. Is he not really an imposter—a fraud who simply wants the title and the wages of a minister? I was in Bujumbura when one of the very first groups of rebels was to be demobilized in a camp north of Bujumbura. A local journalist gave me a lift to the place, which was in the middle of the bush. There we stood, a small group of journalists and photographers and I, waiting for the ex-rebels to arrive in buses, protected by peacekeepers from the South African Defense Force. When eventually they arrived, they certainly did not seem very frightening; they had machetes and a few old hand guns and many of them were only in their early teens. This was seized upon by the gathered journalists who claimed that many of the "so-called rebels" that were demobilized had been recruited only weeks earlier among the rural poor with promises of various demobilization packages. In other words, they were far from the brave warriors that the rebel leaders claimed to command.

This particular group belonged to Alain Mugabarabona's rebel faction of Palipehutu-FNL (Front National pour la Libération). As opposed to the rest of Palipehutu-FNL, under the command of Agathon Rwasa, he had chosen to sign a peace agreement with the government and had been offered several positions in government. However, his leadership and his power base had always been subject to suspicion and contestation. Many took the pathetic state of his "combatants" as evidence that Mugabarabona was a fraud.

Mugabarabona himself had tried to take over the leadership of Palipehutu-FNL the previous year, but had not succeeded. Instead, the movement split in two with him leading one faction. When he claimed to have taken over the movement, various Burundian internet forums were teeming with declarations of support or disavowal.[6] Being clandestine and transnational, the strength and size of such movements are very difficult to assess. This left a large room for interpretation. Anyone could start interpreting the strength of the various factions, and I have found that this was a favorite pastime for Burundians—especially when I was in Bujumbura during those crucial months in 2003, when the first movements were beginning to be demobilized. Neither experts nor the man on the street knew what was actually going on among the rebel groups. Was the fighting around the capital in Bujumbura Rural and sporadically in other parts of the country the doings of this or of that rebel group? Obviously all factions liked to take responsibility, exaggerating their own strength. Some people—especially expatriates and foreign observers—began doubting whether the fighters could actually be qualified as rebels or were simply renegades who no longer obeyed their leaders and had taken to banditry. Several Hutu—especially those who remained in exile—believed that the violence was instigated by the army as an excuse to kill and arrest the Hutu population.

During this period of uncertainty, rumors developed that Mugabarabona had no backing whatsoever and was merely an opportunist, seeking to make the best out of the situation for himself. By claiming to be the leader of a rebel movement, he could negotiate a peace agreement with the government and negotiate for himself and his associates to have influential positions in the government. And Mugabarabona is just one case. Similar stories circulated about the leader of a faction in the CNDD-FDD, Jean Bosco Ngendakengurukiye, who also signed a peace agreement with only a small number of combatants.[7]

I have interviewed close advisers of Mugabarabona and Jean-Bosco who predictably denied the charges and claimed that the factions broke away due to political differences. Whether or not this is the case is not the issue. It is very likely that neither leader had any substantial backing in the population, or many combatants in the forests. However, the stories that circulate about these leaders still have the character of rumors. This is similar to analyzing witchcraft where it does not really make any sense to discuss whether or not a certain person is "in actual fact" a witchdoctor. It is the accusations that are interesting to explore, as Geschiere (1997) points out.

Rumors about corruption also go the other way. When a rebel leader was ousted or at least challenged by another potential leader, it was usually based on charges of mismanagement of party funds. At least this was the common interpretation of the man on the street. Either he was accused of embezzlement of party funds or more generally of misusing the organization for personal means. Most recently, in August 2005, Jean Minani, who has been the unchallenged leader

---

6 I discuss the disputes over his leadership that took place among the diaspora in various internet chat forums elsewhere (Turner 2005a).

7 Pierre Nkurunziza, leader of the remaining CNDD-FDD faction, had at that point in time (July 2003) not signed any definitive agreement with the government. He has since done so and is now president, after winning the lion's share of votes in the 2005 elections.

of what used to be the largest party in the country, FRODEBU, was removed after the disastrous results in the elections. However, he was not ousted because of a lack of political vision or leadership but due to charges of misappropriating party funds. In this way, the individual politician is morally evaluated through the lens of corruption.

The countless conversations, rumors, and jokes about people like Mugabarabona in the streets, homes, and cafés of Bujumbura were about evaluating politics in moral terms. In the confusion of the transition period, as tables were (perhaps?) turning, political parties mushrooming, and lines of conflict shifting, ordinary people in Bujumbura were searching for causalities and connections. Rather than attribute the changes and the insecurity to structural conditions or to chance, they were looking for causalities in the hidden world of corruption, pinpointing the ulterior motives of individual politicians.

Although Mugabarabona is not accused of being corrupt in the conventional sense of breaking the law, he is certainly perceived to be misusing his position of authority and, most importantly in relation to my argument, of having a hidden agenda behind what he officially declares. The rumors unveil his agenda and morally evaluate his political project as self-interested enrichment rather than struggle for the greater, collective cause, which is what "clean politics" ought to be about.

Naïve Politicians and Their Puppeteers

Hutus and Tutsis alike are struggling with the question of whether politicians returning from exile are themselves manipulating the system or are being manipulated by other—more powerful—actors. Are they, in other words, corrupt by default, using the political system for their own selfish gains? Or is it the system that corrupts them morally? This is a dilemma similar to the one concerning the rebels that are being supplied by the president. In the case of Mugabarabona and his likes, it seems that he is manipulating the system for his own sake. In other cases, the rumors seem to claim that the returning politicians are naïve pawns in a power game that they cannot even see. Below I give a few examples.

On one of my first days in Bujumbura, Josiane, a local journalist, and I passed through a part of town that obviously used to be bare field and where massive houses were being built, connected by potholed dirt roads. Josiane points and laughs as she tells me that this is *l'argent d'Arusha* ("money from Arusha"). People in Bujumbura have named the area after the *per diems* that the Hutu politicians received when attending the lengthy peace negotiations in Arusha. "Why do you think the negotiations took so long?," Richard, the driver, grins. This is hardly a narrative, let alone a conspiracy theory. It is simply a place name. And yet it makes people laugh knowingly because—like all good rumors—it insinuates a lot more than it says.[8] The point of this joke about the returning politicians and their houses is to spread doubt about their motivations for joining the peace process. Was it to serve the cause or to build a house? But it also hints at something else, namely that these nouveau riche Hutu are just as naïve as Hutu have always been in the eyes of my interlocutors.[9] The happy-go-lucky, childish Hutu are easily satisfied and hence easily tricked. Give them a big house and a Mercedes Benz and they will no longer complain. The Tutsi, on the other hand, are known to be cunning, secretive, and tricky (Turner 2005). They never speak their mind, I was told in the refugee camp, when I asked how to tell a Tutsi from a Hutu. In this context of ethnic stereotypes, the story of the "money from Arusha" gets a new meaning. Once the Hutu get the money and the houses, they lose focus on the real issues, leaving the Tutsi—who have old money and political experience, due to years of dominance, and who according to these rumors always think strategically—to do what they like.

It may seem like a lot to deduce from one small joke. But the theme of the naïve Hutu returning from exile is pervasive—although, as mentioned earlier, it also is ambiguous. Pascal (a pseudonym), a Hutu living in Denmark, gave me the clearest indication of this at a social gathering for the Burundian Children's Cultural Association (Burundi Børne Kulturforening) in Denmark. The problem, he says, is these "new politicians," referring to the Hutu in the government. They do not have enough experience to know the tricks of the Tutsi. "I know these people. I know what kind of game they are playing," he repeats, referring to the fact that he used to be a high-ranking member of UPRONA (the main "Tutsi" party) during the one-party system. Pascal boasts that he knows Kadege, a Tutsi and vice president at the time of interview, very well from those days. Kadege is shrewd and cunning. "*Il est malign!*," he repeats. As the evening progresses he portrays a picture of Kadege and his ally, ex-President Buyoya, pulling the strings in a number of conspiracies while the new Hutu politicians gladly believe that they have power.

From the perspective of my informant the "new politicians" let themselves be blinded by the titles ("minister of good governance or whatever," he says with contempt), houses, and cars. "They think they have power. But is that power?," Pascal asks rhetorically. We see here how material goods and the symbols of power—titles as ministers and so on—are thought to "blind" the "naïve Hutu," who lived abroad and do not know the hidden agendas of these malign Tutsi. According to the conspiracy theories peddled in exile Hutu circles, the Tutsi produce an optical illusion of power that obscures the real picture of power. The theme of visibility and invisibility is central to this intricate understanding of power. Not only is "real power" assumed to be hidden, it is even assumed that formal, visible power, i.e., the power that is linked to titles and is the result of negotiations and elections, works to obscure real power, which operates behind

---

8 As West and Sanders (2003) claim, conspiracy theories do not necessarily cast light and explain hidden connections. They are content with showing that they exist, leaving them—like the public secret—always on the limit between obscurity and clarity.

9 On such ethnic stereotypes see Malkki (1995) and Turner (2001, 2005b).

the scenes and rests on money and force. In other words, according to some of the more radical Hutu, usually living in Europe, democracy and power sharing can actually worsen the situation for the Hutu. In the "bad old days" when the Tutsi were blatantly in control of the state apparatus you knew where you had them, according to this logic. There was a clear-cut and visible common enemy for the Hutu. Now the Tutsi have introduced a veneer of democracy that obscures the fact that they are really in control and gives them an excellent cover for their diabolical plans. This is what concerns people like Pascal. In other words, power is perceived always to have two sides—a visible and an invisible—and corruption narratives aim to reveal the invisible side of power. With democratic reforms and accountability one might expect power to become transparent and corruption narratives to disappear. However, they seem to continue and even increase, as democracy is perceived as an even better way of covering up the true mechanisms of power. The openness and apparent transparency fill the field of vision so much that they actually "blind" people, allowing corrupt politics to take place in the shadows.

The Deadlock of Concealment

If power relies on secrecy, what then can be done to fight power? Is it possible to uncover secrets and "break the spell?" Or is one forced to play the game—and stick to one's secrets—in order not to be weak? Léandre, a Hutu at Louvain-la-Neuve, a catholic university outside Brussels with a large number of Burundian students, told me how he had attempted to create a study forum where Hutu and Tutsi students might meet and exchange views on the political problems in their home country. This initiative was strongly rejected by his fellow Hutu students who accused him of selling out to the Tutsi. Their main argument was that if they would discuss frankly with the Tutsi, the Tutsi would be able to use the knowledge thus acquired against them. They would be giving away their secrets, so to speak. Undoubtedly, the Tutsi students had the same reservations. I asked him whether the issue of keeping secrets and not speaking openly is a Tutsi vice, as I had been told in the camps. "No it's a problem of all Burundians," he replied and explained that it is also connected to the fear of witchcraft. The logic of witchcraft is that your enemies can use some intimate part of you in their magic and use it against you. Therefore you should always keep a certain appearance and never reveal your whole "self" to anyone. "That is why we always hide something '*dans la poche*' ('in our pockets')." In other words, everyone is forced to have secrets in order to avoid being misused by enemies.

Many Burundians, like Léandre, are aware of this "deadlock of concealment" and believe that it hinders sincere political dialogue and reconciliation in Burundi.[10] Several politicians who took part in the negotiations in Arusha and were later elected members of the national assembly admitted in private that they did not always negotiate with full conviction. As long as they believe that the opponent is playing foul, they will not put all their effort into the negotiations either. They keep something hidden in their pocket in order not to be exposed. Hiding something, moreover, gives you a better negotiating position, as your opponent might believe that you are hiding more than you actually are hiding. The secret expands in their imagination, giving you a lot of "power in reserve." Notions of secrecy—of hiding one's true intentions—are imputed on the leaders in conspiracy theories. But these examples also show that people feel almost forced to adopt such practices of concealment, if they are to achieve anything and in order to protect themselves against the other. Having hidden agendas is necessary for self-protection and access to power.

Concluding Remarks

In the indeterminate political field that exists at present in Burundi, politics and politicians are morally evaluated in rumors and conspiracy theories, spreading like wildfire along *radio trottoir* ("sidewalk radio"). An important element of these narratives concerns corruption, although not always of the conventional, legal type. The fact that returning Hutu politicians build big houses does not necessarily mean that the means to do so are illicitly acquired. Rather, it is perceived as morally corrupting because it allegedly leads them to loose focus on the real, political issues at stake.

Central to the issue of corruption is the matter of secrecy. It is secrecy that links corruption to power, and hence makes it so relevant a topic for rumors. Rumors are, after all, about searching for secrets and partially uncovering them. The issue of secrecy operates at several levels in the cases mentioned above. First, there are the conspiracy theories that seek to explain the fortunes and misfortunes of various political groups by claiming that some of them are paid by the government or the army in an attempt to divide and rule the Hutu. The bribing is therefore the secret behind the apparent power of this or that faction. The power is, however, only external appearance, for the second layer of secrecy involves the secret plans of those who gave the bribes. By paying off one rebel movement to fight another, "they" (whomever they may be) are able to continue to rule the country behind the façade.

---

10 It is not my intention to draw a dystopian picture of the future of Burundi. Most Burundians inside Burundi agree that the political reforms have opened the public space and that everyone can now express their opinions openly. They say that at last most factions are now "putting their cards on the table" and expressing their grievances and interests, which is seen as a great progress compared to earlier when everyone was playing *"cache-cache."*

A similar duality takes place in relation to the rumors about the returning politicians. On the one hand, the rumors and jokes insinuate that Mugabarabona and other returning politicians may have other than purely ideological motives for returning and joining the political process. They are accused of pursuing selfish, economic interests rather than the interests of the people. These motives are obviously kept secret. But their power is still fake and superficial, and they are themselves victims of others' secret plans. Secrecy also operates at a deeper, more dangerous level. This is where someone—sometimes claimed to be ex-president and Tutsi strongman Pierre Buyoya and often simply left unsaid as an incognito "central committee," the puppeteers whose faces we do not know—corrupts the new politicians with material wealth. By blinding the Hutu politicians with wealth, "they" can carry out their plans in secret. This is where "real" power is assumed to reside, hidden far away from the public eye.

So it seems that the issue of secrecy and corruption has permeated political imagination in Burundi both in times of war and in times of peace and reconciliation. While "the Tutsi" were believed to divide and rule the Hutu through bribing certain factions of the rebel groups—effectively destroying the Hutu's ability to unite and hence fight the government army—they are now believed to hide their diabolical plans behind the surface of democracy and political participation. In many ways the latter method is perceived to be even more dangerous than the first, because it pretends to be transparent and has managed to trick the majority of Hutu politicians into believing they have real power while in fact they hold only superficial power. Although most Burundians welcome the transformation and believe that the political field has improved significantly due to the fact that people now dare to express their opinions openly, a small amount of doubt remains. The corruption narratives express this doubt as they attempt to dig below the surface and explore the secrecy that underpins power. These narratives do not simply judge a few "rotten apples" who have broken the law—be it written law or moral norms—but actually make moral evaluations of politics in general. Corruption is perceived to be intrinsic to politics and the question in corruption narratives is not whether it exists but how well it is hidden behind the surface.

References

Appadurai, A. (1999) Dead Certainty: Ethnic Violence in the Era of Globalization. In: B. Meyer and P. Geschiere (eds) *Globalization and Identity—Dialectics of Flow and Closure.* Oxford: Blackwell.

Bastian, M. (2003) "Diabolic Realities": Narratives of Conspiracy, Transparency, and "Ritual Murder" in the Nigerian Popular Print and Electronic Media. In: H.G. West and T. Sanders (eds) *Transparency and Conspiracy—Ethnographies of Suspicion in the New World Order.* Durham, NC: Duke University Press: 65–92.

Campion-Vincent, V. (2001) On Organ Theft Narratives. *Current Anthropology* 42(4): 555–6.

Canetti, E. (1984 [1962]) *Crowds and Power.* New York: Farrar Straus Giroux.

Chrétien, J.-P. (1990) L'ethnisme au Burundi: tragédies et propagandes. *Politique Africaine* 39: 182–90.

Comaroff, J. and J.L. Comaroff (1999) Occult Economies and the Violence of Abstraction: Notes from the South African Postcolony. *American Ethnologist* 26(2): 279–303.

—— (2000) Millennial Capitalism: First Thoughts on a Second Coming. *Public Culture* 12(2): 291–343.

—— (2003) Transparent Fictions; or, The Conspiracies of a Liberal Imagination: An Afterword. In: H.G. West and T. Sanders (eds) *Transparency and Conspiracy—Ethnographies of Suspicion in the New World Order*. Durham, NC: Duke University Press: 287–301.

Copjec, J. (ed.) (1994) *Supposing the Subject*, vol. 1. London: Verso.

Dolar, M. (1998) Where Does Power Come From? *New Formations* 35: 79–92.

Ellis, S. and G. ter Haar (2004) *Worlds of Power: Religious Thought and Political Practice in Africa*. London: Hurst.

Feldman, A. (1995) Ethnographic States of Emergency. In: A. Robben and C. Nordstrom (eds) *Fieldwork under Fire*. Berkeley, CA: University of California Press.

Gahama, J. (1983) *Le Burundi sous administration belge*. Paris: Karthala.

Geschiere, P. (1997) *The Modernity of Witchcraft: Politics and the Occult in Postcolonial Africa: Sorcellerie et politique en Afrique—la viande des autres*. Charlottesville, VA: University Press of Virginia.

—— (1999) Globalization and the Power of Indeterminate Meaning: Witchcraft and Spirit Cults in African and East Asia. In: P. Geschiere and B. Meyer (eds) *Globalization and Identity—Dialectics of Flow and Closure*. Oxford: Blackwell: 211–39.

Lemarchand, R. (1970) *Rwanda and Burundi*. London: Pall Mall Press.

—— (1996) *Burundi: Ethnic Conflict and Genocide*. Cambridge: Cambridge University Press.

Malkki, L.H. (1995) *Purity and Exile: Violence, Memory, and National Cosmology among Hutu Refugees in Tanzania*. Chicago, IL: University of Chicago Press.

Mbembé, J.A. (2001) *On the Postcolony*. Berkeley, CA: University of California Press.

Scheper-Hughes, N. (1996) Theft of Life: The Globalization of Organ Stealing Rumours. *Anthropology Today* 12(3): 3–11.

Taussig, M.T. (1999) *Defacement: Public Secrecy and the Labor of the Negative*. Stanford, CA: Stanford University Press.

Taylor, C.C. (1999) *Sacrifice as Terror: The Rwandan Genocide of 1994*. Oxford: Berg.

Turner, P. (1993) *I Heard it Through the Grapevine: Rumor in African-American Culture*. Berkeley, CA: University of California Press.

Turner, S. (2001) The Barriers of Innocence—Humanitarian Intervention and Political Imagination in a Refugee Camp for Burundians in Tanzania. PhD dissertation. Roskilde University.

—— (2002) Dans l'œil du cyclone. Les réfugiés, l'aide et la communauté internationale en Tanzanie. *Politique Africaine* 85: 29–45.

—— (2005a) Cyberwars of Words: Expressing the Unspeakable in Burundi's Diaspora. In S. Turner (ed.) *Diaspora, Development and Conflict: The Forms and Means of Transnational Engagement*. Bornholm, Denmark.

—— (2005b) The Tutsi are Afraid We Will Discover their Secrets—on Secrecy and Sovereign Power in Burundi. *Social Identities* 11(1): 37–55.

West, H.G. and T. Sanders (2003) *Transparency and Conspiracy: Ethnographies of Suspicion in the New World Order*. Durham, NC: Duke University Press.

White, L. (1997) The Traffic in Heads: Bodies, Borders and the Articulation of Regional Histories. *Journal of Southern African Studies* 23(2): 325–38.

Žižek, S. (1989) *The Sublime Object of Ideology*. London: Verso.

—— (1997) *The Plague of Fantasies*. London: Verso.

Chapter 7

The Orchestration of Corruption and Excess Enjoyment in Western Mexico

Pieter de Vries

The telephone rang. It was Andrés:[1]

> It's over now Pieter, they are coming after me, accusing me of all sorts of things, exactly the same accusations we leveled against Camacho. They want to destroy my reputation, but everyone knows that *they* are the corrupt ones. What hurts me most is that I predicted the whole thing and that I received no support whatsoever from my political friends. They are all a bunch of opportunists and too afraid to take a stance, so they let me bleed. The truth is that we are not ready for democracy in Mexico, most of us are cowards.

This was the final outcome of a conflict that had lasted for almost a year. I visited Andrés a year before in El Grullo, a small city in western Mexico. After the usual small talk, he told me about a political power struggle in which he had been involved. The struggle related to control over the local Water Users' Association, which had been established in 1988 as a pilot project within a new policy that turned over the management of irrigation districts to local farmers' associations. So far, this project was considered a very successful experiment by Mexican standards and had even gained the attention of international institutions such as the World Bank and the FAO (the Food and Agricultural Organization of the United Nations). However, according to Andrés, an engineer and former staff member in the Secretary of Hydraulic Resources, control of the association had been in the hands of a corrupt and undemocratic clique. As he told me, some time ago he had initiated a movement to end the corrupt practices of this administration.

They had been successful in this endeavor, and a few weeks earlier the manager of the association had been forced to resign and Andrés had been appointed as the new manager. He was full of ideas about changing the association's mode of operation and dreamed of converting it into a vehicle for social change for the whole area. This would not be an easy task, he pointed out, since in organizing the change of management of the association he had been compelled to strike an alliance with different groups and characters in the region, the most notorious among them being the treasurer of the sugar refinery, Mr López, who was known as a particularly savvy and unscrupulous *cacique* (political boss).

---

[1] The names of all individuals appearing in the ethnography have been changed.

Now a year later, when Andrés phoned me, he felt depressed, was disappointed with his friends, and feared for his life. He had been forced to resign his post as manager of the Water Users' Association and felt impelled to defend himself against charges of fraud. Andrés was the object of a campaign of character assassination by his erstwhile allies converted into political enemies. Even close friends were having trouble to believe in his innocence. During the last months he had been trying to mobilize all of López's enemies in order to strengthen his position in the Association, but with surprisingly little success.

This article focuses on this political struggle around this Water Users' Association, a struggle in which accusations of corruption played a prominent role. As argued in much of the literature on bureaucratic politics in Mexico (Grindle 1977; Nuijten 2003) no distinction can be made between the political and the bureaucratic arena. Practices labeled as corrupt are seen as an intrinsic part of the administrative process. In the ethnography I contrast two different ways of dealing with the political imperative of bureaucratic action: the bureaucratic strategy in which corruption is viewed instrumentally, as a way of getting things done (exemplified by Andrés's mode of operation) versus the strategy that openly stages corruption as a spectacle that carries all sorts of enjoyments (López's mode of operation). Interestingly, the second way of "performing corruption" is seen by local people as more "transparent" and "accountable," for the reason that it provides an inner glimpse of the murky workings of power (see Turner this volume for a similar argument). This chapter pays special attention to this public performance of corruption by political bosses, or *caciques*, who are very adept in staging spectacles of corrupt transgression in liminal spaces—sites where an imagery of power is constructed as a counterpoint to, and subversion of, official images.[2] I call this practice the orchestration of excess enjoyment. But first a theoretical note on corruption in Mexico.

Corruption and the Imagination of Power in Mexico

As in Africa (see chapters by Turner and Blundo in this volume) corruption in Mexico lends itself to all kinds of spectacular imaginations. Perhaps it not would be too far off the mark to argue that the talk of corruption in Mexico fulfils the same function as that of witchcraft in contemporary politics in Africa in the construction of a distinct imaginary of power (Comaroff and Comaroff 1993; Geschiere 1997). In Mexico, the talk of corruption reflects the public secret that state power is essentially venal and spectacular. The talk, speculation, and imagination of corruption is, in short, a form of state fetishism (Taussig 1997).

---

2 The notion of liminality has been developed by Arnold van Gennep (1909) for the study of rites de passages: "as a temporary and transitional state preparing the way for membership in a recognized and honored category" (Malkki 1995: 6f.). Victor Turner (1974: 47) extends the concept to refer "to any condition outside or on the peripheries of everyday life." Here I wish to concentrate on the role of liminal figures and spaces in the construction of a culture of power.

Since state power permeates the social body everyone in one way or the other is entangled in webs of complicity. Since Mexican citizens are aware that power is everywhere they spend much time on the analysis, dissection, and deconstruction of power. It is thus through the thematization of power as all-pervasive, venal, and spectacular that corruption as a social fact is constructed through the work of imagination. Yet, this does not make it less real, for corruption stands for the everyday workings of power in Mexico. Furthermore, corruption does not only render possible the imagination of power, it also creates subjects of corruption who are involved in its construction, whether as active perpetrators or as passive spectators. In Mexico images of corruption not only haunt the subject, but they also shape part of a person's identity by creating webs of complicity nobody can escape from.

The question is not whether you are corrupt but the extent to which you have been "touched" (*te tocó entrarle al juego*), or to put it in Althusserian terms "interpelated" by corruption. There is no innocent spectator in a game in which all actors are players. If everyone is corrupt, the question to be answered is to what extent one is corrupt and, in a precise sense, what is the grain that tips the scale, thus making one's corruption unacceptable or immoral (see Nuijten 2003). In Mexican bureaucratic contexts there is much talk about "acceptable" and "non-acceptable" corruption (*cuando se vale y cuando no se vale entrarle al juego*). So, the talk of corruption is not only constitutive of social reality, but also creates moral subjects.

The chapter is organized as follows. First, the relation between politics and corruption in a Mexican irrigation bureaucracy is discussed. Second, I present an ethnographic account of the political conflict. Finally, in the concluding section I venture into the theoretical and ethical implications of the chosen perspective.

Corruption and Bureaucratic Politics

Soon after I started accompanying Andrés in his work as general manager of the Association we had an enlightening conversation about the importance of creating a financial reserve in order to win the favors of politicians and bureaucrats. Andrés told me:

> Pieter, you should understand that a good manager must be able to combine his technical expertise with a good insight in political relations. Both are inseparable. If you are not able to gain the support of local politicians, members of congress, and your superiors then you are lost. You must be able to play the political game in order to show your technical and administrative capacities. You need to work on your network within the party [the PRI, which at that moment still was the hegemonic state party] in order to build up a reputation as someone who can get things done, while ensuring political stability. This is our dilemma. On the one hand, we have to protect our institutions from the predatory influence of scores of politicians and corrupt bureaucrats, on the other we need these people in order to do our job well. The question is how to manage these conflicting demands without endangering your reputation.

You should take into account that there are various administrative technologies for creating a financial reserve in the Water Users' Association, but basically they amount to the following two. First, you can start charging the users' additional sums for the services you provide, or renting out machinery and personnel in order to generate a financial surplus. That is what Camacho [the former manager of the Water Users' Association against whom he had been fighting] did with all the consequences that we know. The other way to make a reserve is by negotiating with your providers a lower price than what they put in their invoices. Let's say you buy a truck and have it assessed for a value of 100,000 pesos, but you get a good price from your provider, as little as 80,000, with the understanding that you will buy everything from him. The difference between the agreed price and the invoice you can use to cover your political expenses. The problem with Camacho is that he became too greedy, he was renting out the machinery and pocketing the profits, he was also selling water permits. Furthermore, Camacho did not organize political parties, thus he did not account in political terms for the extra profits he generated through his position. In order not to fall into the trap of being labeled as a corrupt administrator you must be totally sure that you can count upon the discretion of your providers. Still, there will always be rumors and accusations. Therefore, it is important that you spend money "out of your pocket" [this means from the reserve] for political rallies, events, etc. The problem is how to find a balance between the lures of enriching yourself and the demands of the political system.

Andrés told me that over the past years he had had to find funds for: visits of members of the state congress, senators, and other national politicians; contributions to political rallies of local politicians; and financial contributions of a more personal kind, like paying the costs of a mariachi music band playing during the birthday of the regional head of the National Water Agency or presents such as furniture or doors for the new house of the regional head of the Secretary of Agriculture in the state capital of Guadalajara.

Andrés was thus arguing that there is an implicit form of socio-political accountability in corrupt practices based on the knowledge that all important bureaucratic positions offer possibilities and generate demands for kickbacks. In finding a balance between the political and technical exigencies of his job, an administrator with access to public funds has to avoid accusations of corruption by being responsive to the political and personal needs of his followers, superiors, and politicians. I will argue later that such forms of socio-political accountability are facilitated by performative capacities and the celebration of enjoyment. Unfortunately for Andrés, in the end he would not be able to establish such a balance.

Andrés presented a number of convincing arguments for the idea that the legal principles of transparent and accountable administration cannot be enacted. Yet, this does not mean that there is no accountability at all. Only, existing forms of accountability follow a deeply entrenched socio-political logic. As the proverb puts it: "*La Ley se obedece, pero no se cumple*" (the law is obeyed, but not enacted). Here we encounter the classical distinction between the letter of the law and the spirit of the law. In following a Lacanian perspective I argue that the spirit of the law exists by virtue of the gap between what the law says and the everyday practices that unfold in legal and administrative contexts. This gap is precisely the space in which the imagination of corruption is possible. The letter of the Law is a dead letter, a *non sequitur*, as it does not take into account the practical and political circumstances in which it is to be applied.

In spite of all the talk and speculation, the phenomenon of corruption is difficult to pin down in a precise way. Corruption in Mexico always-already is and remains an intractable, intangible fact. Its reality is without doubt, but as a fact it can never be clearly delineated. Acts labeled as corrupt can be interpreted in multiple ways, as political exigencies, as ways of easing up the administrative process, as expressions of personal greed, and so on. Yet, psychological and rational explanations always fall short. There is an excessive, non-rational side to the phenomenon. Corruption can be evoked, symbolized, but not clearly defined. It stands for something that has more to it than itself. As Andrés suggests, there are no right or wrong ways to be corrupt, there is no script for enacting corruption. What do exist are rules that must be transgressed in order to be able to accomplish certain goals. The talk and speculation of corruption does not lend itself to be systematized as a coherent discourse, as an object of knowledge through which the workings of power become legible. Corruption is by definition untransparent, it can be read in multiple ways. Corruption belongs to the realm of imagination and is evoked through narratives, jokes, and story telling. Insofar as it produces knowledge, it is an elusive, partial, spectacular knowledge.

The Political Economy of *Caciquismo* and Sugar in Western Jalisco

A commercial and administrative service center for a predominantly agricultural region, El Grullo is home to roughly 20,000 inhabitants. Among the administrative agencies located in El Grullo are the offices of the Ministry of Agriculture (Secretaría de Agricultura y Recursos Hidráulicos), which includes the National Water Agency (Comisión Nacional de Agua). The area benefits from abundant water flowing from two dams. Having become increasingly important as a cash crop during the last decade, sugar dominates the landscape of the region.

Since the establishment of an irrigation system in the late 1950s, the regional economy has had a boom and bust character. Cotton, melon, and tomatoes succeeded each other as cash crops, each being viable for only a few years due to problems with pest control and marketing. With the arrival of the sugar refinery in the 1960s, a crop was introduced to the region that provided a degree of continuity to the farmers without offering spectacular profits. And with sugar came several organizations linking the state bureaucracy with the *ejidatarios*[3] and the landed

---

3   The *ejido* is a form of corporate land tenure established by the Mexican state after the revolution (1910–1920), in which the land is *de facto* possessed by families but de *jure* remains property of the state. *Ejidatarios* were forbidden to sell and rent out land, or to engage in sharecropping arrangements. However, in practice these rules were not enforced. This ambivalent legal situation conferred the agrarian bureaucracy all kinds of possibilities to engage in "acceptable" and "non-acceptable" forms of corruption. In 1992 the *ejido* regime was liberalized, entitling *ejidatarios* to establish their own rules.

elite: the CNC (Confederación Nacional Campesina) for the *ejidatarios*, and the CNPP (Confederación Nacional de Pequeños Propietarios) for the private producers (van der Zaag 1992).

After the revolution in Mexico (1910–1920), political bosses played an important role in the pacification of rural areas. One such character in western Jalisco was General García Barragán. After playing a central role in the pacification of the region, the general embarked on a successful political career during which he held posts such as the governorship of the state of Jalisco and the secretary of defense in the national government. In the latter position, he ordered the student massacre of Tlatelolco in 1968. In western Jalisco, he is recalled with much awe but little admiration, as he was able to control the whole region through a policy of divide and rule (see de Vries 2002).

The general himself brought the sugarcane refinery to El Grullo, and for more than a decade all important functions within the refinery's organization were monopolized by people close to him. But by the mid-1970s, new leaders began to play a role in the sugarcane refinery. These leaders belonged to a rival political group led by José Guadalupe Zuno Arce, son of a former governor of Jalisco and brother-in-law of president Echeverría (1970–1976), whose regime saw the rise of a distinctively activist form of agrarian populism in western Mexico. Zuno set out to establish a local stronghold, or *cacicazgo*, through the implementation of a regional development program with ample financial support from the president. The organizational structure created for this purpose, the Comisión del Sur, sought to mobilize the popular sectors against the regional power elite through the establishment of a system of collective cooperatives and people's industries. In addition, a network of roads was put in place as well as an airstrip, regularly used among others by the presidential jet.

Zuno enjoyed organizing large rallies (*encuentros*) that were attended by several thousands of families from distant rural areas. During these massive events, people were lavishly treated to food and mariachi music. As the main speaker, Zuno would hold lengthy speeches about socialist solidarity and the anti-imperialist struggle. I was told several times by villagers that Fidel Castro and Mao Tse Tung visited the region in that period. Whether Fidel Castro ever visited the region is not officially known, but that Mao did is impossible as it is known that he never left China.

Zuno himself was a complex character. He was an obsessive worker and an alcoholic although he waged public campaigns against alcohol. He was also known as a lonely man who sought the company of ordinary people when he drank. He expected absolute commitment from his followers, and it was believed that once a village (*ejido*) refused to participate in one of his projects it would be excluded from all other activities. He built a fabulous ranch in the region with a zoo full of imported animals such as zebras and lions that were put on free display to the people. After his downfall, he retired from politics and established himself with his family on this ranch. The cooperatives and people's industries died a quick death. Yet, the peasants in the area with whom I spoke remember Zuno and the Comisión del Sur with gratitude. Thanks to him, they learned to deal with state agencies and with the state-party, the PRI (Partido Revolucionario

Institucional), developing a sense of confidence in the process. He surrounded himself with people of common origin and nurtured their leadership qualities, which he considered to be crucial for the development of the area. Several of his followers later became important politicians elsewhere in Jalisco. It should be mentioned that a principal skill these politicians learned from their master was that of organizing large-scale meetings (*encuentros*, *asambleas*, and *fiestas* or parties). For it was the hallmark of Zuno's populist program that a mass movement had to be forged by bringing people together in large-scale social events and haranguing them so as to create a collective class consciousness.

López, in fact, was one such leader. He started out as one of Zuno's bodyguards or *pistoleros*, a position he credits to Zuno's drinking friendship with his brother. During the first years of Zuno's leadership López would alternate his services to Zuno with periods in the United States where he worked as an illegal day laborer. There he developed a great admiration for the entrepreneurial skills of the Americans. When he returned from the United States, he was assigned to drive one of Zuno's political assistants. At the Comisión, López learned how to address people, giving them a sense of worth. He also learned how to organize mass events and to use a class-based discourse of social justice.

At the end of his term, Zuno sent López to the El Grullo-Autlán region to work on a water distribution system. General Barragán and his family, who held a longstanding feud against the Zuno family, controlled the region. López saw his chance to play a major role in regional politics. He bought *ejido* land, started to grow sugar, and became active in the CNC-cañera (the *ejidatarios* producers organization), which was in the hands of a group of notoriously incompetent politicians. They let the sugar refinery bribe them in return for accepting low sugar prices. López successfully disputed the power of these politicians and was credited by the *ejidatarios* as the person who transformed the CNC into an organization that could defend their interests vis-à-vis the sugarcane refinery. In the process, he benefited from the new laws promulgated by the government. These laws stipulated that the sugar factories were to restrict themselves to the processing of sugar and leave the producers' organizations (CNC and CNPP) to take care of the organization of labor in the fields (mainly the cutting of the sugarcane) and the transport to the refinery. Through control of these tasks, López acquired an enormous power: he controlled people, resources, and, increasingly, land as the CNC acted as an intermediary between the sugarcane refinery and the *ejidatarios* in issuing permits for sugarcane cultivation. At the same time, he introduced a series of benefits for sugarcane producers including a retirement and life insurance scheme, the provision of cheap housing, and jobs in the refinery for sons of *ejidatarios*. He was also, however, accused by his political rivals of using his power in order to enrich himself.

Zuno's *cacicazgo* proved to be rather short-lived. By the end of the Echevarría administration, Zuno could not sustain his stronghold because he had made too many enemies—within the church, the regional elite, and even at the national level—and was not able to secure the support of López Portillo, the new president, who saw in him a dangerous rival. This situation provided Zuno's pupil, López, with the opportunity to establish his own power base in the region.

The Rise of the Opposition Movement

At the end of the 1980s, the Secretary of Agriculture and Water Resources (SARH) was reorganized. This neoliberal restructuring program dictated that the role of the agrarian bureaucracy had to shift from involvement in production toward the creation of an enabling environment for agricultural development. Accordingly, the SARH in El Grullo started to experiment with the devolution of functions to a Water Users' Association. Eventually, in February 1991, the maintenance and operation tasks of the irrigation district were handed over to the Water Users' Association with full financial autonomy, while another institution, the National Water Agency, was put in charge of securing the flow of water from the dams to the irrigation district.

It did not take long before the association was considered a success and regarded as a national showpiece, so much so that even World Bank officials presented it as a successful pilot case and that it was visited by various delegates from Asian countries. Later, at the beginning of the 1990s, the sugarcane refinery in El Grullo was privatized by the government. This refinery, it should be pointed out, was one of the few in Mexico that was profitable, not because it was well-run and efficient but because environmental factors in El Grullo contributed to a high concentration of sugar in the cane. The CNC-cañera bid to buy the refinery, but because it was unable to make a down-payment the refinery was sold to a commercial group from North Mexico. This change from state to private ownership had important consequences for the relationships between the refinery and the Sugar Producers Organizations, especially the CNC, which represented the smallholder *ejidatarios* (the CNPP represents the larger private producers). It should be noted that the Sugar Producers Organizations were officially in charge of transport, field operations such as the cutting of the cane, input supply, and credit and that these organizations feared that a privatized refinery would attempt to extend its activities into these domains or at least force the Sugar Producers Organizations to rationalize their activities by cutting labor costs drastically. As I will show, this rationalization was perceived as a threat particularly by the CNC, while the CNPP as the representative of the larger sugarcane producers held a more sympathetic stance toward these state policies of privatization and liberalization. Thus, whereas in the past both refinery management and the CNC had been able to establish a *modus vivendi* largely based on common political interests, the relationship henceforth was characterized by mutual distrust. In effect, these neoliberal modernization policies threatened the interests of the former secretary and then treasurer of the CNC, Jesús López, while strengthening the interests of his rival, Camacho, the secretary of the CNPP.

It was at this juncture that Andrés started to play an important role in the forging of an opposition movement in the Water Users' Association. The way in which Andrés became a representative of his *ejido* for the association is telling. Andrés, himself a son of one of the most prominent families of El Grullo, had become *ejidatario* on land that his mother had owned. He became the representative of the association's assembly by cooption. Each of the 15 *ejidos* in the area provides two delegates to the association (regardless of the number of *ejidatarios*). According to law, these delegates should be elected by the assembly of *ejidatarios*, but in practice they are chosen by the chairman of the *ejido* committee, the Comisario Ejidal, together with the board of the association. One day a friend of Andrés and member of the association's board approached him to ask whether he would be ready to become part of the association's assembly as "fresh blood" was needed. Andrés's *ejido* is the smallest one of the region, with only eight *ejidatarios*. As Andrés had a great deal of control in the *ejido*, he accepted the offer and became a delegate. At the assembly meetings, Andrés became an active member, posing delicate questions about the use of the association's machinery and the maintenance of the canals and roads. It struck him that no decisions were made at the assemblies and that the association's manager ran the association without rendering any accounts.

The board of the association was composed of prominent (ex-)politicians and members of the elite, and the manager Camacho, as said, was also chairman of the union of private sugarcane producers, the CNPP. They all shared a strong interest in sugarcane production. It soon became clear to Andrés that a large disparity existed between the resources that the association generated and the services that were provided to the users. It also became apparent that no financial accounts existed of the rent from the machinery. His queries remained unanswered and he disliked the lack of administrative accountability manifested by the board. By talking to the water guards and examining the accounting books he later realized that the acquiescence of the delegates was obtained through the provision of services on their farms (road and irrigation works undertaken at their farms under the cost price) by the association's manager. In addition, many of them were late in paying the annual water payments and owed the association money.

Andrés was not the only person who adopted a critical position at the assemblies. There was another recently appointed delegate, Guillermo, who started to ask uncomfortable questions. Guillermo was a wealthy farmer and *compadre* of Jesús López. So far, Camacho and the agrarian elite of El Grullo had been successful in resisting López's attempts to infiltrate the association. As Camacho saw in Guillermo an agent of his dreaded rival, he opposed his nomination. Nevertheless, Guillermo was appointed. Not surprisingly, Andrés and Guillermo coincided in their criticisms. What followed was a strategic alliance between the two, and thus a rapprochement between Jesús López, the secretary of the CNC, and Andrés.

López was especially interested in subverting the legitimacy of his rival, Camacho, for he had good reasons to fear that Camacho was conniving with the new owners of the sugarcane refinery. A plan was designed by López, Andrés, and Guillermo to secure the support of a number of delegates and to persuade the Comisariados Ejidales of a number of *ejidos* to change their delegates. To that end, a campaign was set up by Andrés and Guillermo in which the current board was accused of undemocratic behavior (no elections of the board or the assembly had been held since the establishment of the association in 1989) and of incompetence (maintenance of the system was below standard). Eventually, Camacho was charged with nepotism, favoritism, and outright corruption. He was accused of never having organized an election of the board, of using the association's machinery for his own benefit, of not attending to the office in spite of receiving a full salary as manager, of contracting the services of his brother in the execution of irrigation and infrastructural works, and of selling water to farmers outside the irrigation district. Later, after the downfall of Camacho a number of other accusations of corruption were added by an accountancy office that was hired by the board.

The new opposition movement claimed to hold to the values of solidarity, mutual help, responsibility, and transparency. In effect, the opposition group heavily drew on the "good governance" discourse of the then prevalent social-liberal regime of Carlos Salinas (1988–1994). Salinas argued that the backwardness of Mexican agriculture was due to the paternalism of the state. According to Salinas, this paternalism led to multiple networks of patron-client relations and hence prevented the emergence of a strong civil society that could hold government representatives accountable for their actions. This discourse of civil responsibility, transparency of government, and administrative accountability of the Mexican state in the 1990s was based on international agendas imposing programs of democratization and good governance in countries that were said to be notoriously "corrupt." Yet, as discussed before, in order to function in Mexican bureaucracies, any functionary has to strike a balance between technical competence and political interests. Hence, for survival in the bureaucracy sociopolitical accountability is much more essential than administrative accountability and transparency.

The social-liberal argument put forward by Andrés and Guillermo was that a small elite who represented only a wealthy minority had captured the association. They had been able to remain in power for so long by counting on the passivity of the people, bribing the delegates with small favors, and discouraging the involvement and accountability of the association's members. These views, however, were vehemently countered by the elite politicians of El Grullo who firmly denied that Camacho had been corrupt and supported him to the end. By them he was considered an able manager, who had successfully opposed attempts by corrupt bureaucrats and politicians to appropriate the association. The adoption of the official discourse of democracy, transparency, and accountability by the opposition movement was in itself not surprising. More surprising, was the way in which they combined this discourse with notions of class and leadership mediated through a cultural language of regional identity. As noted, Andrés, the ideologist of the movement, stressed not only the corruption by the board of the association, but also emphasized the bad leadership style of Camacho.

In order to understand the critique on Camacho's personal style in this regional context it is important to delve a bit into his background. Originally from Guadalajara where he graduated as a civil engineer, Camacho came from a family of agrarian entrepreneurs who owned irrigated land in El Grullo. Camacho was able to establish a close relation with the rich landowners in El Grullo and the agrarian bureaucracy in Guadalajara. Thanks to these contacts he was elected secretary of the CNPP and later administrator of the Water User's Association. As chairman of the CNPP, he favored the privatization of the sugarcane refinery and maintained a good relationship with the refinery's management. Yet, in spite of his influence in the region as the head of the CNPP and of the Water User's Association, Camacho never made efforts to become a popular politician. He did not use the organizations he headed to create a political base for himself. To maintain his power over the assembly and delegates, he depended on the influence of the old elite, comprised mainly of politicians who worked under the late general Barragán. In his campaign, Andrés again and again accused Camacho of never going to the field for inspections and of refusing to interact with the *canaleros* (the front-line workers in charge of the distribution of water) or the farmers. As is sometimes apparent in members of the regional elite, Camacho lacked the skill or ability to deal with people outside his class. As Andrés argued, the art of managing people entailed that they should become part of a whole, of a wider design, the creation of one collective will. In Mexico, and particularly in the state of Jalisco, this cohesion should occur in a culturally specific way, which is with food and drink, with musical groups and mariachi. And that was something Camacho never did. During the time Camacho was the manager of the association, he never organized a party. According to Andrés he did not recognize the yearning for a sense of community harbored by the *ejidatarios* and lacked the style of management that was essential in this part of Mexico. In fact, Andrés pointed to the importance of a culture of power that includes the willingness of leaders to engage in personalized relations with the *ejidatarios* and their families (for example by becoming the godfather of their children, or lending them money) and the ability to organize public modes of enjoyment.

The movement against Camacho and the elite politicians was organized and consolidated during festive *encuentros* (meetings) organized by López. Andrés, a good storyteller and the self-appointed chronicler of the region, entertained the crowds with interesting stories. In addition, he had some status as the son of a well-known physician and former mayor and the grandson of the man who was once the richest man in town, who established the first gas station and was the first to own a car. Yet, it was López who provided the enjoyment. In fact, his capacity to orchestrate enjoyment and to perform as a violent character gave him an edge over Andrés, who as argued, clung to the state discourses of good governance, social democracy, and administrative accountability. Next, I explain the notion of the *cacique* in Mexico and the development of López into a figure of regional power.

Caciquismo and Liminality in Mexico

Although there are many studies on the intermediation or brokerage roles of the *cacique*, little attention has been paid to the ubiquity of the figure of the *cacique* in the Mexican political imaginary. Such an approach would imply studying the socio-symbolic processes by which *caciquismo* is imagined as a pervasive, corrupt, and violent but inevitable component of Mexican political culture (de Vries 2002). In Mexico the law is but a dead letter. What makes state power strong is the possibility to engage in all sorts of opaque, illegal activities in liminal spaces that are nevertheless no less part of the state than the formal institutional apparatus that lends it its legitimacy. In these spaces the *caciques* play a central role in the exercise of power. It cannot be emphasized enough though that such spheres are internal to the logic by which the Mexican state operates. In this view, the phenomenon of *caciquismo* is critical in the constitution of a spectacle through which the power of the state is represented, while the *cacique* himself plays a central role in this spectacle as its orchestrator.[4] By focusing on this dialectic between the performance and the imagination of power it is possible to show how the figure of the *cacique* offers a view of the state in its intimate connection with violence and enjoyment.

Let us go back for a moment to the personal trajectory of López. In the El Grullo region López is credited with breaking the hegemony of the Barragán people, first through his involvement in a water distribution project and then through his involvement in the CNC. In the *ejidos*, there is a common knowledge of the stories of López's corruption, but by many he is considered a great social fighter, in the tradition of Pancho Villa and Emiliano Zapata. He is credited for having given back to them the CNC as an organization in defense of smallholders. Some members of the *ejidos* have explained to me that they like the way in which López runs the *asambleas* (assemblies) of the CNC and the public accounts he gives of current problems, negotiations, losses, and benefits. They also like the yearly parties organized at the end of the sugarcane harvest in the best tradition of Zuno. At these yearly parties, which are attended by the *ejidatarios*, typical regional food is served (*birria*) and popular bands play mariachi music. Also, contrary to the views of many of the elite, the *ejidatarios* seem to consider López a spirited speaker, someone who can express their views and aspirations.

The stance of elite members toward López is ambiguous. Several of them have said to me that they despise him for his lack of manners and ancestry. He instills a paradoxical mixture of fear and disgust. Juan, a member of the elite, for example sees López as an uncultured man, but very astute and intelligent, who thanks to his resoluteness and courage was able to accomplish much for the CNC. Yet, López lacks the necessary skills to become a successful politician. Precisely due to his lack of vision and political education, he fell pray to the vices of power. Unable to aspire to higher positions in the political system, López became an alcoholic obsessed with money, power, and women. By some he is seen as an egomaniac who is only able to surround himself by the lowest, most mediocre characters for fear that someone more intelligent would put an end to his power.

Andrés, too, in spite of his contempt for the local elite politicians, can be counted as part of the elite. As a chronicler of the historical events of the region, he describes López in one of his books as an important social fighter who liberated the sugar refinery from the scourge of corrupt leaders. Yet, in private he portrays an image of him as a typical exponent of the Mexican political system, which co-opts and corrupts local leaders. Typically, Andrés sees López as someone who has lost family values and who holds an immoral view of life only dedicated to material joys. As said, Andrés and López knew each other from the Comisión del Sur and both were strongly influenced by the ideas and methods of Zuno. Yet,

---

4 See Debord (1977) on the concept of the spectacle.

while Andrés argues that he is a true follower of the ideology and political project developed by Zuno, López set out to deploy the skills of populist management, while remaining unconcerned with any larger political project.

I will now return to the discussion about the character of *caciques* in Mexico and the liminal spaces in which they operate. Liminal figures such as *caciques* are characters who cross boundaries between the inside and outside of several social domains, thus gaining a certain status as hybrid or ambivalent figures who stand outside the system, and therefore do not abide to the rules of proper behavior. Liminal spaces are sites where an imagery of power is constructed as a counterpoint to, and subversion of, official images. They designate a kind of anti-structure in which the intimate connections between power and illegitimate enjoyment are acted out (Turner 1977). Arguably, the structural characteristics of such liminal spaces render it possible for political bosses, or *caciques*, to act out in ways marked as polluted and corrupt in the public code (Malkki 1995). Such spaces should be conceived as sites in which a network of complicities involving petty politicians, bureaucrats, and *caciques* is forged, the latter being highly skilled in converting these spaces into platforms for political action. It must be emphasized that these political practices are highly gendered by a determined aesthetics of *machismo* (Gutmann 1997) through which particular sexual experiences, such as homoeroticism and promiscuous sexual seduction are celebrated. In this way, politics and power can be represented as something quite different from their portrayals in official discourse: as an intimate and gendered world suffused with all sorts of prohibited desires.

A celebration of the pleasure of "playing the game" can be found in these liminal spaces. *Caciques* and their clients often enjoy talking about, and are proud of, the ways they arrange things outside the law, and they like to celebrate these accomplishments through abundant partying. It is precisely this partying that affords the pleasure in "playing the game," the spectacle of enjoyment, and the performative side of "corruption" and that enables *caciques* to play a role in the cultural representation of power (Gupta 1995; Mbembé 1992). Next I describe the liminal spaces in which López so deftly orchestrates enjoyment.

López's Parties

I base this account on six parties at López's house. Five of these celebrations were held after an assembly of the association and one to honor López on his birthday. López himself was never present at the assemblies of the Water Users' Association, but after each assembly, the group of Andrés and Guillermo and I would go to his ranch in El Grullo where he would receive us in a merry mood and inquire into every detail of the meeting, who was present and who absent and what had been the role of the various participants. At these parties, Andrés typically introduced me as a sociologist undertaking a study of irrigation management turnover in Mexico and as a black belt judoka, hence suggesting that I was in attendance as his bodyguard. López's ranch is situated at a distance of a few kilometers from the sugar mill. A small pathway leads to the ranch, which is surrounded by sugarcane fields. It is built in a typically Mexican style, a patio or courtyard at the heart of a square building with a large kitchen, sleeping rooms, toilets, and a small sitting room. In the courtyard there is also an empty swimming pool.

López owns another ranch and several hundred head of cattle in a neighboring municipality where his wife and children live. It is common knowledge that in El Grullo, he has a steady lover, a former brothel madam called Laura, whom he made his secretary at the CNC. The story goes around that López found a husband for his lover when she was pregnant with his child, bought her a ranch with a large extension of sugarcane on it, and forced his wife to be his lover's *madrina* (godmother) at the marriage.

What is striking in these spectacular stories is their highly gendered nature. López, in fact, never denied their truth value as they heightened his status as a real *"macho Jalisciense"* (a Jalisco stud). It should be noted that western Jalisco is the area where the machista imagery of the typical ranchero is most cultivated, as attested in Mexico's popular culture.

At the parties, the composition of the invited groups differed according to the purpose, but always present were López's *compadre* Guillermo, Andrés, politicians from neighboring towns, and two of López's assistants at the CNC. In addition, two officials of the National Water Agency would attend, as well as local politicians, members of the association of vegetable producers, engineers of the sugarcane refinery, Comisariados Ejidales (chairmen of the *ejidos*), and those delegates of the association who had ingratiated themselves with the opposition movement. Another visitor was a rich farmer nicknamed el Panzón (the big-bellied) who played the role of a buffoon, entertaining López's guests with anecdotes and jokes. A bachelor in his sixties, he was renowned for his laziness and gluttony. He was seen as a spy for López, visiting parties and bars, playing the buffoon, and returning to López with the information he gathered. That López and el Panzón were very close became quite evident during the *encuentros* organized by López, where the latter used to refer to el Panzón as the source of his knowledge about circulating rumors. López would take el Panzón with him on his travels to Cuba[5] and to the United States, where they engaged in forms of extensive partying. Ironically, this close companionship generated the same kinds of suspicions about López's virility which the latter enjoyed so much to cast on his rival.

There is no doubt that López is an excellent host, taking care that everyone should feel at home on his ranch. This is not to suggest that López effaced himself. He liked to be the center of the attention, and he frequently told stories and anecdotes himself. He expected people to laugh at them and partake in his enjoyment. When he sensed that anyone was aloof, he tried to cheer that person up. He encouraged people to eat and drink as much as possible, taking care that everyone's plate was filled with food: barbecue, tortillas, and different kinds of salsas and fried beans. Typically, there was no service personnel. López himself made the barbecue, assisted by his henchmen. Other friends, part of the inner

---

5   There is a special relationship between the Cuban unions of sugarcane growers and the Mexican ones.

circle, would take care of cooking the beans, and of preparing the sauces. Liquor was abundant and all of the best brands were available: tequila, brandy, rum, cognac, and whisky. All liquor was mixed with soft drinks in exactly the same manner as the cheap *mezcal* (a liquor produced out of agave, akin to tequila) from the region. I was the only one who drank whisky pure or with water alone, a habit that motivated a couple of scornful remarks by López in which I was compared with his elitist arch-rival Camacho, suggesting that I shared his inability to comply with the habits of the region. López especially derided Andrés as an imitator of foreign cultures when he suggested that cognac should be drunk warm and plain. López would say that on his ranch everyone should drink and eat as they liked. He would not tolerate any effeminate manners or elite fashions; it was their right to drink expensive Scotch whisky "*a la Mejicana*" (the Mexican way), that is, mixed with cheap soft drinks. At the end of these *encuentros*, we all would be drunk although no one passed out, probably because of the large amounts of food eaten. The gatherings did not continue late into the night. At some point one of López's close friends would leave, a sign that the *encuentro* ought to draw to a close.

Topics of discussion at these parties included politics and gossip about various renowned persons, without exception in a negative way. López was ready to talk ill about anyone, so long as that person was absent. The most frequent objects of gossip and foul speculation were members of the elite. López seemed to enjoy talking about his sexual relationships with the wives and daughters of well-known politicians and bureaucrats in the region. In this regard, he distinguished himself strongly from Camacho who did not advertise or announce his sexuality in public. According to López's own accounts, "respectable" ladies found him irresistible, in part because of the neglect by their "distinguished" husbands. He for example frequently talked about his relationship with the daughter of a member of the board of the association, an ex-mayor and one of his enemies. He narrated the most intimate details of their relationship while reminding everyone about the hatred that linked him to her father, in this way displaying his prowess vis-à-vis his rival not only as a politician but also as a man. López claimed to know the sexual habits of many others, whether heterosexual or homosexual, offering plenty of details about the latter ones. Homosexuality, in fact, was an all-pervasive theme and López referred to it as an expression of weakness, ambivalence, and treacherousness. These stories, whether true or not, served both as sexual rhetoric of self-aggrandizement and as ways of denigrating his rivals and in particular the elite.

In spite of the use of a discourse of social class, López did not discuss wider socio-political issues at the regional or national level. It was Andrés who broached themes concerning the intentions of President Salinas, the nature of social-liberalism, and the future of the PRI at the national level and in El Grullo. López, in contrast, was more concerned with petty politics. In addition, López used the *encuentros* at his ranch to present a view of himself as a wild man whose success could be attributed to the fact that he transgressed all rules. This style encompassed driving his Chrysler Suburban car at excessive speed with a bottle of liquor in his hand and going to his favorite restaurant, the family restaurant Cuatro Caminos, where he would spend a small fortune on mariachis, having them play for hours until deep into the night when everyone had left and he himself had fallen asleep. Neither would he refrain from harassing women he found attractive, most often selecting those who connoted the elegance and self-assuredness associated with women from the elite class. Being snuffed at by them would only reassure him in their public hypocrisy as against their behavior in private spheres.

At one of the *encuentros* I attended, he told me the following story about his acquaintance with the newly appointed head of the Policía Federal de Caminos (the highway patrol), a police department renowned for their corruption. López explained that he met the head of the Policía Federal de Caminos at Cuatro Caminos and asked for a mariachi group to celebrate the acquaintance. Soon a man approached the head of police, asking him for a job for his son at the Policía Federal de Caminos and offering to pay for the position. López then interfered and ordered the man to pay for the mariachi band instead, thus cashing in the reward intended for the head of police. According to López, the more the head of the police drank the more friendly he became, patting and hugging López to the point that López said he eventually felt embarrassed. Finally, the head of police left the group to fetch a present. He came back with a small box with golden rings, bracelets, and necklaces with crosses or Virgins of Guadalupe and let López and his henchmen choose. In telling this story, López commented that such an intimate and sentimental attitude was not manly, thus implying that the head of police was homosexual, an accusation most likely designed to undermine his authority. In this way López was showing that he did not fear outside authorities and that they were as much liable to being denigrated as were members of the elite such as Camacho. Furthermore, in doubting the manliness of the *Federales* (a police corps widely known for its excessive masculinist behavior) and depicting them as sentimental petty thieves (since the jewelry was presumably acquired through extortion) he portrayed himself as the real "wild man," an autonomous being who responds only to rules of his own making and who openly displays and enjoys his excesses, without having to resort to any kind of justification in terms of common social conventions (in this case that of adhering to a shared religious belief).

It is clear that López used the *encuentros* as a setting in which the takeover of the association was prepared. In fact, these *encuentros* served him not only to counter the threat posed by the alliance between Camacho's CNPP and the sugar refinery but also to reinforce his position within the CNC. It would be false to argue, however, that the *encuentros* became a sort of arena leading to the formation of a group or a faction with a distinct identity and common views on how to tackle the problems of the region. Rather, the *encuentros* operated as liminal spaces within which complicities were welded and acted out and where a regional culture of power was enacted. Drink, gossip, the celebration of masculinity, and character assassination played central roles in this enactment.

Even though these liminal spaces were not aimed at the formation of a group with a clear-cut political agenda they obviously responded to a definite political logic consonant with the established system of domination. Yet, we should not idealize these performances as transgressive events constituting a kind of anti-hegemony (Taussig 1997; Tsing 1993). These forms of transgression were not directed at undermining the official, public law. Transgression here is not liberating or confrontational. It does not aim at creating an alternative order outside the present structures of domination. On the contrary, transgression in this context serves as a support of domination. It compensates for the weakness and vulnerability of the public law.

After this intermezzo on liminality as central to the Mexican political and bureaucratic process I wish to return to the political conflict and the face-off between Andrés and López.

The Evolution of the Political Conflict

The power struggle evolved as follows: Andrés and López struck an alliance in order to topple Camacho from the Water Users' Association. For Andrés, acquiring control over the association was a first step in the establishment of a regional popular movement in the tradition of Zuno in the Comisión del Sur and in line with the social-liberal agenda of then President Salinas. López, on the other hand, was interested in reinforcing his position in the face of the new alliance between the sugarcane refinery and the CNPP (thus Camacho). Andrés, López, and his *compadre* Guillermo set out to create a majority within the assembly of the association that would vote for the removal of the sitting board.

The campaign against Camacho was so successful that six months after the rise of the opposition movement the removal of the entire board of the Water Users' Association was achieved. Andrés and Guillermo were elected members of the board, Andrés as manager and secretary and Guillermo as treasurer. In addition, three other loyal supporters of López were appointed to the board. New problems arose, however. Andrés had his own populist ideas with respect to the management of the Water Users' Association and the interests of the producers. These plans did not coincide with López's crusade. López was only concerned with the Water User's Association to defend his interests against those of Camacho and to strengthen his power base within the CNC. In other words he saw the association as an instrument to maintain his political control in the region and he did not tolerate any interference in his line of attack. This meant that he sought new allies among local politicians and the agrarian bureaucracy. These alliances were forged in part during the *encuentros* he organized.

When Andrés's views started to differ too much from López's, the latter decided to use his henchmen in the Association to confront Andrés. At the same time he began a campaign against Andrés accusing him of acting in complicity with the agrarian elite against the interests of the users and portraying him as somebody who did not differ much from Camacho. Andrés confided in me that he resented these accusations and tried to reach an agreement with López through the intermediation of Guillermo.

Guillermo, during the time that he had been on the board of the association, had established a close relationship with Andrés, whom he admired for his engineering skills. That López had no scruples in getting rid of his closest friends is shown by the way in which he treated Guillermo, his *compadre*. Guillermo made several attempts to discuss matters with López, but López avoided talking about the subject with him, while telling friends that he had concerns about the closeness of Guillermo to Andrés. Guillermo upon hearing about these concerns from López's friends grew increasingly desperate. Finally, López accused Guillermo of corruption and of establishing an alliance with Andrés against him. López put so much pressure on Guillermo that the latter decided to resign from the association, in exchange for López's promise that the accusations of corruption against him would be stopped.

Then followed a concerted campaign of intimidation and character assassination against Andrés in which he was accused of engaging in exactly the same corrupt practices as Camacho. Andrés tried to counter this campaign by mobilizing a number of delegates with whom he had established a close relationship as manager of the association. In addition, he sought the support of the political elite with the argument that he was the last bulwark in the association against López and his corrupt supporters. But all these initiatives were to no avail. The way in which Guillermo had been treated proved to be highly intimidating for most delegates, in particular the big ones, all members of Camacho's CNPP (the private farmers' producers union). When Andrés sought an accommodation with the elite in his struggle against López the elite did not support him. In this way he was punished for seeking an alliance with López to oust Camacho. A new assembly was organized, and Andrés failed to obtain the support of the majority for a number of measures he advocated. López, who for the first time attended an assembly of the association, confronted Andrés publicly, accusing him of being a spy of the elite. He also warned him not to get into a fight with him. Andrés, feeling that even his closest allies had abandoned him, could do little else than submit his resignation.

What this political struggle shows is López's total indifference to demonstrating a good reputation in terms of administrative accountability and transparent government. On the contrary, López operates in ways that openly deny the legitimacy of the official system. Here we see the role of the spectacle and the orchestration of enjoyment in the establishment of a regional regime of power by liminal characters such as López.

Conclusion: Everyday Corruption and the Orchestration of Enjoyment

In the introduction an argument was built in favor of viewing corruption in ways that attend to the elusive and imaginative side of the phenomenon, to the excessive enjoyment that the speculation and talk of corruption renders possible. The power of corruption relies on its evocative capacity, on the glimpses it provides into the workings of the state as an amoral, venal, and all-pervasive entity. In this sense corruption both unveils a public secret and mystifies the power of the state, thus contributing to the fetishistic imagination of the state.

Contrary to what the programs of anti-corruption campaigns would claim, it is not a question of defining subjects who are accountable and responsible as opposed to others who are corrupt and transgressive. If everybody is a little corrupt, albeit some more than others, then everybody is complicit in the construction of the obscene object of corruption. What individuals share is their participation in the spectacles that corruption stages, whether as spectators or perpetrators, or more often than not as something in between.

Corruption evokes the obscene side of the state, while mystifying its power. This cohabitation of the "real" and the "imagined," as I showed in the ethnography, renders possible the orchestration of corruption as excess enjoyment by liminal characters or *caciques*. When using the term "excess enjoyment" I am referring to the Lacanian concept of *jouissance*.[6] Slavoj Žižek, the foremost Lacanian of these days, cogently argues that the obscene imaginations and fantasies that the topic of corruption renders possible are inherent to the workings of state power. As he puts it, political subjects come to belong to a "lawful" community by partaking in the "netherworld of unwritten obscene rules which regulate the "inherent transgression" of the community, the way we are allowed/expected to violate its explicit rules" (Žižek 2002: lxi). What makes a political community, then, is not the idea of the existence of a legitimate state, or the principle of the Law[7], but exactly its opposite, the rituals and rules by which political subjects transgress the explicit rules of the Law. The point not to be lost, however, is that the talk and imagination of corrupt transgression is deeply complicit with the workings of hegemony. This, it could be suggested is the "secret of the law."

The Lacanian view on the transgressive character of corruption as inherent to the workings of power helps us explain the obsession of Mexican bureaucrats with the topic of corruption. Everybody knows that it is only possible to put things to work in the public administration by engaging in semi-legal and untransparent circuits. Without the social skills and knowledge about how to break the law very little—if anything—can be achieved. At the same time bureaucrats have to refer and believe in the democratic and accountable operation of the bureaucracy in order to be able to do their work. According to Žižek (1989, 1992) the typical subject of ideology is the cynic who argues that he does not believe in the official discourse of the state but who, following a pragmatic imperative, behaves as if he believes it. As he puts it, ideology does not reside in (false) belief but in reality. The more the subject denies that he is a subject of ideology the more immersed he is in it. This fetishistic disavowal is ideology at its purest. In the case of corruption, the formula of ideology can thus be defined as follows: I know very well that nothing can be done without engaging in acts labeled as corruption, however, in my public performance I act as if it is possible to do away with corruption, thus abiding to the official text of the law. This is a typical case of fetishistic disavowal:

---

6   It should be noted that *jouissance* in French means both enjoyment and sexual orgasmic satisfaction.

7   In Lacanian terms "the Law" stands for the Big Other: a fictive, imagined, authority that guarantees the consistency of the social order. However, since the Other does not exist (for it is a necessary fiction that confers coherence to the symbolic order) the Law is not complete, it needs its opposite, transgression, in order to legitimize itself. Law thus is productive of a transgressive super-ego which entices the subject to engage in all sorts of excessive enjoyments.

"I know very well, but I act 'as if' because that is what is expected from me, this is the way things are actually run."

In this respect, Andrés in his efforts to set up a popular movement based on the Mexican anti-corruption platform, revealed himself to be a typical subject of the ideology of the governmental good-governance agenda. Ideology in this sense refers not to false knowledge, but to the subjects' practical relation to a certain object of enjoyment, as a relation of fetishistic disavowal. As we saw, Andrés was very good in using a language against corruption, and he knew he had to engage in such acts in order to achieve his political goals. Yet, he himself became a victim of corruption as an everyday practice.

But what happens when subjects do not abide by the official text and openly admit how things are run? This is López's strategy. He orchestrates corruption as a public spectacle. He does not engage in the practice of fetishistic disavowal, as he never uses discourses of democracy, accountability, and justice. On the contrary, he displays his corruption in a proud way, thus displaying the inner workings of power. Thus, paradoxically, he engages in "transparent" corruption. This, I argue, explains why López appeals more to the popular imagination than Andrés, because he openly displays the "public secret of the state."

Let us inquire further into the question why López is so respected among the peasants, in spite of his public corruption. There is no doubt that López is credited by the majority for defending the rights of sugarcane growers in the area and having ended the "corruption" of the old politicians. He is also known as a committed union leader who takes care of the problems and complaints of peasant smallholders. The large majority of the peasants are also aware that López was never an altruistic character, the more so because López has always enjoyed displaying ostentatiously and sharing (in parties, and so on) his newly acquired riches. There are no doubts that he, in his capacity of a simple state functionary, could never have gathered so much wealth through honest means. Sure, many peasant sugarcane producers consider that López has gone too far in his hunger to become rich. But, at the same time they appreciate his sharing with others and the transparent character of his corruption.

Not surprisingly, López's deeds are read in different ways by different sections of the population. Peasants' notions of social justice differ from those of the urban middle class or the official statements of the regime. Peasant smallholders are happy to pay bribes to public officials as long as the latter comply with their part of the transaction. Furthermore, they are quite incredulous with regard to public administration reforms destined to make an end to corruption. Dealings with state officials are always fraught with dangers as well as opportunities. Little difference is therefore made between following legal procedures and engaging in so-called corrupt practices. It is at this point that the figure of the *cacique* comes to play a central role as he renders possible the imagining of state power in its intimate connection with violence and enjoyment. Thus rather than arguing that corrupt characters such as Mexican *caciques* are a symptom of a diseased political system and have to be cut out in order to cure the system, it would be more interesting to explore the meanings of their performances and transgressions in establishing a particular regime of power. The dialectical lesson is that if we take the obscene and corrupt underside of the law as the truth of the law then characters such as López should be read against the grain of the official text.

References

Comaroff, J. and J. Comaroff (eds) (1993) *Modernity and Its Malcontents: Ritual and Power in Postcolonial Africa.* Chicago, IL: University of Chicago Press.
Debord, G. (1977) *The Society of the Spectacle.* Detroit, MI: Black and Red.
Gennep, A. van. (1909) *The Rites of Passage.* London: Routledge and Kegan Paul
Geschiere, P. (1997) *The Modernity of Witchcraft: Politics and the Occult in Postcolonial Africa.* Trans. Janet Roitman. Charlottesville, VA: University of Virginia Press.
Grindle, M. (1977) *Bureaucrats, Politicians, and Peasants in Mexico: A Case Study in Public Policy.* Berkeley and Los Angeles, CA: University of California Press.
Gupta, A. (1995) Blurred Boundaries: The Discourse of Corruption, the Culture of Politics and Bureaucracy. *American Ethnologist* 22(2): 375–402.
Gutmann, M. (1997) The Ethnographic (G)ambit: Women and the Negotiation of Masculinity in Mexico City. *American Ethnologist* 24(4): 833–55.
Malkki, L. (1995) *Purity and Exile: Violence, Memory, and National Cosmology among Hutu Refugees in Tanzania.* Chicago, IL: University of Chicago Press.
Mbembé, A. (1992) The Banality of Power and the Aesthetics of Vulgarity in the Postcolony. *Public Culture* 4(2): 1–30.
Nuijten, M. (2003) *The Culture and the Politics of Organization in Mexico.* London: Pluto Press.
Taussig, M. (1997) *The Magic of the State.* New York: Routledge.
Tsing, A. (1993) *In the Realm of the Diamond Queen: Marginality in an Out-of-the-Way Place.* Princeton, NJ: Princeton University Press.
Turner, V. (1974) *Dramas, Fields, and Metaphors. Symbolic Action in Human Society.* Ithaca, NY: Cornell.
Turner, V. (1977) *The Ritual Process: Structure and Anti-Structure.* Ithaca, NY: Cornell University Press.
Vries, P. de (2002) Vanishing Mediators: Enjoyment as a Political Factor in Western Mexico. *American Ethnologist* 29(4): 901–27.
Zaag, P. van der (1992) Chicanery at the Canal: Changing Practice in Irrigation in Western Mexico. PhD dissertation. Wageningen Agricultural University. Department of Rural Development Sociology.
Žižek, S. (1989) *The Sublime Object of Ideology.* London: Verso.
—— (2002) *For They Know Not What They Do: Enjoyment as a Political Factor.* 2nd edition. London: Verso.

State Officials in the Twilight Zone

Chapter 8

Corruption or Social Capital? Tact and the Performance of *Guanxi* in Market Socialist China

Alan Smart and Carolyn L. Hsu

In recent years, near universal disdain for corruption has been paralleled by acclaim for social capital as the new cure for socio-economic and developmental problems, yet the overlap between the two processes is rarely considered. Networks, trust, obligation, and a reliance on informal arrangements: all are part of both phenomena. It is only by assuming that corruption is clearly defined and distinct from social capital that respective condemnation and celebration can be maintained. The argument by Rothstein and Stolle that "the high level of social capital in the Scandinavian countries can be explained by ... the low level of patronage and corruption" (Rothstein and Stolle 2003: 1) takes for granted the clear separability of the two concepts. Concrete cases, however, reveal their fuzzy boundaries.

In China, the term *guanxi* ("relationship," "network" or "connection") encompasses a complex body of informal practices, based on principles of gift exchange, and used for both affective and instrumental purposes. On the one hand, research on *guanxi* has revealed its positive functions for building trust in the absence of adequate formal legal and financial institutions (Yang 1994). *Guanxi* practice has facilitated entrepreneurship in China in the absence of enforceable contracts by engendering sufficient trust for foreign investment (Smart and Smart 1991), informal loans (Tsai 2002), and business partnerships and deals (Hsu 2005; Keister 2002). On the other hand, China scholars have also, often in the same studies, drawn strong links between *guanxi* practice and corruption (*fubai* or *tanwu*) (Smart 1993b; Sun 2004; Tsai 2002; Wank 2002; Yang 1994). Indeed, in China, both official state discourse and dissident rhetoric tend to condemn *guanxi* practice as corruption (Hsu 2001; Liu 1983; Yang 1994: 56–62).

Guanxi has an ambiguous nature: it can either be presented as clearly morally better than corruption or as merging inseparably into it. Ordinary citizens are just as likely to describe *guanxi* practice in neutral or even positive terms, as in negative ones. They find it difficult to articulate the difference between "good" *guanxi* practice and "bad" corruption. Mayfair Yang (1994) describes her interviewees struggling to explain why "reasonable" (*heli*) *guanxi* practice is not corruption. For them, in broad terms corruption is "for selfish, individual-gain purposes, and it is not legal," whereas *guanxi* practice is only used for "reasonable demands" and connotes "'human sentiments' (*renqing*), friendship, long-term personal relationships, and the image of people helping one another" (Yang 1994: 62f.).

In this chapter, we argue that situated performance and the interpretations of others influence whether particular actions and relationships come to be perceived and labeled as corrupt or not. As the introduction to this volume persuasively argues, the definition of corruption cannot be restricted to legal definitions, but also has to take account of contested moral evaluations. Skill is particularly necessary to avoid practices from becoming labeled as corrupt. Inept performance can result in a gift exchange becoming disdained as a bribe.

Skilled performance in exchange was particularly important during the early period of China's economic reforms (1979–1992), when the incorporation of capitalist economic practices into a communist state was facilitated by a large degree of ambiguity and tacit acceptance of things that were (not yet) legal or adequately regulated by administrative guidelines. This situation is epitomized by the saying that "A model worker in Guangdong may be a criminal in Shanghai, a chair of meetings in Hainan may be a bearer of handcuffs in Beijing" (Sun 2004: 3). The experimental and geographical diversity of the reform process resulted in high levels of uncertainty about what was legal, as well as about what was moral, since newly legalized practices such as the dismissal of workers were often seen as immoral. The rectification and clarification process is still ongoing, but preparation for and accession to the World Trade Organization has greatly increased the degree of legal transparency in contemporary China.

This chapter will concentrate on *guanxi* practices that might be defined as corrupt, but which participants would prefer to have seen as legitimate, such as the exchange of gifts and favors. An ethnographic perspective encourages us to explore how the social relationships involved in *guanxi* practice and corruption are seen by local actors. Benefiting from one's position in government or business is not always inherently perceived as *fubai* or *tanwu* (corruption or bribery); becoming characterized as "dirty" involves complex processes of performance and interpretation. Tactful performance in social interaction is a crucial but under-examined element of these processes. We use examples from our field research to illustrate the tactful management of morally ambivalent demands, and then discuss more widely the significance of tact in social interaction.

We draw upon research conducted at what could be considered the People's Republic of China's (PRC) two opposite poles: Guangdong in China's far south, and Heilongjiang in its far north. Their geographic difference is mirrored in their divergent experiences in market reform. Guangdong has consistently been an early mover and innovator, frequently "pushing the envelope" far beyond what the central government had explicitly sanctioned or envisioned. Heilongjiang, with its heavy economic reliance on state-owned enterprises, experienced its golden age of economic prosperity under the socialist planned economy and therefore has been much more reluctant to embrace the market. In Guangdong, where Smart's research concentrated on foreign investment, pioneering capitalists, most of whom in the first years of reform were from Hong Kong, navigated ambivalent waters that relied on social legitimacy to overcome numerous breaches of Chinese law. Exchanges that were more or less "corrupt" were ubiquitous in the management of the new capitalist enterprises and the local governments that facilitated their expansion. In order to cope with the incompatibilities between Chinese communist rule and capitalist logic, social relationships lubricated the clashing gears of the two, making it possible to take advantage of potentially lucrative "factor complementarities."

In the city of Harbin in Heilongjiang, Hsu's research reveals, *guanxi* connections were an integral part of business practices because contracts could not be enforced through legal means. Harbin businesspeople reacted to the inadequacy of formal institutions by confining their business transactions to "friends" and avoiding "strangers." Through *guanxi* practice based on gift exchange, these businesspeople could expand their networks of "friends" promiscuously, allowing entrepreneurship to flourish. In Harbin, everyone seemed to engage in *guanxi* practice and seemed to consider it a normal daily activity, and yet under certain circumstances, *guanxi* practice was strenuously condemned as corruption.

This chapter tackles the complicated relationship between *guanxi* practice and corruption from a variety of angles. The first section examines the historical and ideological roots of current Chinese cultural conceptions of the two phenomena. We analyze the historicized narratives that lay behind the contested, but relatively dichotomized view of "reasonable" *guanxi* practice versus condemnable corruption. The second section describes China's political and economic trajectory in the post-1979 market reform period, and its influence on *guanxi* practice and corruption. The third section examines the particular ways in which social actors strive to enact "reasonable" *guanxi*, rather than "corrupt" activities. It looks at how, under these circumstances, actors negotiate the complex but necessary activities of gift exchange, building trust, utilizing networks, and constructing favorable relationships. We explore the role of tact as a crucial dimension in performing acceptable *guanxi* practice and avoiding labels of corruption. In the last section, we return to the macro level and discuss different predictions for the future that scholars have made about the relationship between *guanxi* and corruption.

Guanxi and Corruption in Historical Context

Contemporary China scholars, especially those in the West, tend to see *guanxi* and corruption as intertwined phenomena. Our informants were also quick to condemn certain forms of *guanxi* practice as corruption. However, in the lived experience of Chinese citizens, "reasonable" *guanxi* practice and corruption were attached to two different sets of associations and evoked two different sets of "historical" narratives. The term *guanxi* connotes "human sentiments" (*renqing*), warm generosity, and close relationships, while "corruption" (*fubai* or *tanwu*) elicits stories of immoral officials exploiting and abusing those whom they are supposed to serve.

Local understandings of both *guanxi* practice and corruption are rooted in what Westerners call "Confucianism," and what Chinese informants would probably term "traditional Chinese culture." This worldview purports to explain the nature of human beings and human society by focusing on the centrality of relationships. The five Cardinal Relationships are seen as the central organizing principles of society: affection between parent and child, righteousness between ruler and subject, distinction between husband and wife, order between older and younger brothers, and sincerity between friends (Lo and Otis 2003: 136). In Confucian ideology persons were primarily defined by their social roles and responsibilities in relationships. If everyone acted out his or her social role correctly, society would prosper. These relationships were generally hierarchical and complementary, and based on the two central institutions of dynastic China: the patriarchal family and the imperial court. Family relationships were the subject of *guanxi* discourse, while corruption rhetoric focused on the relationship between the court and its subjects.

To understand how *guanxi* is practiced, we must understand the role of material gifts and favors in Confucian relationships. In contrast to the Western ideology of relationships, in which instrumental considerations taint "pure" emotional ties (Carrier 1999), in Chinese Confucianism expressive relationships were supposed to be manifested through the exchange of useful goods and helpful actions (Lo and Otis 2003). To put it another way, in Western Judeo-Christian tradition, the ideal friend is one who lays down his life for his friends, the antithesis of the false friend who "uses" friends for personal gain. In contrast, in Confucian ideology, "using" friends for personal gain is lauded as the path to true friendships. In this view, genuine relationships are built through transactions that benefit one individual more than the other, since this type of interaction puts the first person in debt to the second and sets up the rationale for further interactions.

At heart, *guanxi* practice is based on the logic of gift exchange (Mauss 1967). In a gift exchange, the "relationship must be presented as primary and the exchange, useful as they may be, treated as only secondary" (Smart 1993a: 399). Therefore, each transaction must be treated as a step in a series of interactions designed to deepen the relationship. The rule of thumb in *guanxi* practice was to respond to any gift with greater munificence: "You honor me with a foot; I honor you with a yard" (Hwang 1987: 954; Yang 1994: 143). We can contrast gift exchanges to market transactions, which are isolated and discrete interactions where both parties exchange items of equivalent value. In *guanxi* practice, a gift that clearly and blatantly paid off the debt and thereby ended the relationship of obligation between the two parties would be considered shockingly offensive.

In pre-communist *guanxi* practice, people outside the extended kin network were strangers (*shengren*), unconstrained by obligations or affection and therefore not eligible for gift exchange or *guanxi* ties. In interactions between strangers, there was no basis of trust, and both parties were assumed to be motivated solely by self-interest. However, certain non-kin had the potential to become pseudo-kin through *guanxi* gift exchange. These were people who shared a "*guanxi* base" such as the same surname, the same hometown, the same workplace, or the same class in school (Tong and Yong 1998). A *guanxi* base can be seen as a latent connection that could be activated into a *guanxi* relationship through the commencement of gift exchange.

Although *guanxi* practice is understood through the discourse of warm relationships and emotional connections, it has also always been a technique for instrumental gain. In gift exchange, when people do favors or offer gifts to their "friends," kin, or pseudo-kin, they cannot act as though they expect something in return. However, the norms of reciprocity do obligate the recipient to do something in return (Hwang 1987; Lo and Otis 2003; Smart 1993a). This contradiction between the "unconditional" gift and the binding obligation that results was the central principle that allowed the practice of *guanxi* to function. Indeed, the Chinese term *guanxi* can be translated not only as "relationship" but also as "obligation." (When thanked, Chinese people respond, "*Meiyou guanxi*," or "No obligation!"—an act of misrecognition or of tactful denial.)

In the Communist era under Mao Zedong (1949–1978), the pressures of a redistributive economy and an intrusive state forced *guanxi* practice to change. Confucianism was condemned, and the power of the patriarchal clan was significantly undermined. No longer centered on the family, *guanxi* practice became a "modularized" practice for individuals (Lo and Otis 2003). *Guanxi* practice became untied from *guanxi* bases, and people could build *guanxi* ties with anyone, just by starting a series of favor exchanges. The most common way to meet new *guanxi* contacts was through introductions through mutual "friends." Consequently, one of the best favors a person could offer a friend (or potential friend) was an introduction to someone who might potentially help them out someday. Moreover, since people could still obtain favors from "a friend of a friend of a friend," they could reach out to a substantial population of useful contacts. Despite the fact that *guanxi* practice networks could and did expand greatly in their new, modularized form, these "friendships" were still materially manifested through gifts and favors. And despite official propaganda campaigns condemning *guanxi* practice (Gardner 1969), these behaviors continued to be associated in popular talk with the language of cordial emotional ties. To be a human being with "human sentiments" (*renqing*) was to practice *guanxi*, and a person who defaults on *guanxi* obligations was a person with no face (*mianzi*). Failing to meet expectations that one would reciprocate past kindness or favors could result in accusations of lacking "conscience" (*liangxin*) (Oxfeld 2006). As a result, Chinese could talk about *guanxi* without shame, unlike corruption.

It is useful to think of *guanxi* as occupying the middle of the space of social relationships, ranging from purely instrumental to purely affective. *Guanxi* combines instrumental utility with respect for maintaining and enhancing a relationship, and avoids the polar ends of conformity to impersonal rule systems or blatant extraction of tribute (Smart 1993b).

In contrast to the positive rhetoric associated with *guanxi*, the discourse of *fubai* (corruption) and *tanwu* (bribery) is thoroughly negative. The words themselves elicit disgust: the "*fu*" in *fubai* means "decayed" or "corroded," and can be used to refer to rotting food, while the "*wu*" in *tanwu* is "filth" or "pollution." During the middle and late imperial periods, corruption figured prominently in historical narratives about the rise and fall of dynasties (Huang 1981; Lui 1979). These narratives focused on the reciprocal relationship between ruler and subject, understood through the Confucian concept of the Mandate of Heaven.

Political leaders are given the mandate to rule (by heaven) because of their moral rectitude, wisdom, and sincere desire to care for their subjects. If an emperor and his court abandon the path of righteousness and become corrupt, his subjects are no longer morally obligated to submit to his rule. Indeed, they are morally obligated to overthrow the decadent dynasty and place an upright man upon the throne. According to the Chinese historical narrative, this new dynasty will also eventually succumb to corruption, and the cycle will begin anew.

We should note that, according to Chinese discourse, corruption is inextricably associated with political power and its abuse. Moreover, it is a crime of morality. Whether an act is considered corrupt or not depends not on its category but on its context: the attitude of the perpetrator and the effects of the action. In late imperial China, officials were so under-funded that they were compelled to collect illegal fees and surcharges above the official tax quotas in order to run their offices and do their jobs. Most of these officials probably also added a little padding to improve their standard of living. As long as the amounts did not exceed "reasonable" levels, soliciting bribes for these purposes was considered socially acceptable (Lui 1979: 3). However, if local officials exploited their jurisdictions to the point that the subjects suffered and were in danger of losing their subsistence, their behavior would be considered intolerably and criminally corrupt (Lui 1979: 4–8). Kevin O'Brien and Lianjiang Li (2006) have traced parallels between these traditional patterns and what they describe as "rightful resistance" in rural areas, using central policies and allies against corrupt local officials (O'Brien 2006).

Although *guanxi* and corruption are associated with two separate discursive narratives, in practice they involve overlapping activities. Despite the rhetorical distinction between "warm human sentiments" and exploitation, the behaviors they describe are often identical: the exchange of gifts and favors for instrumental purposes. Indeed, a flourishing culture of *guanxi* transactions creates conditions that facilitate bribery and corruption. Bribery violates the basic foundation of *guanxi* gift exchange by making instrumental gain the sole purpose of the interaction, and the relationship between the participants is ignored or even damaged in the process. However, actors indulging in bribery interactions can adopt the forms and expressions of *guanxi*, although savvy participants may be well aware that the substance of the transaction is a sham.

If a *guanxi* transaction involves state functionaries, elicits "unreasonable" gain, and harms the people these functionaries are supposed to serve, people would generally accept that this is an act of corruption. Thus, *guanxi* and corruption can be understood as separate but overlapping phenomena. Yet, this also means that the definition of corruption depends on the definitions of "state," "reasonable gain," and "harm to the people." As a result, the relationship between *guanxi* practice and corruption has been dynamic and the site of contestation.

When Mao Zedong and the Communist Party of China (CPC) came to power in 1949, the state expanded far beyond the size and scope of the late imperial government. The irrationalities of the command economy and the traumas of disruptive political campaigns increased the importance of *guanxi* interactions for daily life (Yang 1994), at the same time that *guanxi* practice was becoming decoupled from the patriarchal family. *Guanxi* practice became a technique necessary for obtaining everything from bicycles, foodstuffs, and train tickets to desirable job assignments. Meanwhile, the ever-growing population of party-state cadres, as gatekeepers in the redistributive economy, found themselves in an excellent position to benefit from gift and favor exchange practices. Ironically, although corrupt behavior may have been on the rise, the talk of corruption was relatively suppressed in the socialist era. After all, the traditional Chinese corruption narrative claims that every regime inevitably succumbs to inner degradation and collapses, while Mao's regime insisted that it was radically different from everything that came before, a perfect new system for a perfectible new China. In the 1950s, 1960s, and 1970s, behaviors that could have been considered "corrupt" were commonly labeled "feudal," "counter-revolutionary," "capitalist," or "bourgeois" (Hsu 2001).

Beginning in 1978, Deng Xiaoping's "Reform and Opening Up" movement transformed the institutional landscape of China once again, which in turn reshaped the practice of *guanxi*, the definition of corruption, and the relationship between the two. Under these new conditions, how do social actors negotiate the boundaries between "reasonable *guanxi*" and corruption, and how do their actions shape society?

Economic Reforms, *Guanxi*, and Corruption

It is impossible to generalize about "reform China," not only because of its geographic and socio-cultural diversity but also because the period after 1979 has lasted almost as long as the prior Maoist era, and has resulted in complex transformations in society and in the reform process itself. At the risk of over-simplifying, the period from 1979 to 1992 involved trends toward engagement with the capitalist global economy and "deep" decentralization, with localities and provinces not only increasing their share of revenues, but gaining powers to innovate in often radical ways. Successful local experiments were often adopted by the central government and implemented nationally. Opening up occurred earliest in the new Special Economic Zones and in the southeastern provinces of Guangdong and Fujian. Reforms generally affected the countryside more quickly than the urban economy, and the coast before the interior. After 1992, reforms spread more broadly, affecting the cities and state-owned enterprises to a greater extent. The leadership, moreover, started to acknowledge market reforms more explicitly than before. Despite the deepening of the economic reforms, however, there was an accompanying recentralization of the state, with the center substantially increasing its share of revenues and developing a more effective "regulatory state" (Yang 2004). Preparation for and accession to the World Trade Organization in 2001 swung the pendulum definitively back to centralized and more universal "rules of the game" for the economy.

However, despite this complexity, we can still make two general statements about *guanxi* and corruption in the reform era. As the market made consumer products and services widely available, it became less necessary to use *guanxi* to get daily necessities, such as train tickets or special food items. Instead, *guanxi* practice "colonized" new areas of scarcity, particularly relating to permissions and access (Yang 2002), and became integral to doing business in the PRC. Second, corruption, which in terms of public attention had been relatively unimportant in the Maoist era, surged to the forefront of public consideration as one of China's most dire social problems. Needless to say, these two phenomena were related.

From the earliest stages of the reform era, *guanxi* practice was used to bypass the obstacles to doing business in China. In 1979, taking the "capitalist road" was still a shocking and dangerous path. Reforms then were intended to strengthen the Communist Party and China so it could compete economically with its class enemies. Since much that was central to the new system was in contradiction to the "socialist road," reformers avoided referring to capitalism. Initially the new system was spatially delimited to the new Special Economic Zones. For local officials to forge tactical alliances with foreign capitalists was a daring and risky strategy. The results often had very rich returns, as new wealth was created at a rapid rate in the 1980s, but the situation had to be handled very carefully if it were not to create political problems. Gifts, in the forms of patriotic contributions from ethnic Chinese "compatriots" in Hong Kong to "building a strong China," were acceptable in a way that capitalist investment was not. It was relatively safe to "build an export-oriented factory," but much more dangerous to "make deals with foreign capitalists." By adopting the correct labels and discourses, it was possible to move ahead in ways that "pushed the envelope" of acceptable practice. Achieving this often involved a multitude of—often *guanxi*-related—practices that could be labeled as corrupt according to the letter of the newly enacted laws. In the absence of encouragement for innovation and the underdevelopment of clear guidelines in almost all aspects of early reform, collusion was often the most effective way to promote local development.

Chinese business practices developed in contexts where the legal and financial institutions were inadequate and often antagonistic to Chinese entrepreneurs. Contracts were difficult, if not impossible, to enforce through legal means (Chen 1999). Small business owners had no recourse against police harassment. Banks generally refused to loan any capital (Tsai 2002). *Guanxi* practice, then, served to functionally replace contracts and other formal institutions. Through ever-expanding networks of "friends," aspiring business owners could raise capital, form partnerships, seek suppliers, gather information, and conduct relatively secure transactions. In Harbin, Hsu met only one entrepreneur who was able to secure a loan from a bank, and he had strong *guanxi* ties with the bank officer. Most aspiring business owners in Harbin and elsewhere relied on an array of informal financial resources, based on *guanxi* practice (Tsai 2002). Business transactions were not conducted through formal, written agreements, but instead generated through meandering conversations over multi-course banquets. It was common practice in Harbin, for *guanxi* "friends" not only to lend each other money and share news, but also to offer each other retail space and introduce potential clients. Thus it was possible for a person with very few resources, except "friends," to start and sustain a small business.

Guanxi practice also facilitated foreign direct investment. *Guanxi* practice (in somewhat different forms) had become an integral part of business workings in Chinese communities in Taiwan, Hong Kong, Singapore, and elsewhere throughout the world, creating a type of capitalist practice many scholars consider to be distinct from the Euro-American form (Hamilton 2000; Redding 1990, 2000; Tong and Yong 1998). Drawing upon these *guanxi*-based practices, investors from Chinese diaspora communities were able to make connections and build cooperative relations with actors in the PRC. These investors were willing to put their capital in China, despite the lack of legal protections, because they could rely on *guanxi* as their basis of security (Chen 1999; Hsing 1998; Smart 1993a). Mobilizing *guanxi* networks allowed them to penetrate the Chinese market more quickly and successfully than other investors. As China began to integrate into the capitalist world economy, these "overseas compatriots" became key sources of finance, connections, and information. Ironically, insecure property rights and ambiguous or lax legal regulations for Hong Kong investors in China, along with widespread distrust of the state, encouraged reliance on personal relationships, which helped produce one of the fastest growing economies in history.

Even if relationships that Transparency International, for example, would label as corrupt did serve to promote economic growth in China, we would need to balance this with the negative consequences of *guanxi*, including its tendency to facilitate corruption. The use of networks and social capital helped resolve many problems, but also created a context that was conducive to wasteful venality that undermined not only archaic red tape but also other inconvenient laws, such as protections for labor and the environment (Pun 2005). Another consequence was that market reforms initially enhanced the power of local cadres, who could use their access to state resources to strike it rich on the market—and use their authority over licenses, tax breaks, and property to exploit entrepreneurs.

China's export boom, a critical element in supporting the "rise of China" (Keith 2005), has been significantly facilitated by social relationships between foreign investors and local officials that are frequently categorized as "corrupt" by critics such as those in the anti-sweatshopping movement. Local expectations that rules can and should be "flexibly adjusted" to suit the needs of economic growth parallel Peter Evans's (1995) argument that successful developmental states are characterized by "embedded autonomy" of an internally cohesive state bureaucracy and state connectedness with private sector entrepreneurs. A shift one way leads to kleptocracy and predatory states but overemphasis on the other direction leads to an isolated state apparatus that fails to mobilize national competitive advantages. Even in classic examples of embedded autonomy, the interpenetration of bureaucracy and private sector could be considered either as corrupt or as the concentration of social capital, and changes in ruling parties or factions have often resulted in corruption charges against those considered praiseworthy at an earlier point in time.

By the late 1980s, fiscal imbalances and partial reforms had resulted in high levels of inflation, central government deficits, and poor investment practices. Officials were enriching themselves at an escalating rate by brokering between the dual pricing system for the market and planned economies. Meanwhile ordinary urban citizens suffered from stagnating state-controlled wages and "red-eye disease" (jealousy), gazing upon the nouveau riche and their new, appalling habits of conspicuous consumption. They wondered, "Why should taxi drivers make several times the income of engineers? Why should teenagers lucky enough to get jobs in a joint-venture hotel make more than most senior professors?" (Calhoun 1994: 248).

Chinese political dissidents offered an answer to these questions: the problem was political corruption. Economic inequality, excessive and decadent consumer consumption, and even inflation were not random, inexplicable occurrences; they were the direct results of the sinful actions of a thoroughly corrupt political elite. A handbill at Tiananmen Square during the 1989 student protests declared:

> These people's public servants have used the blood and sweat of the people to build palatial retreats all over China ... to buy foreign luxury vehicles, and go abroad on pleasure trips with their children, and even with the children's nannies! ... While the country suffers, a tiny handful benefit, and the people end up shouldering the debt. (Han 1990: 275)

The evocation of the traditional historical narrative of corruption was a powerful and effective strategy. At the Tiananmen Protests, it was the most popular platform for attracting the support of urban citizens (Calhoun 1994: 248; Gates 1991: 241). The Chinese party-state was forced to respond with a series of high-profile anti-corruption campaigns and arrests. Well into the late 1990s, the majority of Hsu's interviewees in Harbin still declared "corruption" to be China's most serious social problem (Hsu 2001).

At the same time, China scholars also became interested in the problem of corruption (Ding 1994; Holmes 1993; Kwong 1997; Lo 1993; Lu 2000). However, we should note that the popular definition of corruption used by ordinary citizens was not necessarily the same as the scholarly definition. For people of modest means, the problem of corruption was not one of conflating the public and the private, or of exchanging gifts for favors. Instead, corruption was defined as "excessive" gain by political elites at the expense of the common people they were expected to work for. A small business owner in Harbin, interviewed by Hsu, offered a typical view:

> Nowadays cadres are corrupt, don't work for common people. Let me give you an example: [a state enterprise] is laying off workers. It's in big trouble right? But the cadres are still eating big, carrying on. They're not even considering what they're eating, how many people's salaries is that? They're not even considering that. How can the common people believe cadres? How can they believe leaders? They're too corrupt, these leaders.

For her, corrupt cadres were those who failed to take care of their workers and indulged in conspicuous consumption, not necessarily those who took bribes or did anything illegal. To use her words, these cadres consumed people's salaries by "eating big" (at expensive banquets) while workers lost their jobs.

Negotiating the Boundaries of *Guanxi* and Corruption: the Importance of Tact

In the reform era, *guanxi* practice had evolved to become an integral part of doing business. At the same time, public awareness of (and disgust at) corruption was raised to new heights. As we discussed above *guanxi* and corruption were discursively separate phenomenon but in practice often involved the same actions: the exchange of gifts and favors for useful benefits. On a micro-level, then, how did social actors negotiate these practices so that their actions could be categorized as "reasonable" *guanxi* rather than corruption?

We argue that the distinctive feature of *guanxi* is the way in which it incorporates both genuine sentiment (*ganqing*) and a series of techniques for getting things done. These techniques include creating a sense of shared identity, invoking obligation and the use of gift exchange to build a long-term relationship. To emphasize the self-serving strategies at the expense of the emotional connection, or vice versa, is to miss the critical point about *guanxi*: its ambiguous fusion of the two dimensions. The ambiguity of *guanxi* allows it to adapt to dramatically different types of situation by changing its features and practices. It is crucial, then, that *guanxi* not be considered to be invariant or uni-dimensional. *Guanxi* is better seen as an interactional idiom (Wank 1999: 30), a set of discursive forms within which people interact and which they can use to accomplish things and build relationships. One result is that the outcomes and characteristics of the practices of *guanxi* vary considerably by context and occasion.

When networks cross boundaries as burdened with difference, separation, and conflict as those between capitalist Hong Kong and socialist China, the connections, linkages, and practices that result are naturally fraught with ambivalence and contradictions. The ambivalent dimensions of cross-border relations make it desirable that much that is central to these exchanges and to the *guanxi* networks must be tactfully excluded from the performance. The introduction to this volume usefully emphasizes the role of secrecy in corruption, but it is important to recognize that what is not made explicit may not necessarily be secret to the local community.

Cultivating *guanxi* is not just the usage of customary forms to disguise what might otherwise be recognized as corrupt exchange. Instead, the exchanges are used to cultivate and strengthen relationships that are expected to continue. The Chinese Communist Party encourages the strengthening of trustworthy social relationships between Hong Kong investors in China and mainlanders since these relationships can encourage patriotic investment in the motherland on the part of diaspora Chinese (Smart and Smart 1998).

Reliance on *guanxi* to get things done is not an automatically successful strategy, but depends considerably on the skill involved in the actual interactional performances. Because the narrative underlying *guanxi* practice claims that the primary purpose of the interaction is to strengthen the relationship, rather than instrumental gain, treating one's partner simply as a means to an end is likely to undermine the transaction and even the *guanxi* tie itself. On the other hand, according to the traditional narrative of corruption, benefiting from one's government position (or social connections to government officials) is not necessarily a bad thing. Instead, the label "corruption" is determined by complex processes of performance and interpretation. An act is considered corrupt if it benefits the principle parties at the expense of others. If, however, a potentially corrupt action is understood as serving the collective community in addition to enriching the principle actors, then it can be seen in a much more positive light. Sun (2004) terms this second practice "collective bribery," where corrupt practices undertaken in the interest of the rural collective or state-owned enterprise incur far lighter penalties than those that are undertaken exclusively for private benefit. Since collective bribers usually also benefit personally, the difference between "reasonable" *guanxi* practice and an act of corruption hinges on managing perception.

Since the style and specifics of the interaction will have an impact on how it is perceived by those involved, tact is of the utmost importance. Tact involves indirect and obscure circumlocutions in describing events (Bayraktaroglu 1991; Brown 1987: 10) that nevertheless allow cognoscenti to understand what is being alluded to (Chang 1999). Tact is particularly crucial in contexts where there are high levels of distrust of the prevailing institutions, so that tactics of cultivating personal, non-official relationships are relied on instead.

For example, foreign investors face major difficulties due to limited accountability and transparency of policies and enforcement actions. A given policy legislated by the central or provincial government can be interpreted in diverse ways by local administrative units. Interpretations by the same administrative unit can change over time. Ambiguity and insecurity are compounded when one considers the same process being repeated at each of the levels of implementation, enforcement, and dispute settlement.

During Smart's fieldwork in Guangdong in 1989, there was a surprise visit from several well-dressed men and women who spoke Putonghua, or Mandarin, the northern Chinese dialect which is China's official national language. (Cantonese is the local dialect spoken in Hong Kong and Guangdong, although Guangdong residents would learn Mandarin in school.) They were led by a man who identified himself in accented Cantonese as someone from a department within the local administrative government. This particular official was not known to any of the Hong Kong personnel at the factory, even the manager assigned to the factory as a liaison with the local administrative unit did not know him by name or in person. All the same, their request for a tour of the factory was honored. The guests showed a great deal of interest in the finished products, all of which were produced for export to Hong Kong and elsewhere.

When the visitors left, they were all carrying one or two boxes of shoes and Smart saw the visiting local official counting out money to one of the Hong Kong investors. A subsequent interview with the Hong Kong investor revealed that the visitors' request for a tour had been accepted as good public relations without any cost to the factory. When the visitors expressed interests in the shoes, he suggested that they could pick out what they wanted for a token charge that covered the cost of material only. He said he was not prepared to give away any shoes for free since the visiting party was unknown to him. Even if he had known them, he would still have charged the shoes at cost so that other officials would not flood to his factories with visitors for free shoes. There would be no end of visitors if it were known he gave away his products for free.

The investor managed to refuse implied demands for a gift of the shoes, but did so in a tactful manner that still indicated a concession and favor on behalf of the manager. An inept performance might have offended the visitors, or even have resulted in long-term problems. The response could be seen as following the implied hint, even if it was not exactly the outcome that the visitor had intended. By being tactful, the manager had avoided a precedent that could have been very troublesome and costly over the longer term. Yet, he also skillfully offered enough "gifts and favors" to indicate that he was willing to engage in an ongoing relationship with the official, a relationship which could provide benefits (or least prevent discomfort) for all the people involved in the factory. Through his tactful performance, he transformed a potential act of corruption and exploitation into a "reasonable" *guanxi* transaction.

This is only one example that could be given where tact served to deflect unwanted attempts to extract graft, or where failures of tact made corruption or conflict unpleasantly apparent. Yet, tact as performance and interpretation has rarely been considered at any depth in relation to corruption and the legal/illegal dichotomy. Can tactful performances reduce the likelihood that acts will be socially constructed as corrupt or at least unjustified to local participants? To what extent can we see the outcomes of local corrupt practices as mediated by the skill, or otherwise, of execution?

Erving Goffman pioneered politeness studies with his examinations of how interaction rituals preserve people's public image or "face" (Goffman 1959). Subsequent study of politeness has almost exclusively been developed by linguists, who have focused on trying to explain the pervasiveness of politeness as a form of discourse that seems to deviate from the assumption that human communication is "rational, purposeful, and goal-directed" (Mao 1994: 453). Instead of clearly communicating the purpose behind an interaction, polite discursive forms are more likely to be indirect, to avoid offense, and to adopt formulae that are often largely empty of new information.

In common usage, politeness is often thought to consist of conforming to social rules about proper behavior (Fraser 1990: 220). There are problems with this common-sense view, however. Most importantly, it misses out the crucial skills involved in knowing when rules should not be followed, or when it is safe to break them. As Janney and Arndt point out:

> Within a given culture, almost any normal adult can be polite in impolite ways, or be impolite in polite ways. The former is politeness from a social point of view, and the latter is politeness from an interpersonal point of view ... we will refer to the former as "social politeness" and to the latter as tact. (Janney and Arndt 1992: 22)

Fraser argues that politeness should be seen as involving a tacit "conversational contract." In a social interaction, "each party brings an understanding of some initial set of rights and obligations that will determine ... what the participants can expect from the other(s)" (Fraser 1990: 232). Following formal rules of etiquette in a context of individuals with a close social distance can thus be interpreted, not as politeness, but as a deliberate attempt to mock or humiliate, as Garfinkel's students found when he set them the task of acting like a boarder while at home with their families (Garfinkel 1967). Being polite, then, consists not of simply following a general set of rules but in operating in an effective way within expectations, able to cope with lapses of tact and interactional breaches. Impoliteness is a socially constituted event, apparent only after subsequent interaction has failed to reinterpret it as conforming to expectations. In a similar way, the corruptness of a transaction may only be set in the subsequent enactments.

Tact is one kind of politeness behavior, characterized by Leech (1983: 132) in his Tact Maxim: "(a) Minimize cost to other [(b) Maximize benefit to other]." For example, when A offers to give B a ride, and B responds by inquiring if it won't cause some inconvenience, one response in conformity with the Tact Maxim is to deny any inconvenience because A is going in that direction anyways (Gu 1990: 244). This response is tactful because "it makes it easier for B to accept A's offer" by "minimizing the debt B owes A" (Gu 1990: 244).

In Chinese culture, the operation of tact can be seen in the interaction ritual where invitations to a meal are at first rejected, but the inviter (A) continues to insist and attempts to reject the excuses proffered by the receiver (B) of the invitation. In an Anglo-American context, "A might appear downright imposing, while B would act hypocritically, i.e. making fake refusals" (Gu 1990: 253). In the Chinese context, though, it would be either an immediate acceptance of an invitation or a failure to repeat the invitation that would be impolite. A skillful invitee can use his language in such a way as to accept the invitation while still appearing in accord with Chinese expectations of polite behavior. Gu (1990: 254) demonstrates how B's response "*bu lai (le), tai mafan*" ("No, I won't come. It is too much trouble for you") accomplishes this. The reason for declining is not convincing since it only offers concern for A's costs and efforts, rather than one related, for example, to schedule conflicts. Rather than the repeated insistences that ensue being impolite impositions on B, they are tactful responses that allow B to feel less indebted ("it is only a simple meal and it is already prepared anyways") and less greedy by accepting immediately.

Janney and Arndt (1992: 22) argue that there are important differences between tact and politeness:

> whereas the function of social politeness is essentially to coordinate social interaction—to regulate the mechanical exchange of roles and activities—the function of tact is quite different: namely to preserve face and regulate interpersonal relationships. Metaphorically, we might say that social politeness is somewhat like a system of social traffic rules, while tact is more a matter of interpersonal driving styles and strategies. In fact, it is probably not social politeness that enables people to avoid most everyday interpersonal conflicts, but tact.

This analysis offers a perspective on social interaction that is too focused on the constructive dimensions. Tact is a set of techniques that can be used in a variety of different ways, with an assortment of potential outcomes, many of them destructive. It can be used in order to get people to agree to things that may not be in their self-interest. It can be used to say offensive things that need to be said. It can be used to promote collusion that injures many others, or to protect those who engage in graft from easy discovery.

Rather than simply following maxims of polite practice, the politics of polite interaction generate subtle and complex interpersonal "tugs of war" (Mao 1994: 484). Chang (1999) points out a puzzle about Chinese discourse in comparison to Western discourses. On the one hand, role relationships and status hierarchies are more clearly defined and stable than in the West. On the other hand, "while Western speakers tend to fashion meanings clearly in verbal utterances, Chinese speakers emphasize listener interpretation of received messages" which are more "imprecise and ambiguous" (Chang 1999: 536). There is, then, a "puzzling conflation of two apparently contradictory qualities of speech: more well-defined role relationship systems lead to less direct verbal discourse" (ibid.). Chang concludes that the resolution of this contradiction lies in the way that ambiguous and indirect utterances produce "an indeterminate linguistic space ... which allows interactants considerable flexibility in negotiating relational position and role behavior within the confines of a relational system" (ibid.: 537).

This space "allows interactants to negotiate their relational status without directly challenging the well-defined cultural rules of relationship ... by utilizing ambiguous messages" (Chang 1999: 542). Chang's accounts show how "verbal skill in manipulating obligation and social expectation" can serve to undermine utterances from a husband's mother that would appear to lessen the wife's status but without having to disrupt familial harmony (ibid.: 552). Tact here allows ambiguous digs at the other that cannot be objected to because the alternative interpretation is completely acceptable: a polite way of being impolite. It also allows the desire for a bribe to be communicated with plausible deniability.

An ethnographic understanding of *guanxi* and corruption in China needs to attend to the ways in which social performances influence whether or not transactions are perceived by its participants as being corrupt or not. This is a distinct process from that of labeling, where those with the power to impose "performative utterances" label or define certain instances as being corrupt despite their similarities with other instances that might not be sanctioned in the same way. Ordinary members of society often see legal acts as corrupt. They may also reject the label of corrupt applied by legal functionaries to other practices seen by these ordinary people as socially acceptable.

A successful tactful performance requires the voluntary complicity of all the parties involved, including outside observers. *Guanxi* transactions involving state actors are at risk of being re-emplotted as stories of corruption. If we return to the example of the officials' visit to the Guangdong shoe factory, imagine the consequences if an observer (such as a tactless social scientist) began loudly asking questions at an inopportune moment: "Why are those men taking those shoes? Did you give them to them for free? What are you hoping to get in return? Do you often bribe officials like this?" Because even tactful *guanxi* interactions are vulnerable to this kind of re-interpretation, it is important to persuade all relevant parties that the transaction was "reasonable." Moreover, if a party has a vested interest in de-legitimizing the state actors involved, they have a powerful weapon with which to do so. This was the case in the intellectual dissident movement of the late 1980s that culminated in the Tiananmen Protests. The protestors argued that conspicuous consumption (palatial apartments, European cars, designer clothes) and social dislocations (layoff, inflation) should be read as evidence of corruption (Hsu 2001). They claimed that the entire cadre corps was so rife with corruption that the fallback assumption should be that any and every state official was indulging in corrupt acts.

In Harbin, in the late 1990s, this type of dissident rhetoric had penetrated popular discourse and had become a useful tool for disrupting "tactful" *guanxi* performances. Hsu's interviewees quoted dissident mantras like "Out of ten officials, nine are corrupt" (*Shige dangguan, jiuge tan*). A 42-year-old entrepreneur described a hypothetical gift-exchange incident re-emplotted as a tale of rent-seeking corruption:

> If you send them money [as a gift] of course they'll take it. If they would just do things according to the law, there would be no corruption. For example, if I were the superior in some department ... You come to my office because you need something done. I can do it for you, or I cannot do it for you. I can tell you to come back tomorrow, or the day after tomorrow. So you're frustrated. You think, is it that you need to send me two boxes of cigarettes? So you give me the cigarettes the next time you see me, and oh! I'll be happy to help you. If there was law, there wouldn't be this problem. You would say, according to the legal regulations, you have to do this for me today. If you don't do it, sorry, but you're demoted. But in China, it's no way. There's no possibility of it.

Even cadres complained about cadre corruption. A thirty-five-year old low-ranking cadre in a government agency complained about the corruption of enterprise cadres but at the same time she admitted that it would be difficult for a highly positioned cadre to avoid suspicious entanglements altogether without being very tactless.

> Even if you don't want it, people will give it to you. It's hard to resolve. Especially since the people sending the gifts are all close to you, really good friends, asking for favors. Can you find a way to help me? And then if you achieve their task, they give you presents. Do you take it or not? The people giving aren't strangers. Even if you don't want to take it, you can't not take it. You don't even try, and you get rich. You say, "no, no," and wealth just comes ... And it's also, well, if I help you out, people feel that they have to show their appreciation, take you out to eat, send a little present. Or you feel embarrassed. Or you feel disgraced in your relationship.

Even though corruption discourse offered a way for Harbiners to disrupt tactful performances of *guanxi*, a counterbalance was offered by *guanxi* discourse, reminding people that anyone with "human sentiment" would find themselves complicit in "reasonable" *guanxi* transactions involving the exchange of gifts and favors. Significantly, Hsu's interviewees rarely used corruption discourse to condemn *guanxi* transactions by officials who were familiar to them, unless they genuinely believed that those officials had harmed them or people they knew. Otherwise, Harbiners tended to believe that the cadres they knew were "reasonable," while corruption was a problem among cadres elsewhere. This seems to indicate that tactful performances of *guanxi* transactions were generally successful at deflecting corruption accusations, as long as people did not believe their livelihoods were threatened.

Tact is not everything. Some local officials are seen as rough but honest, with "their heart in the right place." Even when not following the formal rules, and while being perhaps rather inept in describing their actions in politically acceptable forms, they are believed to be acting in the best interest of the community. Villagers might be offended when such "rough gems" get caught up in anti-corruption campaigns while slicker individuals manage to package their self-interested grasping in safer forms. Ultimately, people are good at seeing through the Emperor's clothes of charm. But at the margin, where individuals operate in landscapes of grey rather than black or white, tact can make a significant impact on whether informal breaches of procedure are seen as corrupt or as "reasonable" responses to, for example, inappropriate regulatory constraints.

Guanxi and Corruption in Market Socialist China: Possible Trajectories

An analysis of tact provides a glimpse of the micro-level, allowing us to see how social actors negotiate the slippery boundary between "reasonable" *guanxi* and corruption on a daily basis, both as practitioners and as outside observers. What can it tell us about the macro-level relationship between *guanxi* practice and corruption in market socialist China? In this section, we examine three different possible trajectories.

Douglas Guthrie has argued (*contra* Mayfair Yang 1994) that the significance of *guanxi* has actually declined in China since 1978, as a direct result of market reforms (Guthrie 1998, 1999, 2002). His research on state enterprise managers in Shanghai in 1995 suggests that although *guanxi* connections are still important, the "practice and technique of using and manipulating these relationships for specific ends" have become less significant and acceptable (Guthrie 1998: 262). The managers he interviewed insisted that while relationships are still important in China, the use of connections to circumvent official procedures and rules is increasingly rare. Guthrie concludes that *guanxi* practice is an imperfect practice that arises under conditions of inadequate formal institutions. As formal institutions, especially the rational-legal system, become more complete, *guanxi* practice becomes increasingly risky and decreasingly useful. Consequently, according to Guthrie, as rational institutions become established, irrational *guanxi*-based practices fade in importance.

This argument is important and reflects sentiments that are very prevalent in China. However, we are skeptical about some of the dichotomies that appear to be taken for granted in Guthrie's argument: between instrumental and expressive (sentimental) ties, and between efficient "rational-legal" market procedures versus inefficient *guanxi*-related practices. He, moreover, ignores research indicating that *guanxi* practice is common in ethnically Chinese societies with flourishing economies (Singapore, Taiwan, and so on). The most serious problem with Guthrie's conclusions, however, is his data. In formal interviews at their workplaces, Guthrie asked state enterprise managers whether they participated in *guanxi* practice. Under these conditions, there was no way for them to discreetly admit to tactful uses of *guanxi*-related practices. In other words, he had framed the question so that it was about potentially corrupt or at least suspiciously unreasonable behaviors, not about "reasonable" *guanxi* interactions.

In addition, other authors disagree that *guanxi* has declined in significance, and see the overlap between *guanxi* and corruption as having increased. In reaction to the economic strains of the 1980s and the debacle of the Tiananmen Protests, the state imposed greater fiscal authority and political control, cooling reform until 1992. More radical reforms after 1992 were ironically accompanied by a reversal of the trend of decentralization. Greater market discipline required a more influential central state. The central government's share of total budgetary revenue had dropped from 40 per cent in 1983 to just over 20 per cent in 1993. As a result of a new tax assignment system, the center's take soared to almost 60 per cent in 1994; although a substantial portion of this was reallocated to the provinces, the new system still gave Beijing much more effective power (Yang 2004: 74).

Beijing's reactions to the 1997 Asian Financial Crisis resulted in strengthened regulation of banks, securities markets, and the insurance industry. In 1998, huge scandals prompted a crackdown on smuggling that eventually encouraged a series of administrative reforms that substantially changed the landscape for corruption. The scandals revealed the extent to which smuggling had been organized by the Public Security Bureau, the People's Liberation Army, and other governmental agencies. Smuggling was not a minor inconvenience, since over 20 per cent of total government revenues accrued from the Customs Administration. The year after the 1998 crackdown, customs revenue increased 81 per cent (Yang 2004: 122).

Although the fiscal decentralization of the 1980s had certainly facilitated all manners of corruption, Kang Chen has argued that recentralization in the 1990s did not end corruption, but instead transformed it into a much more destructive form (Chen 2004). The previous tax system had provided incentives for local officials to promote local development since they would share in the proceeds. This produced what Chen describes as "helping hand" corruption (Chen 2004: 1002), such as the "collective bribery" that is done in the interests of the locality or collectivity, even if the official personally benefits as well. The recentralization reforms of the 1990s undermined this incentive structure, encouraging the development of more illicit "extra-budgetary funds" and resulting in "short time-horizon, grabbing-hand behavior that was uncoordinated and more opportunistic, and which inhibited private sector development and economic growth, and so contracted the local tax base for both budgetary and off-budget taxes" (Chen 2004: 1002).

Similarly, Yan Sun concludes that prior to 1992, bribery and associated activities "did not result in overwhelming harms that strangled reform" (Sun 2004: 80). While rampant bribery resulted in unfairness in access to resources and contributed to income inequality, it also contributed to the flow of goods and information, and played an overall constructive role in the system (Sun 2004: 80). After 1992, however, bribery could no longer "be seen as individual efforts that chip away at a dominant planned economy and circumvent formal barriers to equal access. Rather, it undermines a dominant market and thus the reform program itself, making unequal ... competition the rule of the game" (Sun 2004: 86).

Although we find the "grabbing hand" model worth serious consideration, our analysis of tact does offer some possible evidence of countervailing forces against a total descent into corruption. The importance of tactful performance in the practice of *guanxi* at the turn of the century reveals that social actors felt real pressure to present the image of "reasonable" *guanxi* rather than exploitative corruption, to show that they were acting on behalf of the collective good rather than selfish gain. After all, outsiders had the power to discursively transform the actions they observed (or just heard about) into narratives of corruption—and in the context of the anti-corruption campaigns of the 1990s, accusations of corruption could have serious consequences. Consequently, social actors had a real incentive not only to look like they were acting for the collective good, but also to actually do so, at least to the extent that they could tactfully persuade all the relevant parties involved that they were engaging in an act of "reasonable" *guanxi* rather than selfish corruption. In other words, there were genuine social constraints against a thorough descent into utter corruption, although those constraints might have been weak.

An alternative scenario is that corruption may have become more significant even while *guanxi* has become less important, if Sun is correct in arguing that commercialization has meant that an ever smaller proportion of bribers have "direct affective ties to officeholders" (Sun 2004: 72). Potentially, this could result in a clearer distinction between networking and corrupt practices, a pattern that could be described as the "domestication," or "taming" of *guanxi* so that it conforms to the rule of law, which has been the case in Singapore and Hong Kong (Manion 2004). After all, *guanxi* is still important in Hong Kong and Taiwan; rather than fading away, it can be seen as having been domesticated in such a way as to be more or less limited by the rule of law and concerns about economic efficiency. In other words, the boundary between corruption and "reasonable" *guanxi* may become more distinct and sharp-edged.

Conclusion: The Continuity between Corruption and Social Capital

There is an odd form of schizophrenia current in public policy studies, where great attention is being paid to both social capital and corruption, with the former hailed as the solution to myriad developmental problems and the latter the cause of just as many developmental dysfunctions (Bukanovsky 2006; Li 2006). Despite the overlap between them, one concept is seen as an almost unmitigated public good and the other a completely unmitigated public "bad."

The case of *guanxi* practice and corruption in China reveals a much more complicated picture. *Guanxi* practice and corruption can be seen as a culturally dynamic set of concepts and practices which actors could draw upon to negotiate the unstable and complicated world of China in the early market reform era. *Guanxi* practice allowed actors to construct social networks and build relationships of trust, which encouraged investment and facilitated the rise of small businesses, but also created a conductive environment for rent seeking, bribery, collusion, and exploitation. These complex and multiple forces are played out at the level of micro-interactions, where self-interest, emotional feelings, communal benefit, and personal reputation are performatively negotiated.

The analysis here concentrated on a relatively neglected dimension that is of considerable significance for both exchange performances and their interpretation: tact. If all of the actors involved (including outside observers) are willing to tactfully behave as though the transaction were primarily about "human" sentiment and/or the collective good, then the interaction can be coded as "reasonable" *guanxi*. In contrast, if actors wish to cast a suspicion of corruption upon the transaction, they can expose the self-interest and exploitative aspect of the interaction. This importance of performance for the labeling of practices also implies that tact can serve to effectively disguise corruption, manipulation, and exploitation.

With respect to the developmental implications of either high levels of social capital or pervasive corruption, our point is that we cannot begin with assumptions but must examine what actually happens on the ground. Furthermore, if we are to be consistent, insistence on corruption as anathema implies that we will need to be very cautious about policy approaches that rely heavily on the promotion of social capital. Effective understanding of both phenomena requires us to remember the continuity between the two when diagnosing practices as either corruption or social capital – and demands us to be conscious in the prognosis of the longer-term developmental effects of these practices.

References

Bayraktaroglu, A. (1991) Politeness and Interactional Imbalance. *International Journal of the Sociology of Language* 92: 5–34.

Brown, P. (1987) *Politeness: Some Universals in Language Usage*. Cambridge: Cambridge University Press.

Bukanovsky, M. (2006) The Hollowness of Anti-corruption Discourse. *Review of International Political Economy* 13(2): 209.

Calhoun, C. (1994) *Neither Gods Nor Emperors: Students and the Struggle for Democracy in China*. Berkeley, CA: University of California Press.

Carrier, J.G. (1999) People Who Can Be Friends: Selves and Social Relationships. In: S. Bell and S. Coleman (eds) *The Anthropology of Friendship*. Oxford: Berg: 21–38.

Chang, H. (1999) The "Well-Defined" Is "Ambiguous"—Indeterminacy in Chinese Conversation. *Journal of Pragmatics* 31: 535–56.

Chen, A.H.Y. (1999) Rational Law, Economic Development and the Case of China. *Social and Legal Studies* 8(1): 97–120.

Chen, K. (2004) Fiscal Centralization and the Form of Corruption in China. *European Journal of Political Economy* 20: 1001–9.

Ding, X.L. (1994) *The Decline of Communism in China*. New York: Cambridge University Press.
Evans, P. (1995) *Embedded Autonomy*. Princeton. NJ: Princeton University Press.
Fraser, B. (1990) Perspectives on Politeness. *Journal of Pragmatics* 14(2): 219–36.
Gardner, J. (1969) The Wu-fan Campaign in Shanghai. In: A.D. Barnett (ed.) *Chinese Communist Politics in Action*. Seattle, WA: University of Washington Press:477–539.
Garfinkel, H. (1967) *Studies in Ethnomethodology*. Englewood Cliffs, NJ: Prentice-Hall.
Gates, H. (1991) Eating for Revenge: Consumption and Corruption Under Economic De-Reform. *Dialectical Anthropology* 16: 233–49.
Goffman, E. (1959) *The Presentation of Self in Everyday Life*. Garden City, NY: Doubleday.
Gu, Y. (1990) Politeness Phenomena in Modern Chinese. *Journal of Pragmatics* 14(2): 237–57.
Guthrie, D. (1998) The Declining Significance of *guanxi* in China's Economic Transition. *The China Quarterly* 154: 254–82.
—— (1999) *Dragon in a Three-Piece Suit*. Princeton, NJ: Princeton University Press.
—— (2002) Information Asymmetries and the Problem of Perception: The Significance of Structural Position in Assessing the Importance of *Guanxi* in China. In: T. Gold, D. Guthrie, and D. Wank (eds) *Social Connections in China*. Cambridge: Cambridge University Press: 37–56.
Hamilton, G.G. (2000) Reciprocity and Control: The Organization of Chinese Family Owned Conglomerates. In: H.W.-C. Yeung and K. Olds (eds) *Globalization of Chinese Business Firms*. New York: St Martin's Press: 55–74.
Han, M. (ed.) (1990) *Cries for Democracy; Writing and Speeches from thee 1989 Chinese Democracy Movement*. Princeton, NJ: Princeton University Press.
Holmes, L. (1993) *The End of Communist Power: Anti-Corruption Campaigns and Legitimation Crisis*. New York: Oxford University Press.
Hsing, Y. (1998) *Making Capitalism in China: The Taiwan Connection*. Oxford: Oxford University Press.
Hsu, C.L. (2001) Political Narratives and the Production of Legitimacy: The Case of Corruption in Post-Mao China. *Qualitative Sociology* 24(1): 25–54.
—— (2005) Capitalism Without Contracts Versus Capitalists Without Capitalism: Comparing the Influence of Chinese *Guanxi* and Russian Blat on Marketization. *Communist and Post-Communist Studies* 38: 309–27.
Huang, R. (1981) *1587: A Year of No Significance*. New Haven, CN: Yale University Press.
Hwang, K. (1987) Face and Favor: The Chinese Power Game. *American Journal of Sociology* 92(4): 944–74.
Janney, R. and H. Arndt (1992) Intracultural Tact versus Intercultural Tact. In: S.I. Richard, J. Watts, and Konrad Ehlich (eds) *Politeness in Language: Studies in its History, Theory and Practice*. Berlin/New York: Mouton de Gruyter: 21–41.
Keister, L. (2002) *Guanxi* in Business Groups: Social Ties and the Formation of Economic Relations. In: T. Gold, D. Guthrie, and D. Wank (eds) *Social Connections in China*. Cambridge: Cambridge University Press: 77–96.
Keith, R.C. (2005) China as a Rising World Power and its Response to "Globalization." In: R.C. Keith (ed.) *China as a Rising World Power and its Response to "Globalization."* New York: Routledge: 1–18.
Kwong, J. (1997) *The Political Economy of Corruption in China*. Armonk, NY: M.E. Sharpe.
Leech, G. (1983) *Principles of Pragmatics*. Longman: London.

Li, T. (2006) Neoliberal Strategies of Government through Community: The Social Development Program of the World Bank in Indonesia. In: Institute for International Law and Justice Working Paper 2006/2: New York University.
Liu, B. (1983) People or Monsters? In: P. Link (ed.) *People or Monsters? And Other Stories and Reportage from China after Mao*. Bloomington, IN: Indiana University Press: 11–68.
Lo, M.M. and E.M. Otis (2003) *Guanxi* Civility: Processes, Potentials, and Contingencies. *Politics and Society* 31(1): 131–62.
Lo, T. Wing (1993) *Corruption and Politics in Hong Kong and China*. Philadelphia, PA: Open University Press.
Lu, X. (2000*)* *Cadres and Corruption*. Stanford, CA: Stanford University Press.
Lui, A. (1979) *Corruption in China During the early Ch'ing Period: 1644–1660*. Hong Kong: Center of Asian Studies Occasional Papers and Monographs.
Manion, M. (2004) Anticorruption Reform in a Setting of Widespread Corruption. In: M. Manion (ed.) *Corruption by Design*. Cambridge, MA: Harvard University Press: 1–26.
Mao, R.L. (1994) Beyond Politeness Theory: "Face" Revisited and Renewed. *Journal of Pragmatics* 21(5): 451–86.
Mauss, M. (1967) *The Gift: Forms and Functions of Exchange in Archaic Societies*. Trans. I. Cunnison. New York: Norton.
O'Brien, K.J. and L. Li (2006) *Rightful Resistance in Rural China*. Cambridge: Cambrige University Press.
Oxfeld, E. (2006) Liangxin: The Idea of Conscience in the Moral Discourse of a Rural Chinese Community. Society for East Asian Anthropology conference, Hong Kong, 2006.
Pun, N. (2005) *Made in China: Women Factory Workers in a Global Workplace*. Durham, NC: Duke University Press.
Redding, G. (1990) *The Spirit of Chinese Capitalism*. New York: Walter de Gruyter.
—— (2000) What is Chinese About Chinese Family Business? and How Much is Family and How Much is Business? In: H.W.-C. Yeung and K. Olds (eds) *Globalization of Chinese Business Firms*. New York: St Martin's Press: 31–54.
Rothstein, B. and D. Stolle (2003) Introduction: Social Capital in Scandinavia. *Scandinavian Political Studies* 26(1): 1–26.
Salaf, J.W. and S. Wong (1998) Network Capital: Emigration from Hong Kong. *British Journal of Sociology* 49(3): 358–74.
Smart, A. (1993a) Gifts, Bribes, and *Guanxi*: A Reconsideration of Bourdieu's Social Capital. *Cultural Anthropology* 8(3): 388–408.
—— (1993b) The Political Economy of Rent-seeking in a Chinese Factory Town. *Anthropology of Work Review* 14(2/3): 15–19.
—— (1998) Guanxi, Gifts, and Learning from China: A Review Essay. *Anthropos* 93(4–6): 559–65.
Smart, A. and J. Smart (1998) Transnational Social Networks and Negotiated Identities in Interactions between Hong Kong and China. In: M.P. Smith and L.E. Guarnizo (eds) *Transnationalism from Below*. New Brunswick, NJ: Transaction Publishers: 103–29.
Smart, J. and A. Smart (1991) Personal Relations and Divergent Economies: A Case Study of Hong Kong Investment in China. *International Journal of Urban and Regional Research* 15(2): 216–33.
Sun, Y. (2004) *Corruption and Market in Contemporary China*. Ithaca, NY: Cornell University Press.

Tong, C.K. and P.K. Yong (1998) *Guanxi* Bases, Xinyong and Chinese Business Networks. *British Journal of Sociology* 49(1): 75–96.

Tsai, K. (2002) *Back-Alley Banking*. Ithaca, NY: Cornell University Press.

Wank, D. (1999) *Commodifying Communism: Business, Trust, and Politics in a Chinese City.* Cambridge: Cambridge University Press.

—— (2002) Business-State Clientelism in China: Decline or Evolution? In: T. Gold, D. Guthrie, and D. Wank (eds) *Social Connections in China*. Cambridge: Cambridge University Press: 97–116.

Yang, D. (2004) *Remaking the Chinese Leviathan. Market Transition and the Politics of Governance in China*. Stanford, CA: Stanford University Press.

Yang, M.M. (1994) *Gifts, Favors and Banquets: The Art of Social Relationships in China.* Ithaca, NY: Cornell University Press.

—— (2002) The Resilience of *Guanxi* and its New Deployments: A Critique of Some New *Guanxi* Scholarship. *The China Quarterly* 170: 459–76.

Chapter 9

Corruption in the US Borderlands with Mexico: The "Purity" of Society and the "Perversity" of Borders

Josiah McC. Heyman and Howard Campbell

Introduction: Corruption in an Ideologically "Pure" Setting

A key theme of this book (notably the introduction), as well as the literature that leads up to it (Heyman and Smart 1999; Nuijten 2003; Schneider and Schneider 2003; Abraham and van Schendel 2005)[1] is that a strict division between the clean and the corrupt—the legal, bureaucratic, and rational versus the illegal, informal, and irrational—is excessively simple. In our view, it is better to begin by analyzing social-political processes that produce characteristically mixed or perverse outcomes in government activities, containing both elements of formal policy adherence and other elements, of policy incompleteness, subversion, and hidden agendas, including (but not limited to) corruption. It is likewise important to understand how such ambivalent realities are justified and mystified by ideologies of good versus bad, clean versus corrupt.

We take this perspective in examining corruption on the US side of the US-Mexico border. The standard journalistic and law enforcement framework is that Mexico is the source of illegality and corruption, while the US is the target of these illegal activities and itself is clean. Yet, there is significant evidence of corruption on the US side, not just in the sense that Mexican smuggling organizations subvert US state operations (though this is certainly true) but also in the sense that within the US rules are ignored and bent through a variety of transactions and relationships. It is interesting how these phenomena occur and are understood in a context of strong ideologies of rationality and cleanliness.

Corruption is commonly viewed as a flaw, a limitation, or a failure of isolated individuals—the "bad apple" explanation. This is particularly important in maintaining the ideological purity of the US side. The individual component of corruption exists, without question. But our perspective is that individual acts of corruption occur within and are revealing of wider social processes. First, we

---

1 See also the extensive literature review on corruption in Harris (2003: 1–32).

show that acts of corruption happen repeatedly, in patterned ways, rather than rarely and idiosyncratically. Second, and more important, we demonstrate that individual and overt cases of corruption in the US are surrounded by systematic processes undermining the letter and spirit of the law and connecting the legal and the illegal. By paying attention to this "penumbra" of corruption, we come to understand the recurrence of corrupt acts on the US side of the border.

Relatively clear acts of corruption (for example, US border officers accepting or extracting favors for overlooking law violations) form part of a wider universe of phenomena, that also includes tolerated illegalities (for example, employment of undocumented labor), ambiguously legal actions (for example, under-enforcement of the law), and legal activities with questionable connections (for example, the use of "mysterious" money in commerce and banking). Corruption in this perspective emerges within a network of fluid transactions and arrangements along the border. We explore why the US-Mexican border has this particular character, not because it is a strange and stigmatized place, but because it has a particular role in a division of labor with respect to the interiors of the United States and Mexico.

Our attention is drawn to the movement of money, commodities, and people between the two nations and the role of the borderlands in mediating such flows. Side-by-side with these flows, we note the density of the state apparatus in this region, the enormous material and symbolic performance of law and bureaucratic power, and the constant presence of police agencies that people in the borderlands simply take for granted. To combine those two perspectives, we take apart the seemingly massive and reified US state apparatus, viewing it as fractured and interpenetrated by other forms of social organization and action (see Abrams 1988; Hansen and Stepputat 2001; and the introduction to this volume). The relationship of the state to the processes and bearers of cross-border flows ends up being fragmented and contradictory rather than characterized by a coherent rational legality.

We also suggest that the visibly flawed and extreme qualities of the border do important symbolic work for the rest of US society in understanding itself as pure. When we look at representations of border corruption in a "rational" society, we see first, that corruption is treated as deviance rather than an outcome of wider processes; second, that the border and Mexico are represented as source of corruption, a kind of anti-state, rather than the necessarily ambiguous part of larger wholes; and third, that the bureaucratic machinery of the US state at the border is a bastion of order (subject to inexplicable moments of deviance) poised against these anti-state forces rather than a complex mixture of both opponent and participant in these processes. Corruption, then, should not happen according to the "rational" view, yet in reality it has to happen, for two definite reasons: to carry out transactions demanded by the larger society and to provide a contrastive, deviant label (the sinful border, the broken border, the corrupt border) to protect the self-view of US society and state. To explore the paradox of corruption in a supposedly rational state, then, is to draw attention to wider issues, including the incompleteness of strong states and strong societies, the presence of ambiguity, fluidity, and transactionality in them, and the particular roles of border cultures and social relations in such formations.

We begin this chapter with an overview of the US-Mexico border, and then sketch the major ways in which the US interior is linked to various illegal and ambiguous flows across this boundary. We then look more locally at the agencies of the US state, the kinds of laws they do and do not actually enforce at the border, and the interactions of the national state with local society in the US borderlands. We take particular note of the way that "mysterious" financial and interpersonal transactions are constitutive of this region. After presenting our analytical overview, we offer several case studies, partly ethnographic and partly journalistic, to demonstrate two points: that corruption on the US side of the border is systematic rather than a matter of a few "bad apples," and that individual patterns of corruption are linked to regional and national/binational processes. We finish by returning to our main analytical themes considering the paradoxical relationship of strong states/societies with their frayed outer edges.

The US-Mexico Border Context

The US-Mexico border is almost 2,000 miles in length. Parts of it are densely urbanized, with binational metropolitan complexes of many hundreds of thousands, and in two cases (San Diego/Tijuana and El Paso/Ciudad Juárez) several million, in population. On the other hand, long sections of the border are quite remote, spanning rugged desert and mountain country, broken by small twin cities at minor crossing points. It is worth emphasizing that most crossings are surrounded by a settlement on both sides, rather than being lonely bureaucratic checkpoints some distance from settled towns, and that we can thus properly speak of a distinctive regional border society in each nation. In part, this is because substantial economic complexes are located along the border, depending directly and indirectly on daily border crossing. These include the *maquiladoras* (the massive band of global export assembly plants on the Mexican side of the border), many legal as well as undocumented migrants commuting between the two nations (but more from Mexico to the US), tourism and shopping, and import/export commerce.

The scale of daily crossing is quite impressive. The single port of El Paso, for example, in 2005 had 7.6 million pedestrian entrants, 29 million passengers in 16 million personal vehicles, 740,000 trucks, and 144,000 rail containers.[2] Mixed with the vast volume of legitimate trade and visiting are substantial flows of illegal commodities (for example, drugs) and entrants who violate the terms of their visas (for example, by working without authorization) once inside the United States. In addition, sections of the border between official ports of entry are subject to illegal entrances (mostly to the US) of an unknown number, but certainly numbering in the millions. The border region is thus host to a huge state

---

2   Data accessed (20 December 2006) on the searchable website of the Bureau of Transportation Statistics (http://www.transtats.bts.gov/bordercrossing.aspx).

presence in both nations, but especially in the United States. This state presence is fundamentally inspectorial and regulatory, and thus concerned with law enforcement in a broad sense, but it must address the examination, registration, and authorization of enormous legal flows as well as interdict a large variety of illegal acts and goods. The standard perception of the US-Mexico border as the location of a huge punitive police apparatus is correct, then, but also misleading insofar as it neglects the equally large regulatory apparatus in this region.

The boundary between the United States and Mexico arguably represents the most extreme border juxtaposition of wealth and poverty in the world, with a ratio of per capita gross domestic product (in purchasing power parity terms) of 4.5 to 1. Nevertheless, both countries are marked by class inequality. There are substantial wealthy and middle-income populations in Mexico, including in the booming northern border cities, and substantial poor populations in the US, notably in its southern border communities, which have the lowest average incomes in the nation. Cutting across this is a dense web of interpersonal ties, which have developed over time for a variety of reasons: commercial and financial relationships, school and university attendance, intermarriage, and above all, the long-term, steady migration of Mexican-origin people into the United States. Most US-side border communities are 80 per cent or more of Mexican origin. They are also substantially bilingual and bicultural communities (particularly on the US side) and are comfortable in operating in a fluid, negotiable fashion between the laws and cultural patterns of the two nations.

The US side of the border is thus complex and contradictory in practice. It is the home of a vast armed police apparatus designed to interdict movements of people and goods from Mexico, but also to inspect them and let them in. It is the locale for a dense web of personal and commercial ties, across a heavily controlled boundary. Symbolically, however, the border represents danger to the nation, in terms of immigration, drugs, and other scary threats (terrorists, epidemics, etc.) that need to be sealed off in such a fashion that the absolute distinction between inside and outside is preserved from the ever-present threat of dissolution (see Heyman 1999; Nevins 2002). This is part of a pattern through which nationalist ideologies construct each other as polar opposites, ignoring their deep cultural and economic intertwining.

For North Americans generally, Mexico is a corrupt, poverty-ridden, backward, Third World nation. By comparison, North Americans tend to see their own country as democratic and law-abiding, wealthy, modern, and progressive. Yet, Mexicans also view the United States with trepidation. For many Mexicans, the US is a racist, materialistic, and hypocritical imperial power unlike their own country, which is tolerant of ethnic diversity, spiritually-oriented, sincere, and respectful of the sovereignty of other nations (Miller 1985: xi–xiii; Riding 1986: ix–xi, 3–29). It is of particular importance to this chapter that US idea-producers construe the US as the home of pure-hearted law enforcement and Mexico as the source of violence and illegality—think, for example, of the talented and widely read non-fiction author Charles Bowden and his *Down by the River* (2002) about the murder of a US Drug Enforcement Agent (possibly) by a Mexican drug smuggling organization. Likewise, a typical journalistic account of corruption in the US borderlands such as that by James Pinkerton (2006), "Border's bribery culture seeps into small towns," views corruption as "seeping" from "third-world" Mexico to the United States.[3]

The next two sections will, however, show that there are systemic practices of corruption (and its penumbra of questionable activities) on the US side, brought about by socio-political forces in both countries.

The United States-Mexico Relation and the Limitations of Perfect Law

In the following two sections, we begin with general societal patterns that surround US officials, and gradually work our way down to the work lives of those officers and the corrupting scenarios they face. We start by making two crucial points: that Mexico and the US are interwoven rather than separated when considering the contexts of corruption, and that the laws involved (on drugs, migration, and so on) are by no means absolutely clear and definitive.

To begin, it helps to recognize that the societies and economies of the US and Mexico are thoroughly integrated, though in highly unequal ways.[4] Just as Mexico draws on US sources of guns, cash, and non-licensed and non-tariffed consumer goods ("*fayuca*"), the US demands from Mexico, as a source or transshipment route, many unregulated or extra-legal goods, services, and people. The most obvious ones are unauthorized migrant labor, illicit drugs, cheap pharmaceuticals, and the sex industry. There is a dense flow of money (cash, wire transfers, credit, and so on) back and forth across the border, with many, often obscure, sources and destinations. Donovan Corliss (2000) offers a telling example of how movements across the border undercut formal legal control: among the Mexican export manufacturers (*maquiladoras*) in Baja California are furniture finishing businesses using highly polluting volatile organic chemicals that moved south of the boundary to avoid US air control regulations, while still serving the US-side market. Any given illegal or questionable cross-border practice thus involves coordinated webs of activities and constituencies in both nations (Naim 2005), some of them open and legal in their home nation.

Law enforcement at the border, whether it is relatively effective or not, largely accounts for the profit to be made in crossing the international boundary. Either one complies with various burdensome regulations and pays various tariffs, or one undertakes the risk and gains the benefit of smuggling. In other words, law enforcement and smuggling are locked in a dance of mutual justification, even if

---

3   To be fair, Pinkerton also mentions the long Texas border history of wealth, bribery, and power.

4   An ironic but emblematic example of the degree of interpenetration of societies on the US-Mexico border is the fact that uniforms worn by US Border Patrol agents carry the label "Made in Mexico" indicating their place of manufacture. In the *El Paso Times* of November 28, 2005, T.J. Bonner, president of the 6,500 member Border Patrol union, complained: "It's embarrassing to be protecting the US-Mexico border and be wearing a uniform made in Mexico."

we take for granted the purity of law (which obviously we do not). Agencies of the US state at the border, then, depend on the continued activity of smuggling to justify their existence, while smugglers likewise depend on the state for their profits.

Trumpeting the threat and power of commodity, drug, and human smuggling, while maintaining a steady rate of arrests to prove effective law enforcement, is the primary way that US border agencies obtain budgetary allocations. An important secondary source of money and resources for law enforcement agencies is asset seizure, taking cash, vehicles, and buildings away from smugglers and smuggling organizations; an experienced investigator told one of us that inter-organizational politics in US border agencies substantially concerned the divvying up of seized assets. Thus, in broad organizational terms, the state and the anti-state are mutually dependent, and, as we shall see, this is reproduced at the level of specific officers and operations (Andreas 2001: 21–6).

The ambiguity of US law extends down to the experiential level of officers. Officers, as a rule, firmly believe in the perfectionist US ideology that law should be absolutely respected and enforced. But in their work, they encounter many laws that are either ignored or only partly enforced, and likewise come to recognize, to some degree or another, that law violations along the border are caused and countenanced by hypocrisies within US society. This realization of the limits of law is crucial in taking up various attitudes, of optimism and persistence, but also of pragmatism, cynicism, and apathy. The latter attitudes may lend themselves to corruption. To understand their experience, we therefore have to delineate the incompleteness of "law" in the US in general, and specifically in the border setting. Interdiction of drugs and unauthorized immigrants are laws that are trumpeted as central to the US state image and are explicitly and extensively enforced. But officers quickly realize that segments of US society are complicit in these illegal flows, in the employment of unauthorized labor and the consumption of forbidden drugs. As one officer wryly put it:

> It's a dog and pony show and it's not really working. Essentially they have taken the teeth out of what we can do—like a dog that has all those sharp canine teeth taken out. They are trying to reform it. When I got here 13 years ago they—the senior management— told me: "There was an immigration problem when I got here. There will be an immigration problem when I leave." For the first few years I was like a Robocop. I put people in jail everyday. But then one day I stopped, "Why should I do this ... its just a drop in the bucket?" It reminds me of Vietnam, it's just a political issue.
>
> We are very aware, very cognizant that we are apprehending only a small percentage of the people who come into the country with drugs. It's depressing. It's a vast border—2,000 miles—there is no way in hell we can put a Border Patrol agent every hundred yards. It's a mission impossible.

Thus, the officers come to recognize consciously or implicitly that public policies are limited and perhaps even fail, not just at the border but in the vast interior from which they quickly start to feel alienated. They feel that they have been set to do a valuable task but without real backing or understanding from the larger North American society. Their response to this awareness of failure varies widely:

from maintaining high standards of personal effort, through relaxing and being only partly effective, to becoming frustrated, cynical, and ineffective, or some complex mixture of all of these responses.[5]

Officers also quickly learn that some aspects of the law to which they are ostensibly dedicated are in fact quite discretionary and can be neglected with little effect (see Lipsky 1980; Maynard-Moody and Musheno 2003). The volume of people and goods transiting the border means that in almost all cases US law enforcement officers *could* stop and intensively inspect many more crossers than they actually do. Indeed, if all laws and regulations were addressed in a reasonably thorough fashion, billions of dollars of commerce at the border would grind to a halt; even modest efforts at additional inspections after 9/11 (opening at least one compartment of every vehicle) resulted in near gridlock along the border. Under such conditions, officers learn to ration their effort to focus on the "most important" violations and the more stigmatized violators—for example by concentrating on drug smuggling offenses and neglecting minor food smuggling violations. Other laws and regulations are largely unenforced, in part because of influential constituencies for illegal flows within the US.

A classic example of a weakly enforced law is the widespread use of local border crossing cards ("laser visas") by Mexican residents to work without authorization in the United States (as domestics, gardeners, day laborers, and so on), which violates the rules governing their entry.[6] This practice covertly favors their US employers, who largely come from the prosperous and influential sectors of the region (Quintanilla and Copeland [1983] 1996), and is also tacitly supported by commercial outlets on the US side of the border that favor easy access for shoppers to these crossing cards and thus do not want a strict approach to their regulation. Port management tolerates this illegal practice because it lacks logistical capacity to enforce the law and also does not want to offend local influentials, although this is difficult to prove (see Gilboy 1992). Border card bearers enter legally, so that it is at the port inspector's discretion to let them through or interrogate them about their intentions. There are certain ritualized ways to negate the rules: if the inspector asks, "where [in the US] are you going?," the commuter replies "*voy de compras*" or "*voy a la Wal-Mart*" ("I am going shopping" or "I am going to Wal-Mart"), statements that provide cover for all parties to enact an illegal practice. Since preventing border card users from taking up paid work in the US is largely discouraged, this case forms a striking example of the limitations of perfect law enforcement to border officers.

Formal law thus fails for a variety of reasons. Formal laws can be practically unenforceable or only partly enforceable in the realities of the border; they can involve different degrees of moral stigma, which allow for neglecting some rules as trivial; and they may be mutually contradictory or otherwise unworkable. But as the case of the commuting undocumented maids and gardeners illustrates,

---

5 Heyman (1995) documents this extensively.

6 These passports allow approved Mexican border residents to cross the boundary to visit and shop for up to 25 miles and 72 hours, but not to work.

economic and political influences weaken or altogether negate key laws, and US border officers cannot help but notice this.

Finally, widespread activities and relationships of questionable legality, largely taken for granted in everyday life, pervade the US side of the border, as well as Mexico's borderlands. By "questionable legality," we mean flows and activities that may have important illegal connections but which on the surface appear to be normal and legal and about which people may gossip but never really know. The most powerful and pervasive "fuzzy element" in the borderlands is mysterious money. By this we mean the widespread liquid cash, luxurious consumption, and booming accounting businesses and law offices amidst a depressingly weak (low-employment, low-wage, no-benefits) US border economy. Mysterious money is generally assumed to be laundered money from drug trafficking and other kinds of smuggling, as well as capital flight money from Mexico.[7] It moreover has a particular social-cultural role on the US side, where overt illegal enterprises are not openly displayed or tolerated, hence making it the main US-side symbol of illegal cross-border flows. The peculiar role of money as a device of mystification is also important; money tells no stories and raises few questions, and is accorded profound legitimacy in the United States. The presence, indeed normality, of this easy money and glittering consumption, and the sense that it likely (but not provably) flows outside and around the law, certainly sets the stage for corruption among officers of the US state.

In summary, the US legal landscape is not simply a predictably rational order occasionally subverted from outside. Rather, law fades into extra-legality and illegality in three ways: in the overall national contradictions affecting high-priority law enforcement goals (interdicting drugs and illegal migrants); in the under-enforcement of other laws; and in the taken-for-granted everyday landscape of questionable money, and unclear activities and relationships in the borderlands. At the same time, the ideology of pure legality is strong in the United States, despite enormous lacunae. In the way that the discourse of absolute corruption has social force of its own in Mexico above and beyond material acts of corruption (Nuijten 2003), so too do US law enforcers and US society engage in a fetishistic discourse of legal formalism as they carry out acts that vary widely between law and extra-legality. Hence the US society as a whole maintains a variety of socially-necessary hypocrisies, while borderlands officers and residents negotiate actual and ambiguous practices, all the time maintaining a surface ideological fetish of law on the US side of the border and an equally fetishized contrast with corrupt Mexico.

---

7 The illegal drug trade across the US border, controlled by massive Mexican narcotics cartels, generates revenues of hundreds of billions of dollars each year. The Mexican cartels grow marijuana and opium (for processing into heroin), manufacture amphetamines, and import cocaine from South America. Three of the largest cartels—the Juárez Cartel, the Arellano Félix Cartel (Tijuana/San Diego area), and the Gulf Cartel (Matamoros/Brownsville)—are headquartered on the border and the other cartels must bring their merchandise through the region in order to sell it in the US (Blancornelas 2003).

The Specific Borderlands Setting of Corruption

In delineating the ambiguity and incompleteness of US law and state, we have touched on a number of features characteristic of US borderlands society. We now turn to that setting, emphasizing how agencies of the central state are "localized," politically and culturally. Note, however, that the US federal structure creates a complex hierarchy of cooperating and competing law enforcement agencies at local (city and county), state, and national (civilian and military) levels, and that the national (or "federal") agencies have structures involving both national and field level management.

Though the US borderlands vary, their economy is generally characterized by dependency on other parts of the US and, ironically, Mexico, the much poorer country. Historically, this area has offered low wage labor to manufacturing investors from outside the region. Such manufacturing has, however, recently departed for even lower cost areas of the world, including for the Mexican side of the border. Low wage agriculture, however, continues to be important in some sections of the US borderlands. Because the Mexican side of the border is economically very dynamic, with world-class assembly plant industries and large sums of money made from border commerce and smuggling, the US side depends substantially on commerce and investments from Mexico. Finally, the wages and other expenditures of the police-military apparatus of the US state are important in this region. The US-side local elite, then, tends to seek rents within these economic structures (for example, offering banking and real estate services to customers with unaccountable cash) rather than developing autonomous patterns of capital accumulation.

The greatest asset of US-side elites is binational, bicultural social relationships that facilitate the flow of commodities and money across the border. They thus have a particular interest in facilitating the free movement of shoppers from Mexico and in partaking of inexpensive if extra-legal labor services characteristic of this region. On the other hand, law enforcement agencies are an important source of external funds and employment, and do help suppress violence and visible lawlessness. Thus, as Schneider and Schneider (2003) show with regard to Palermo, local elites and federal police agencies condition each other, resulting in a complex balance of laws and legal targets that are enforced, half-enforced, and not enforced at all. For example, political bosses along the border are an important source of corruption, both in local law enforcement operations and in their penetration of the federal agencies; this is discussed at greater length as a "scenario" below.[8]

As we burrow down the level at which specific corrupt acts occur, it is important to place US officers in the context of face-to-face society and culture,

---

8   Another point relevant to understanding the local conditioning of the state in the US borderlands is that there is not a neat contrast along the international boundary between the bureaucratic and political culture of the two nations. Rather, practices, habits, and idioms are readily transferred between the two sides, as several of our case studies show.

by examining how they are recruited and how their work is socially organized. All US law enforcement agencies and units of the military that are concerned with drug, immigration, and other border or US-Latin American issues recruit heavily from the southern US border region, where there are a large number of bilingual, bicultural people. Although we are not attributing corruption specifically to officers of borderlands background, the particulars of recruiting from this region and the effects of assignment into areas of active trafficking are worth noting. Recently, US soldiers on an anti-narcotics detail from El Paso to Colombia engaged in substantial (if short-lived) cocaine smuggling themselves. Interestingly, a key figure in the group was a son of poor, migrant farm workers from border Texas who joined the army at a time that it was targeting Spanish speakers for anti-drug operations. A key element that emerged in his trial was his arrogance and naiveté, perhaps sparked by a sudden climb in rank; due to his role as a border Spanish speaker in anti-drug operations, he rose in three months, with little preparation, from private to sergeant (Roberts 2006).

It is telling of the role of the borderlands as the operating zone of both state and anti-state, that ironically enough military and police officers as well as smugglers are recruited from substantially the same heavily minority and marginalized border populations. Although we do not have comprehensive statistics about region of origin for all regional US police agencies, Heyman's study in 1991–1992 found that 56 per cent of Border Patrol officers and a notable 89 per cent of port of entry inspectors grew up in border counties (Heyman 1995: 272). Origin in the region sometimes offers interpersonal (kinship or friendship) connections to people who are directly or indirectly involved in illegal activities; but conversely, we have encountered cases of non-borderlanders who become sucked into friendships of toleration and even into conspiracies because they were naively impressed with the easy and fast life of illegal activities at the border. Recruitment, whether of local people or outsiders, brings people into another set of factors that produce and shape corruption: the work setting of public organizations that operate along the border.

While Border Patrol officers enforce laws forbidding border crossing *between* official entry points (and thus usually have to deal with undocumented immigrants and drug smugglers), inspectors enforce laws and apply regulations to people and goods *at* the official ports of entry. These are the two main front-line federal border enforcement positions. Ports of entry do the most local recruitment and their work is highly integrated into the regional social and political setting (Heyman 2004a, 2004b). Daily, many tens of thousands of trucks, cars, and pedestrians cross each of the large ports on the border. The job involves enormous speed and pressure; the standard for clearance in primary inspections (enter the country/send for further inspections) is 30 seconds per vehicle in El Paso, and this is monitored and enforced by management. An inspector told one of us that everyday he felt like he stood at the bottom of a looming mountain of traffic. There is substantial inconsistency among inspectors, as measured in time spent on the initial ("primary") inspection (Ward et al. 2007), and an officer told us that she feels different inspectors apply the laws differently and with varying degrees of effort. The possibilities for individual discretion are extensive, from small favors to lucrative corruption. Management can tell if an inspector is being overly picky by local standards (for example, halting many dozens of women as possible undocumented maids for further questioning) but cannot tell if they have overlooked a violation since the potential violator rapidly leaves the inspection area for the US interior, with no further "quality control." Also, management is visibly deferential to local commercial and political elites, so that line-workers get the message that discretion is part of the job—they are not to offend people who are well-connected.

The Border Patrol operates away from the allowed border crossings, often in remote farm and desert areas. Officers often function outside of close supervision, in small workgroups (partners or small sets of officers), in areas where movement has a substantial likelihood of being smuggling or another kind of illegal activity. In these settings, a tight sense of insider solidarity tends to emerge, often in opposition to perceived bad outsiders, as well as an alienating sense of being the only group to understand the real struggles of the border.[9] Still, Border Patrol officers do form part of border society and there are cases of them having been suborned by smugglers (see for example, Maril 2004: 188ff.). In such a context, the Border Patrol is particularly susceptible to the characteristic police behavior of covering up abusive and corrupt practices (see Maril 2004: 304; more generally, see Maas [1973] 1997; Stoddard 1975).

Although not a case of corruption as such, group silence about misconduct is part of the broader pattern of non-"Weberian rationality" in the US state, and can contribute to facilitating specific corrupt acts. Group silence in the Border Patrol is illustrated by recent testimony about Patrol officers covering up the shooting of an alleged smuggler in the back. Seven officers, most of them junior, covered up for two senior officers who fired the shots. One of the officers, who eventually testified with immunity after the case was broken open in Mexico, explained that he did not want to be known as a "snitch." The Assistant US Attorney referred to police in-group behavior by describing this as a "thin green line"[10] (Gilot 2006a).

There are also a set of investigative arms of the state, including the Drug Enforcement Agency (DEA), Federal Bureau of Investigations (FBI), Immigration and Customs Enforcement (ICE), and military intelligence agencies.[11] On the one hand, these agencies are the most selective and professionalized arms of the US state in the region, and operate with higher degrees of self-scrutiny and internal standards (for example, many officers have to obtain advanced security clearances before being allowed access to secret surveillance and communications). On the other hand, such organizations often work closely with criminal informants and other illicit inside connections that can and do result in a reversal of commitments (for example, officers covering for or indirectly serving the aims of criminal actors).

---

9 Heyman (1995: 277) terms this sense the "besieged esprit de corps." See also the corroborating ethnography in Maril (2004).

10 This refers to green being the color of the Border Patrol uniform and a "thin blue line," which is the cliché for police cover-ups.

11 Both authors have, at different times, gathered field material from these agencies, though not concerning their covert operations.

Furthermore, the work of law enforcement investigations often places officers in extra-legal domains of easy money, high lifestyle, drugs, commercial sex, and so forth, which thrive on the border.

Finally, we should take note of the US consulates in Mexico that do visa processing, where Mexican employees, who are paid less than their US colleagues, process high volumes of applications from fellow Mexican citizens, with limited (and high-speed) double-checking by a small staff of US officers, themselves with varying degrees of connection into Mexican society.[12]

Work, of course, is not all of life: US officers live within border society and culture. Sometimes they feel isolated, but connections and influences penetrate them nonetheless.[13] As border culture contains significant symbolic codes and relational frameworks for melding opposites, for making "arrangements," for getting things done, for tolerating incongruities, and for pretending not to know about all of this in public, one can readily imagine how this might affect a would-be "rational" bureaucracy.

We must keep in mind when analyzing border culture that stunning resources and arrangements, often tied to mysterious money, exist beside tremendous poverty, suffering, and daily insecurity in this poorest of all US regions, with an even poorer nation next door. Though officers themselves are somewhat removed from these two extremes, being well-paid and well-insured civil servants, some of them come out of poverty[14] and all of them are surrounded by the socio-cultural frameworks rooted in this setting. In summary, we have mentioned two contexts for corruption, one being broad forms of political and economic contradiction in US law and society, and the other being the immediate border cultural setting and specific local political favoritism. These should not be radically separated from each other, because the borderland's cultural idioms of being connected and getting things done have developed historically as a crucial regional pattern for the carrying out of wider covert flows and relationships between the US and Mexico.

We should emphasize in closing that isolated, professionalized, rational bureaucratic performances are very much present in the US-side border agencies. To simply turn the ideology of cleanliness upside-down would be as misleading as the pure ideology itself is. Rather, the normal features of rational bureaucracy are rendered incomplete, contradicted, and conditioned by other processes operating at scales from transnational (US-Latin American) relations, through the internal US society and economy, to the immediate border region.

Corruption in US Border Law Enforcement Agencies: Aggregate Evidence

Actual statistics on corruption in US border law enforcement agencies are difficult to obtain. The US Department of Homeland Security's Office of the Inspector

---

12 A recent rule change requires final sign-off on all visa applications by a US citizen employee of the Consular Service.
13 Maril (2004) delineates moments of both isolation and local connections.
14 See life histories in Heyman (2002).

General produces semi-annual reports to Congress that contain statistics on allegations and investigations concerned with "waste, fraud, and abuse" and "misconduct"—a term, along with "malfeasance," used by agency officials we interviewed rather than "corruption." Unfortunately, statistics are presented in an aggregate fashion—lumping together figures from disparate entities such as the FBI, DEA, Federal Bureau of Prisons, and others—that make it hard to determine how many cases specifically concern border matters. According to one source (Tobin 2005), "20 employees of US Customs and Border Protection were arrested, indicted or convicted of crimes from April 2004 through March 2005." In Douglas, Arizona, between 1991 and 1996, five different Border Patrol agents were arrested for transporting cocaine into the US (Ruiz 1998: 176). Full details on many of these cases, however, are not available.

Interviews with representatives of border law enforcement agencies also proved inconclusive because of the unwillingness of agency officials to disclose information or because hard statistics on number of "misconduct" cases in specific agencies simply did not exist.[15] One reason for this is the well-known pressure against whistle blowing and a culture of silence in border agencies (Rotella 1998: 108). Interagency rivalries may also impede corruption investigations. In our interviews, government spokesmen repeatedly asserted that few cases of "misconduct" occurred: "Agents have been accused of misconduct, and investigations have been conducted, but it does not happen often." When pressed to provide numbers US border spokesmen were either unable or unwilling to comply. Furthermore, although US state authorities are well-aware that border corruption is a serious matter, they have shown little understanding of the mechanisms through which corruption develops, nor do they appear to have the means to stop or control it. Following Abraham and van Schendel (2005: 23), we argue that "For the state, the meanings of routine practices in the borderlands are difficult to comprehend." A government investigator looking into corruption may recognize taking large monetary bribes as serious misconduct, but many forms of coercion and favoritism we discuss below are likely to escape recording. It is likely that the penumbra of informal activities surrounding specific acts of corruption evades the eyes of border authorities.

An example of the patterned blindness of government officials, even those operating directly on the border, is the touching faith in classroom training as a measure against corruption and other forms of misconduct. Officials stated that thorough training of Border Patrol agents and other front-line officers prevented extensive malfeasance. The actual Border Patrol Academy consists of 91 days of paid training at Artesia, New Mexico. During these 91 days, "Twenty-five to fifty hours of ethics and law related to corruption is taught at the academy," according to one official. Subsequently, each Border Patrol agent must attend at least one hour-long class annually concerned with ethical issues. For agency insiders,

---

15 According to a Notimex (Mexican news service) report in *El Diaro* of May 31, 2005, based on information obtained from Michael Shelby, a federal prosecutor in the Laredo/Brownsville area of Texas, criminal accusations of corruption increased from four in 2001 to 17 in 2004.

"misconduct" is only a minor problem committed by "bad seeds" because the Border Patrol incorporates "a modern bureaucratic form that employed a highly efficient methodology, combined with numerous internal and external checks and balances ... in an agency ... deemed the most high profile law enforcement agency in the United States" (Talavera, n.d.: 8).

Yet, a study of newspaper accounts of actual border corruption cases and interviews with an unusually forthcoming "misconduct" investigator revealed a more complex and problematical scenario. In the last five years news stories about law enforcement corruption and other activities in its penumbra have appeared from all major US-Mexico border-crossing areas. Events have included agents killing or harming immigrants, accepting large bribes from drug traffickers, smuggling or helping smugglers pass contraband, selling visas to known criminals, obtaining information for underworld figures, and so on. A recent investigation by *Los Angeles Times* reporters found that:

> Bribery of federal and local officials by Mexican smugglers is rising sharply, and with it the fear that a culture of corruption is taking hold along the 2,000-mile border from Brownsville, Texas to San Diego. At least 200 public employees have been charged with helping to move narcotics or illegal immigrants across the US-Mexican border since 2004, at least double the illicit activity documented in prior years, a *Times* examination of public records has found. Thousands more are under investigation. (Vartabedian, Serrano, and Marosi 2006: 1)

According to an investigator who has handled several high profile cases, not only is "misconduct" a serious, on-going problem but rumors and allegations about corruption are a pervasive feature of daily life in border law enforcement—a scenario which makes it even harder to catch "bad apples" because their reputed actions may disappear within a swirl of rumors. According to one Border Patrol spokesman, approximately one third of Border Patrol agents who quit or are forced to resign from the Patrol do so because of unethical behavior they committed.[16]

Government officials, investigators, and researchers do not know with certitude the extent of corruption on the border but all agree that the potential for misconduct and legal transgressions to go unreported in the vast desert expanses and mountainous hinterlands of the 2,000-mile border is considerable.[17] As the Border Patrol rushes to add 10,000 new agents in the next five years the potential

---

16 If we accept this figure and the 5 per cent annual attrition rate (for 2004 and 2005) provided by the same official, then of a total approximate Border Patrol force of 12,000 we would expect there to be about 200 agents who would be likely to be terminated for unethical behavior each year. This obviously rough estimate only refers to unethical behavior of which the agency is aware.

17 Schneider and Schneider (2005: 518) note that "gangsterism" and other illicit activity, of the sort embodied in border drug cartels, has "identifiable geographies:" "Generated out of the violence of asymmetrical power—for example, enclosures, occupations, abrupt disinvestment, and commodification—they also appear to flourish in terrain that is very expensive if not impossible to police."

for abuse increases exponentially. A spokesman of a union that represents Border Patrol agents notes that "People are slipping through the cracks [in the hiring process] that possibly should never have been hired" (Mike Albon quoted in Tobin 2005).

Our argument is that corruption and related activities are specific events, involving particular individuals (a position that is consistent with the "bad apple" explanation) but that the repeated recurrence of these practices in the same settings begs for systematic generalization and explanation. In the section that follows, we offer a preliminary inventory of corruption scenarios that occur in border law enforcement agencies—developed in a dialogue with an investigator whose job is to detect and catch corrupt officials. Examination of these scenarios reveals systemic processes that go beyond the aberrant behavior of a few individuals.

The scenarios are presented as a portrait of how corruption is sometimes played out on the border but also as examples of the idioms in which local people describe such occurrences. That is to say that there is a local discourse (generated by law enforcement agents and civilians) surrounding corruption that heavily emphasizes border culture. Though we recognize the richness and complexity of border culture, we consider the primary causes of corruption to lay elsewhere, with the structural conditions created by unequal border development, supply and demand dimensions of global political economy, and the complex interpenetration of political systems and societies that produce and consume illegal drugs. Such contexts historically interact with regional societies and their cultural sets, so that there is no particular point in talking about causes in terms either of cultural essence or of entirely external forces (cf. Schneider and Schneider 2003, 2005).[18]

Dense social networks, fluid migration patterns, a generalized de-sensitivity to drug-trafficking because of its ubiquitousness (Campbell 2005), and a tendency to view smuggling as an "illegal" rather than "illicit" activity (Abraham and van Schendel 2005) form the substrata within which border corruption flourishes. Drug cartels—rooted in border society—consciously manipulate local cultural and social norms in order to achieve their aims. But the existence of these corrupting entities and their corrupting processes stem from the huge profits made possible by US prohibition of certain drugs and their interaction with agents of the US state. Ultimately, the political economy substantially affects the local cultural patterns. All observers note the propensity of wealthy smuggling organizations to bribe officials with large sums of money, and the susceptibility of relatively low-paid agents (often with low morale) with enormous discretionary power to succumb to lucrative bribes (Tobin 2005).

---

18 Nor do we by presenting actual border corruption cases mean to fall into the trap identified by Gootenberg (2005), invoking James Scott, of "talking like a state"—that is, of naively reproducing state discourse about "illegal" border activities.

Border Corruption Scenarios

Cross-Border Ties, Daily Face-to-Face Interaction, and Corruption

Residents of border towns often have extensive family, social, and business ties on both sides of the border. Consequently, the most innocuous-seeming social events (weddings, *quinceañeras*, birthday parties, bar parties, and so on) may become settings in which an agent may be approached and asked to provide help in smuggling narcotics or illegally crossing friends.[19] Furthermore, intra-family pressure may be applied on an agent to get him or her to cooperate with drug cartels or other underworld organizations. Given that the drug economy is, de facto, one of the most lucrative border enterprises, tens of thousands of local residents are involved in the trade; this often includes associates, neighbors, casual acquaintances, and former high school friends or relatives of border law enforcement agents. Densely crowded downtown border crossings facilitate intimate interactions that can lead to corruption. People who cross the border frequently (or spotters planted on bridges near border-crossing points) become familiar with specific agents, their schedules, habits, and so on and, vice versa, agents become aware of particular people who cross and their behaviors. This local knowledge and close contact easily evolves into corrupt arrangements.

US immigration officials on the border are under great pressure to do "favors" that would allow relatives or friends into the US legally or quasi-legally.[20] Thus, we see a pattern of strong interpersonal obligations and face-to-face favoritism that is widespread among border people. An appeal from a stranger to a border officer on the basis of shared ethnicity is likely to be harshly rejected, but one from a cousin or childhood friend would be hard to refuse. Hence, whatever the ethnic identity of the US state agents may be, the extremely dense, close-knit, face-to-face social interactions in border settings is fertile terrain for corruption. Close relationships between border law enforcement officials and those they

---

19 Award-winning journalist Sebastian Rotella illustrates the physically dense and intimate nature of border social interactions in Tijuana as follows: "In the movie *Casablanca*, everybody went to Rick's Café Américain. In Tijuana, the Mexican border city that has taken on a cinematic air of intrigue, everybody goes to Bob's Big Boy (El Big). Cops, journalists, spies, lawyers, gangsters, entrepreneurs, political bosses, human rights activists, former, current and future government officials—they all haunt the diner with the statue of the short fat guy in front" (Rotella 1998: 13).

"The diner is thick with talk about sinister topics: after the latest scandal, shootout or gangland murder, reporters hit Big Boy to work their sources, sift through versions, swap theories. If someone draws on a napkin, it usually involves homicide scenes ... Drug trafficking is usually to blame, but there might be other motives: political feuds, corruption debts, smuggling of immigrants or guns or contraband, a deadly cocktail of the above. Did they kill him because he took the money or because he didn't? Is it riskier to do business with the bad guys or stand up to them?" (ibid.: 15).

20 Another related border corruption scenario is that drug trafficking organizations plant people as agents in border law enforcement agencies. According to an inside source this is rumored to occur, though to date there have been no proven cases.

surveil stem from neighborhood and community connections (growing up in the same barrio or *colonia*), family and kin ties, shared experiences in schools and churches, socializing at *fiestas* and ceremonies marking rites of passage (baptisms, *quinceañeras*, weddings, funerals), shopping in the same stores, and miscellaneous leisure activities. These relationships span the border such that a generalized common lifeworld overlaps the strict international boundary. Furthermore, thousands of local residents cross the border line every day. Migrants may come into contact with the same Customs, Immigration, or Border Patrol officials day after day and gradually socialize and develop informal relationships. Thus, a high degree of personal and social intimacy facilitates cross-border business and communication. These connections encourage and promote under-enforcement of laws, tacit allowance of questionable activities, illegality and corruption couched in an idiom of friendship or favors to family.

As US border law enforcement agents constantly interact with their Mexican counterparts and with professional colleagues and clients on both sides of the border, these relationships may evolve from strictly professional relationships into business partnerships involving illegal activities.

In a high-profile El Paso case, the local FBI director (not originally from the border region) abruptly resigned after complaints from Mexican officials (Valdez and Gilot 2003). Mexican authorities alleged the director maintained inappropriate, close personal relationships with a wealthy businessman and a priest in Ciudad Juárez. Complaints surfaced after the FBI director held a press conference at a Juárez racetrack, owned by the businessman, in which the director defended his Mexican friends against accusations of money laundering. The Mexican government accused him of meddling in their internal affairs. The FBI director met the businessman when he interviewed him as part of the investigation into the visa scam described in the next scenario. Subsequently, the businessman allegedly gave the FBI director's wife a high-paying job at the racetrack and provided the family with other benefits. Although we are not alleging bribery was involved, clearly the elements of mysterious money, the high lifestyles surrounding it, and binational elite networks were involved in this case. The former FBI director was ultimately convicted in federal court for making false statements in an Office of Government Ethics Public Financial Disclosure Report submitted to the FBI regarding gifts he received from the prominent Mexican businessman mentioned above (*El Paso Times* December 16, 2006; Gilot 2006b).

Border Transnationalism and Mexican Culture

One of the most dramatic recent border corruption cases involved a clerk in the US Consulate in Ciudad Juárez who sold or speeded up visas for dozens of Mexican nationals in exchange for money. A lengthy investigation disclosed in 2003 that the employee, a fluent Spanish speaker whose family is from Mexico, sold visas to a prominent Mexican businessman. The visas were ultimately used by drug traffickers and a famous boxer who is a known associate of a major drug cartel. An investigator who interviewed the consular employee observed that the employee did not think she had done anything wrong. According to the investigator, "it is just part of the culture ... what she did was accepted there [Mexico]." The businessman, who is one of the richest men in Mexico, was also implicated in the influence peddling investigation involving the director of the FBI office in El Paso. At about the same time as the Juárez case, a US government investigation in the Nuevo Laredo alleged that consular officials sold visas for as much as $1,500. According to a newspaper report of these cases, "visa fraud is far from an unusual occurrence. In fact, the Diplomatic Security Service, part of the State Department, opened 250 visa fraud investigations worldwide since October [2002], officials said" (Gilot 2003).

Favors and the reciprocity they entail may appear as "normal" operating procedure in Mexican government offices—located less than a mile away on the other side of the border. When they occur on US soil or in, for example, the US Consulate Office in Ciudad Juárez, they may be viewed by US authorities as corruption. One possible explanation for corruption could therefore be the influence of Mexican culture across the border.

Yet, the cultural scene we are describing includes both Anglo-Americans (and members of other US ethnic groups) and Mexicans/Mexican-Americans. Intermarriage is common. Proven cases of corruption have involved Anglos,[21] Hispanics, African-Americans, and so on, with no single ethnic group having primacy. Moreover, the interpenetration of "Anglo" and "Hispanic" cultures in Northern Mexico and the US Southwest is so extensive and has been going on so long (since the sixteenth century) that it is often difficult to separate one cultural tradition from the other. Latinos are now the largest minority group in the US; thus Latino/Mexican culture is also part of the US society and state, not an external alien force. Finally, when agents of the US state engage in corrupt actions, whether they are Hispanic, Anglo, African-American, or otherwise they are ultimately US citizens first and foremost, and their actions cannot be attributed to a "foreign" culture.[22]

US consular offices in Mexican border towns are often staffed by "Hispanic-Americans' who are fluent in Spanish and conversant in Mexican customs. Mexican clients of these offices may expect and pressure these co-ethnic officials to extend to them the kinds of reciprocity and culturally-stylized preferential treatment that occur all around them in the same border city. That is, the clients

---

21 A few examples of corrupt activities involving Anglo law enforcement include the cases of Raymond Allen (El Paso INS agent convicted of drug smuggling), Guy Henry Kmett (San Diego Customs Inspector convicted of immigrant smuggling), Presidio, Texas County Sheriff Rick Thompson (convicted of cocaine trafficking), and Charles Vinson (San Diego Border Patrol agent convicted of sexual assault on an immigrant). There are many other examples. Frequently smuggling rings include both Anglos (and members of other ethnicities) and Mexicans in the same organization (Gilot 2006c).

22 We are anticipating a possible argument here, or even a misreading of our own argument. No one that we know of has blamed US corruption on Mexican culture as such, given the politically correct climate of our times. But it is certainly implicit in the commonplace blaming of US-side corruption on the effects of Mexican smuggling organizations, paying no attention to the combined roles of both societies in illegal flows (for example, the otherwise strong journalistic account of Vartabedian et al. 2006).

make little distinction between the customs associated with the US office and other Mexican offices in border cities because they view them as part of the same, undifferentiated cultural world.[23]

Thus, the border region is a space of considerable shared, transnational, and hybrid culture. This cultural complex includes values and practices such as obligation, reciprocity, *confianza*, *respeto*, and patron-client relations, which are highly appreciated in Mexico.

These cultural elements combined with differing laws and customs on each side of the border facilitate actions that in one national context may not necessarily be viewed as corruption but are seen as corruption in the other. For example, long-time border residents may engage in behaviors, such as *fayuca* (non-tariffed consumer goods) smuggling, that emically appear as one single, continuous process but through crossing the border become international.[24] Part of the process (smuggling goods into Mexico) entails actions that are technically illegal yet permitted through systematic, rule-bound, and widely known informal arrangements (*mordidas*—"bribes"). The other part of the process, smuggling goods out of the US, may involve legal violations (such as preparation of false invoices by American shop owners) as well, but since the destination of the goods is Mexico and such *fayuca* smuggling is deeply rooted in border life, the US state turns a blind eye to it, tacitly allowing illegal activity to occur.

Bridge inspectors and other border agents are confronted with various scenarios in which issues of obligation, respect, reciprocity, and other cultural values may be invoked in ways that facilitate corrupt activities. For example, border cultural values grant considerable respect to the elderly. Elderly people, especially grandmothers, at times may be insulated (through social pressure and implicit cultural values) from certain kinds of questioning that may be viewed as invasive or disrespectful. Hence, older people make excellent drug smugglers, especially of small amounts of heroin carried across bridges. Similar issues pertain to women. Values regarding proper respect toward women and their bodies, modesty, etc., may inhibit male inspectors from thoroughly investigating or searching women. Yet, as one female border inspector told Campbell, "women have balls [i.e., spaces]

---

23 Border residents frequently interact simultaneously with both (Mexican and US) state bureaucracies and may apply a common logic to both states. For example, when one of our informants worked as a counselor in the retraining program for US garment workers (almost all of whom were of Mexican descent) laid off as a result of the North American Free Trade Agreement, most of her clients (who often lived in Mexico) gave her gifts. They did this—as they would have in Mexico—to try to establish personal ties and reciprocal bonds. Even though our informant explained to her clients that they had a right to the benefits, they insisted she take the gifts. Out of respect for her elders and because of cultural pressure she was bound to accept them, even though this was technically a violation of US law. The clients explained that they felt it was only fair and appropriate for them to give something since they were receiving support. According to US law these customary "gifts" were illegal, yet they were a normal feature of life within the agency.

There are many other examples of how in border settings two "cultures of the state" intertwine.

24 On the processual dimensions of corruption see Blundo (this volume).

everywhere where they can hide contraband." Relatives, godparents, and fictive co-parents may, on occasion, also be shielded from thorough inspection because of unspoken cultural values concerning respect and dignity.

Contrary to the information presented above—in which local cultural knowledge provides a vehicle for corrupt activities—some observers suggest that the opposite may also occur. Ironically, Mexican-American officials of the US government often consciously strive to separate themselves from Mexican nationals and wield a citizenship ideology in doing so (Heyman 2002; Vila 2000). In a different vein, lack of familiarity with border culture may make newly recruited border agents from outside the region especially vulnerable to corruption. According to several sources within law enforcement agents, corrupt agents tend to be unsophisticated individuals unfamiliar with the border region who fall prey to unfamiliar border cultural arrangements.[25] Pressure to conform to illegal arrangements by more connected colleagues in the workplace also contributes to corruption. So, both local cultural knowledge and lack of familiarity with border culture may be factors in corruption scenarios. In either case, the critical factor is the ever-present availability in the border zone of opportunities to profit from association with narcotics or human smugglers.

Gender and Sexuality Inequalities and Manipulations

Male US border agents habitually flirt with women as they cross the border. According to an agency investigator, inspectors "pull women out of cars just to look at their bodies." The inspectors may "pass them a [phone] number and say 'give me a call.'" Female smugglers, aware of this, manipulate it to their favor. This may entail little more than smiling, winking, and in other ways acting seductive—sufficient to distract the inspector from doing a thorough search. In other cases, the inspector may solicit sexual favors in return for allowing the woman into the US or not scrutinizing her vehicle, luggage, or packages. By merely giving the inspector her phone number or agreeing to meet him later at a hotel or a party, the smuggler may accomplish her task.

Once the female smuggler has successfully crossed several loads in this fashion, she has considerable leverage over the inspector because she can blackmail him by threatening to report him for sexual harassment or for complicity in passing loads of contraband. It should be noted that this type of corruption involves the conscious manipulation of cultural stereotypes by women who are aware that they may be viewed as sexually available or sexually proficient, strictly on the basis of their ethnicity. It may also entail women skillfully managing *"macho"* behaviors to their advantage. In turn, however, male smugglers also attempt (often successfully according to an informant) to flirt with female inspectors in order to obtain preferential treatment.

---

25 A counter-view voiced by a Border Patrol agent was that corrupt agents tend to be former *"cholos"* (gang members; as evidenced by specific tattoos on their bodies) from border towns who, after becoming US agents, renew ties with the drug-smuggling friends in gangs.

US law enforcement agents may engage in socially-taboo sexual relations on the south side of the border (where brothels, massage parlors, and other forms of sexual commerce abound) unbeknownst to relatives and colleagues.[26] If such behavior is observed by "friends" or associates on the Mexican side of the border it may be used to blackmail them into cooperating with smuggling organizations. Extortion through sexual blackmail may occur as a result of serendipitous observation of "deviant" behavior or through deliberate entrapment. Coerced sex may also be initiated by Border Patrol agents who capture undocumented women in remote border regions. As one Patrol officer[27] told us:

> I have personally seen videos of such incidents at court trials. Some women we capture are extremely beautiful. There have been incidents in the Lower Rio Grande Valley where a Border Patrol agent was caught essentially with his *manos en la masa* [with his hands in the dough, or idiomatically, caught red-handed]. He pulled this attractive female from a bus going north at a checkpoint. He pulled her off the bus. The code for an unaccompanied female is 1097. That code means you are by yourself with a single female. He played with the Motorola radio to act like he was calling it in but he didn't do it ... He acted like the radio was defective.
> He picked up the woman off a Greyhound bus. He took her to his house in Brownsville for two or three days. He took her to his house to have sex with her. It was consensual but the deal was he said to her, "If you stay with me for a few days I'll take you up north." But he got caught [with her] traveling down a dirt road late at night.

In a recent case, an official of a US federal border law enforcement agency was arrested and charged with illegal use of government information for private gain and various other crimes. According to an investigator we interviewed, the official actually sold information to drug traffickers in the border region. He did so after being blackmailed by the traffickers who threatened him with revelations about his covert sexual life on the Mexican side of the border. This information did not appear in the local news media but, according to the investigator, was the real impetus for the official's corrupt activities.

Local Capture of the State: Corrupt Political Bosses

The US border region has a long history of political patronage and bossism, due to its poverty, limited public services and infrastructure, and large immigrant and minority population (Anders 1982). Political bosses, especially in remote non-urban counties, are often county sheriffs or otherwise control or influence local law enforcement. Such positions are well suited for corrupt facilitation of smuggling because of an inside position in law enforcement and their location

---

26 In general, law enforcement ironically places its officers more heavily than the average civilian in connection with or awareness of extra-legal domains—worlds of easy money, high lifestyle, drugs, commercial sex, and so forth that thrive on the two sides of the border.

27 For another, corroborating case, see Department of Homeland Security (2006: 18).

on isolated smuggling corridors and transit routes. Moreover, because of the multi-level (federalist) structure of US law enforcement, it is difficult for national and state agencies to avoid dealing with local bosses. Higher-level political actors tolerate the corruption of such bosses because they deliver cash and votes in a region largely characterized by enduring clientelistic politics, until major patrons are no longer willing or able to protect the bosses.

In 2000, Ronald "Joe" Borane, Justice of the Peace and City Magistrate of the small border city of Douglas in Cochise County (Arizona)—one of the largest counties in the US with nearly a hundred miles of boundary with Mexico and one of the most important smuggling corridors along the border—pled guilty to drug racketeering and money laundering charges brought about by a federal sting operation. It turned out he had been operating as a corrupt collaborator of smuggling operations for a long period before then, despite widespread rumors about his involvement. Fifteen years earlier one of us doing fieldwork in Douglas, Arizona, heard that his local nickname was "Joe Cocaine."

Joe Borane was a "power broker" in this poor and sparsely populated county. He was a "prolific fundraiser for the Democratic party" and also, by ethnographic observation, a key figure in delivering votes from the largely Mexican American constituency. He also had extensive connections inside municipal and county law enforcement. He and his brother Ray Borane (the current Mayor of Douglas, and not known to be involved in smuggling) came from an intermarried Lebanese-Mexican family, and had excellent cultural brokerage skills in both nations. At the same time, he seriously abused the vulnerable in favor of local business constituents, running what the prosecutors described as a "debtor's prison" by "repeatedly jailing poor laborers who were unable to settle debts with local property owners" (Dillon 2000). As a result, "he bought nearly 200 houses, ranches, and businesses that made him the county's largest landowner, with assets he declared in February 1999 at $5.9 million," a value believed to be a substantial underestimate (ibid.). There was little question that Joe Borane had operated outside the accepted bounds of law and practice for many years, but while he had law enforcement opponents who brought him down, he also had key protectors and friends, concerning whom there is considerable, unsubstantiated speculation. Though he was outrageous and abusive, his corruption was not merely a case of a bad apple official, but rather a result of the political boss phenomenon in this region, as many other cases from all along the border would show.

Widening the Definition of Corruption

The above inventory of scenarios, constructed through conversations with smugglers and border agents, newspaper reports, and official documents only describes the most direct forms of corruption found in US agencies on the border. It does not address the penumbra of corruption (normally blamed on Mexican citizens or authorities but not possible without US complicity) including tacit acceptance of illicit practices or unproblematic engagement in actions of questionable legality. This is the case, as noted earlier, for the allowance of thousands of Mexican border residents to use "border crossing cards" to come to the US side to work as maids, gardeners, construction workers, and so on. In cities like El Paso, particular main city bus lines cater almost exclusively to such people and their presence is quite visible and obvious to all but the least observant, yet there is no immigration crackdown. The same can be said in relation to the hundreds of individuals and businesses who purchase and transport large amounts of *fayuca* on the US side and smuggle it into Mexico (Chaparro 2005; Ruiz 2005).[28] It would be disingenuous for US authorities to deny knowledge of such practices. Surely, investigating such actions would uncover legal violations on the North American side of the border.

Another domain that should be considered corrupt in a wide definition is the US connection to Mexican drug smuggling violence. The US blames Mexico and other Latin Americans for producing and distributing drugs yet it is very ineffective at preventing consumption (without which a large drug market would not exist) or distribution in its own territory.[29] US authorities criticize "Mexican drug violence" yet sometimes contribute to it or tacitly participate in it by tolerating the murders of their paid informants because the killings occur on Mexican soil.

A very dramatic current case involves an informant on the Juárez drug cartel for the US offices of Immigration and Customs Enforcement (ICE) and the Attorney General. The informant shared extensive knowledge of Juárez drug killings (including US citizens as victims) with the North American government, but ICE and the Attorney General's office did nothing to stop the murders. Subsequently, the informant continued to engage in drug deals while supposedly under US government protection. In one transaction, the informant sent another man to collect money at a fast-food restaurant in El Paso. This man was murdered when he went for the money, allegedly by the Juárez Cartel. Victims' families allege that the US government knew about the danger to their relatives but rather than interrupt the flow of information from the drug informant allowed the homicides to occur (Gilot 2005). In other instances, the US arrests Mexican

---

28 There are numerous other examples of "illegal" or ambiguous activities that are tolerated in border settings such as the phenomenon of informal vendors of goods on international bridges that connect Mexico and the US. Vendors are a ubiquitous feature of, for example, the Paso del Norte bridge between El Paso and Juárez. From time to time the US port authorities send officials to chase the vendors back to Mexico but they invariably return. Clearly, the US government, with the "right" degree of force, could permanently ban such activity, but it does not do so. Consequently, these vendors, who follow their customers (in cars crossing into the US from Mexico) into US territory often to within ten yards of the inspection point at the port of entry, are a permanent part of local culture. Such informal, tacitly accepted border social arrangements can be a breeding ground for "corruption."

29 A parallel example is, of course, the knowing employment of undocumented Mexicans and Central Americans workers, which is against US law. There are various mechanisms in the law used to avoid responsibility and to provide plausible deniability of the illegal act. Again, system of illegal employment is often disproportionately blamed on law violators coming from south of the border, though there is some public discourse within the US of internal self-criticism.

narcotics traffickers, uses them as informants, and then deports them to Mexico where they face almost certain death at the hands of Cartel members or their police associates. The US blames the resultant deaths on Mexico but they would not have occurred had the US provided protection or asylum for their witnesses.

In such scenarios, corruption on the Mexican side of the border is connected in hidden ways to passive, shadow corruption by the US. This activity is not viewed as "American corruption" but is indeed a kind of slippery slope tacit acceptance of illicit activity. Consequently, our definitions of what constitutes corruption and where it is located should be widened to include the aforementioned practices. They tarnish the US' clean self-image and expose US hypocrisy on and across the border.

Conclusion: Borders—Peculiar and Revealing

Our task in one regard has been to demonstrate that corruption among US border officers is significant and systematic. To do this, we have analyzed a number of specific cases and the general patterns, or "scenarios," into which they fit. Beyond the flaws of US government agencies and the peculiarities of the US-Mexico border, we tried to draw attention to two wider concerns, which should be of interest to scholars of corruption across many settings. The first is to explore the patterns of corruption in settings that pretend to be ideologically pure and clean. The second is to reflect on the relationship of borders and transnational flows to national interiors (also see van Schendel 2005).

The US state along the Mexican border is not universally corrupt—we do not want to invert the ideology of cleanliness in an effort to demystify the subject. Much official work is done according to formal, public rules, with a small range of interpretation and discretion. However, the ideology of perfect law hides more complex distributions of practices, some of them rule-bound and rational and others not so. Along the US border, the law is compromised in a number of ways, including the penetration of the state by local social networks and political influences, aspects of the law that are systematically unenforced or under-enforced, and the hypocrisy of tolerated domestic demand for undocumented labor and illegal drugs. Every officer, and not just a few problem officers, learns which features of law must or may be ignored or bent, as well as those that must or may be handled in formal and rational terms. Within this space of systematic ambiguity, explicitly corrupt acts form one end of a range of possibilities, occurring frequently enough to be understood as a patterned outcome. Admittedly, our work is preliminary, and in particular we have not fully addressed why some acts are explicitly considered corrupt while others are simply tolerated and even encouraged as part of the normal ambiguity and hypocrisy of US law. Nevertheless, we have made progress in understanding corruption in ostensibly clean settings by demonstrating that such settings actually contain a range of questionable practices, and that corruption needs to be examined within these contexts rather than as a peculiar perversion of a perfect state and society (see also Harris 2003).

These sorts of ambiguities in law, state, and society are of course quite general and pervasive, and can certainly also be found deep in the US interior. But it is our argument that they are heightened along the US-Mexico border, and more importantly, that they are heightened precisely because of the border's role vis-à-vis US society as a whole. In this perspective, extending Mary Douglas's classic symbolic analysis of external boundaries (1966: 114–28), we can say borders are places of transaction between outside and inside, and symbolic repositories for the dangerous and unclean. Such outer edges do the dirty work of hypocrisy and absorb its negative connotations in a society wedded to an ideology of pure cleanliness but profoundly addicted to illegal transnational flows.

This analysis explains much beneath the surface of border culture and its relationship to corruption: the border comes to have a specialized role as place of ambiguity, zone of toleration, locus of transaction and personal brokerage, supplier of the shameful, illicit, hidden. The border ends up bearing the weight of exported factories and imported cheap labor, forbidden drugs, human smuggling, guns, anything-for-sale night life, and mysterious money—just as it did for prohibited alcohol and gambling in the past. At the same time, it bears the weight of intensive police recruiting, residence, and operations, in no small part because it focuses politically powerful if empirically ludicrous fantasies about the invasion and decay of the nation. It is simultaneously a criminal space and a police space, in ironic but intimate contact. Surely these contradictory mandates from the larger society cannot help but shape, indeed twist, "border culture" at the experiential level for officer and civilian alike. In summary, US-Mexico border corruption gives us insight into borders generally and also into the inherently contradictory notions of perfect law and perfect national society, by becoming in both conceptual and bitterly practical terms their dialectical opposite.

References

Abraham, I. and Schendel, W. van (2005) Introduction: The Making of Illicitness. In: W. van Schendel and I. Abraham (eds) *Illicit Flows and Criminal Things: States, Borders, and the Other Side of Globalization*. Bloomington, IN: Indiana University Press: 1–37.

Abrams, P. (1988) Notes on the Difficulty of Studying the State. *Journal of Historical Sociology* 1: 58–89.

Anders, E. (1982) *Boss Rule in South Texas: The Progressive Era*. Austin, TX: University of Texas Press.

Andreas, P. (2001) *Border Games: Policing the US-Mexico Divide*. Ithaca, NY: Cornell University Press.

Blancornelas, J. (2003) *Horas Extra: Los nuevos tiempos del narcotráfico*. Mexico City: Plaza Janés.

Bowden, C. (2002) *Down by the River: Drugs, Murder, and Family*. New York: Simon and Schuster.

Campbell, H. (2005) Drug Trafficking Stories: Everyday Forms of Narco-Folklore on the US-Mexico Border. *International Journal of Drug Policy* 16(5): 326–33.

Chaparro, R. (2005) Revelan red para traer mercancía china de EP. *El Diario* December 2.
Corliss, D. (2000) Regulating the Border Environment: Toxics, Maquiladoras, and the Public Right to Know. In: L.A. Herzog (ed.) *Shared Space: Rethinking the US-Mexico Border Environment*. La Jolla, CA: Center for US-Mexican Studies, University of California, San Diego: 295–312.
Department of Homeland Security (2006) Office of Inspector General, Department of Homeland Security, Semiannual Report to the Congress, October 1, 2005–March 31, 2006. Washington, DC: Government Printing Office.
Dillon, S. (2000) Small Town Arizona Judge Amasses Fortune, and Indictment. *New York Times* January 29.
Douglas, M. (1966) *Purity and Danger: An Analysis of the Concepts of Pollution and Taboo*. London: Routledge and Kegan Paul.
Gilboy, J.A. (1992) Penetrability of Administrative Systems: Political "Casework" and Immigration Inspections. *Law and Society Review* 26: 273–314.
Gilot, L. (2003) Visa Fraud is Big Business around World. *El Paso Times* June 27.
—— (2005) Families Hire Lawyer who Sued over Juárez Deaths. *El Paso Times* November 28.
—— (2006a) Trial May Expose Agency's Inner Code. *El Paso Times* February 26.
—— (2006b) Sentencing Delayed for ex-FBI Official. *El Paso Times* November 29.
—— (2006c) Smuggling Rings Dismantled. *El Paso Times* January 10.
Gootenberg, P. (2005) Talking Like a State: Drugs, Borders, and the Language of Control. In: W. van Schendel and I. Abraham (eds) *Illicit Flows and Criminal Things: States, Borders, and the Other Side of Globalization*. Bloomington, IN: Indiana University Press: 101–27.
Hansen, T.B. and F. Stepputat (eds) (2001) *States of Imagination: Ethnographic Explorations of the Post Colonial State*. Durham, NC: Duke University Press.
Harris, R. (2003) *Political Corruption: In and Beyond the Nation State*. London and New York: Routledge.
Heyman, J. McC. (1995) Putting Power into the Anthropology of Bureaucracy: The Immigration and Naturalization Service at the Mexico-United States Border. *Current Anthropology* 36: 261–87.
—— (1999) Why Interdiction? Immigration Law Enforcement at the United States-Mexico Border. *Regional Studies* 33: 619–30.
—— (2002) US Immigration Officers of Mexican Ancestry as Mexican Americans, Citizens, and Immigration Police. *Current Anthropology* 43: 479–507.
—— (2004a) United States Ports of Entry on the Mexican Border. In: A.G. Wood (ed.) *On the Border: Society and Culture between the United States and Mexico*. Lanham, MD: Scholarly Resources: 221–40.
—— (2004b) Ports of Entry as Nodes in the World System. *Identities: Global Studies in Culture and Power* 11: 303–27.
—— and A. Smart (1999) States and Illegal Practices: An Overview. In: J. Heyman (ed.) *States and Illegal Practices*. Oxford: Berg Publishers: 1–24.
Lipsky, M. (1980) *Street-Level Bureaucracy: Dilemmas of the Individual in Public Services*. New York: Russell Sage Foundation.
Maas, P. ([1973] 1997) *Serpico*. New York: HarperCollins.
Maril, R.L. (2004) *Patrolling Chaos: The US Border Patrol in Deep South Texas*. Lubbock, TX: Texas Tech University Press.
Maynard-Moody, S. and M. Musheno (2003) *Cops, Teachers, Counselors: Stories from the Front Lines of Public Service*. Ann Arbor, MN: University of Michigan Press.

Miller, T. (1985) *On the Border: Portraits of America's Southwestern Frontier*. Tucson, AZ: University of Arizona Press.
Naím, M. (2005) *Illicit: How Smugglers, Traffickers and Copycats are Hijacking the Global Economy*. New York: Doubleday.
Nevins, J. (2002) *Operation Gatekeeper: The Rise of the "Illegal Alien" and the Making of the US-Mexico Boundary*. New York: Routledge.
Nuijten, M. (2003) *Power, Community, and the State: The Political Anthropology of Organisation in Mexico*. London: Pluto Press.
Pinkerton, J. (2006) Border's Bribery Culture Seeps into Small Towns. *El Paso Times* December 25.
Quintanilla, M. and P. Copeland ([1983] 1996) "Mexican Maids": El Paso's Worst Kept Secret. In: O.J. Martínez (ed.) *US-Mexico Borderlands: Historical and Contemporary Perspectives*. Wilmington, DE: Scholarly Resources: 213–21.
Riding, A. (1986) *Distant Neighbors: A Portrait of the Mexicans*. New York: Vintage Books.
Roberts, C. (2006) Sergeant Succumbed to Greed in Drug Trafficking Case. *El Paso Times* February 6.
Rotella, S. (1998) *Twilight on the Line: Underworlds and Politics at the US-Mexico Border*. New York: Norton.
Ruiz, C. (2005) Aprovechan franquicia ambulantes del centro. *Norte de Ciudad Juárez*. December 8.
Ruiz, R. (1998) *On the Rim of Mexico: Encounters of the Rich and Poor*. Boulder, CO: Westview Press.
Schendel, W. van (2005) Spaces of Engagement: How Borderlands, Illicit Flows, and Territorial States Interlock. In: W. van Schendel and I. Abraham (eds) *Illicit Flows and Criminal Things: States, Borders, and the Other Side of Globalization*. Bloomington, IN: Indiana University Press: 38–68.
Schneider, J. and P.T. Schneider (2003) *Reversible Destiny: Mafia, Antimafia, and the Struggle for Palermo*. Berkeley: University of California Press.
—— (2005) Mafia, Antimafia, and the Plural Cultures of Sicily. *Current Anthropology* 46: 501–20.
Stoddard, E.R. (1975) The Informal "Code" of Police Deviancy: A Group Approach to "Blue-Coat Crime." In: J.H. Skolnick and T.C. Gray (eds) *Police in America*. Boston, MA: Little Brown: 260–75.
Talvera, V. (n.d.) The Disconnect: Perceptions of Corruption by Law Enforcement on the US-Mexico Border. Unpublished seminar paper, files of Campbell.
Tobin, M. (2005) Guardians of the Line. *Arizona Daily Star* November 27.
Valdez, D.W. and L. Gilot (2003) City's FBI Chief Out. *El Paso Times* November 9.
Vartabedian, R., R. Serrano, and R. Marosi (2006) Rise in Bribery Tests Integrity of US Border. *Los Angeles Times* October 23.
Vila, P. (2000) *Crossing Borders, Reinforcing Borders: Social Categories, Metaphors, and Narrative Identities on the US-Mexico Frontier*. Austin, TX: University of Texas Press.
Ward, N.D., P.L. Gurian, J.M. Heyman, and C. Howard (2007) Observed and Perceived Inconsistencies in US Border Inspections. Paper presented at the 86th Annual Meeting of the Transportation Research Board, January, Washington, DC.

Index

Aceh 55, 71
  see also Indonesia
amakudari 78
anthropology of corruption 4–6, 19, 27–8, 48–9, 54, 62
anti-corruption consensus 2, 3, 4, 5, 14, 16–7, 38, 41
  campaigns and policies 33, 56–7, 64–5, 80, 94–5, 160, 162, 176, 185, 203
  discourse 5, 17, 162
Arusha 133, 134, 136, 138

Barthes, Roland 61–2
Bataille, Georges 11
biographical trajectories 6, 26, 33, 35, 43, 44, 46–8
Blom Hansen, Thomas and Finn Stepputat 5, 10
Border Patrol *see* United States of America
Bourdieu, Pierre 10, 61, 62
Bretton Woods institutions 8
  see also International Monetary Fund, World Bank
bribery 1, 4, 5, 15, 19, 37–8, 53, 56, 67, 69, 168, 171–2, 178, 184
  on the border 195, 204, 207
  versus gift giving 4, 78–94
Bujumbura 132, 134–6
bureaucracy 3, 6–10, 37, 39, 46, 53, 55, 58, 64–5, 68, 77–8, 87–8, 144–7, 150, 152, 159, 161, 175, 192–3, 202, 204
bureaucrats 3, 7–10, 48, 57, 59, 61, 64–5, 67, 81, 87, 92, 94, 145, 152, 155, 157, 161
Burundi 19, 125–40
  see also CNDD
Buyoya, Pierre 137, 139

camorra 14
China 13, 17, 167–86
  see also Confucianism, CPC *guanxi*

Ciudad Juárez 193, 207, 208
cleanliness *see* discourses of corruption
clientelism 9, 45, 152, 209, 212
CNDD (Conseil National pour la Défence de la Démocratie) 131–2, 135
Comaroff Jean and John Comaroff, 19, 127, 144
Communist Party of China (CPC) 172, 174, 177
Confucianism 169–71
conspiracy theories 2, 4, 12, 17–19, 93, 99, 128–30, 134, 136, 137, 139, 200
corruption
  accusations 2, 12, 18–19, 31, 39, 43, 49, 108, 119, 130, 132, 134–6, 138–9, 143–4, 146, 149, 151–3, 158–60, 171, 183, 185, 203, 207
  and culture 33, 46, 78–80, 170
  definitions of 5–8, 13, 28–9, 53, 120, 168, 172–3, 176, 212–13, 214
  as deviance 28–30, 38, 61, 91, 93, 192
  economic approaches of 4, 6–7, 19, 35–6
  and gender 63, 65, 155–6, 201, 209–11
  indices, polls and statistics 6, 8, 35–6, 78, 202–3,
  petty versus grand 6, 29, 34, 36–8, 40, 44–5, 47, 53–4
  political science approach of 4, 7, 19, 35, 57
  rumors 12, 18–19, 31, 39, 54, 106, 125, 127–39, 146, 156, 204, 206, 212
  scandals 19, 31, 34, 38, 40, 78, 94, 184, 206
  systemic 2, 16, 53, 54, 57, 61, 63, 65–6, 69–73, 192–3, 195, 214
criminality 12, 29, 32, 42, 78–9, 82–83, 85, 86, 87, 90, 168, 172, 201, 204, 215

Daishinin court 14, 79–95,
  see also taikasei
development, developing countries 3, 8, 40, 57, 148–50, 167, 174–5, 184–6, 205

discourses about corruption 15, 36, 39, 172, 177, 179, 181–2, 205, 198
  critical 57–9, 61–3
  legitimizing 53, 55, 59–65, 72
  purity, cleanliness versus impurity, dirt 55, 58, 63, 64, 79, 126, 130, 132, 133, 136, 168, 191, 196, 202, 214, 215
  see also language
Drug Enforcement Agency (DEA) see United States of America

East Timor 55, 70–71
Eigen, Peter 3
El Grullo 143–63
embezzlement 1, 19, 32, 34, 37, 53, 62, 135
enjoyment 18, 19, 103, 143–63
ethics 1, 16, 27–8, 30, 38, 103, 145, 203–4, 207
extortion 6, 32, 36, 37, 41–2, 53, 57, 60–62, 67, 158, 211

FAO (Food and Agricultural Organization of the United Nations) 143
Federal Bureau of Investigation (FBI) 201, 203, 207–8
Foucault, Michel 10, 55–6, 62, 65
Friedrich, Carl 6, 7

gift giving 4, 14, 17, 29, 31, 33–4, 37, 44, 56, 60, 77–80, 84–9, 91–5, 167–79, 182, 207, 209
global politics 2–8, 55, 57–8, 71, 193, 205
governance 3, 5, 8, 9, 49, 53–4, 69, 72–3, 83, 85
  good 3, 5, 7, 57–8, 152–3, 162
Goya, Francisco
  The Sleep of Reason Produces Monsters 11
Greene, Graham
  The Heart of the Matter 1, 18–19
Greimas, Algirdas 105–7, 111
guanxi 17
  in historical context 169–73
  and performance 177–83
  possible trajectories of 183–5
  in reform era 173–6
Gupta, Akil 10, 28, 36–7, 45–7, 77

Harbin 169, 174, 176, 182–3

Haller Dieter and Chris Shore 5, 13, 28
Heilongjiang 168–9
  see also Harbin
Hong Kong 168, 174, 175, 177, 178, 185
Huntington, Samuel 6, 8, 9, 69
Hutu population 125, 130–31, 133–40

IMF see International Monetary Fund
Immigration and Customs Enforcement (ICE) see United States of America
impurity see discourses
India 37, 45–7
Indonesia 14, 17–18, 53–73
  Commission of Four 56, 57
  non-budgetary finance in 53, 66–71
  see also KKN (*Korupsi, Kolusi dan Nepotisme*)
International Monetary Fund (IMF) 58
  and Indonesia 54, 68, 71
Italy 13, 42, 57, 99–124

Jacquemet Marco 103, 105–6, 110
Japan 77–96
Juárez Cartel 213
judge in court 14, 41, 60, 77, 78, 79, 80, 81–96, 108–18,

KKN (*Korupsi, Kolusi dan Nepotisme*) 57, 61, 63
Kobe Metropolitan Government 87
Kompas 58
Kumejima, Shinji 87–8

Lacan, Jacques 146, 161
language and corruption
  in Africa 18, 30, 32–3, 42, 47, 49,
  in China 171, 177–83
  in Ghana 18
  in Indonesia 17–18, 55, 59, 60–63
  in Italy 106, 109
  in Japan 78
  in Latin America 18
  in Mexico 18, 162, 209
  see also discourses
  see also metaphors
laughing and irony 17, 43, 56, 60–65, 136, 156
lawyer 14, 56, 99–120
legal plurality 2, 13–15
Lockheed Corporation 78, 92

Index

Malkki, Lisa 132, 137, 144, 155
Mani Pulite, Clean Hands 42, 57
Mao Tse Tung / Zedong 148, 171, 172–3
Mbembé, Achille 9, 18, 128, 155
Megawati Soekarnoputri 55, 63–4
Meiji Government 80–81, 83–4, 88
Mexico 9, 10, 18, 143–63,
methodology 6, 27, 30, 32, 35–43, 54, 101–5, 204
  description 27, 33–5, 41
  narratives 40–43
  observation 35–40
  see also biographical trajectories
metaphors 18, 58, 60–64, 105, 118, 180
Mohammad Hatta 56
Morality 1–2, 29, 34–5, 77–9, 86, 94, 126, 172
Mugabarabona, Alain 134–5, 136, 139

Naples 14, 99–119
  see also Piovra clan
narcotics 200, 214
Nye, Joseph 6, 7, 28

organized crime 38, 99, 100, 102, 105–10, 117–19
Olivier de Sardan, Jean-Pierre 5–7, 10, 27–8, 40, 47

patronage 4, 9, 79, 87–8, 167, 211–12
performance and corruption 17–18, 33, 84, 103, 110, 144, 154, 158, 161, 168, 177–81, 192, 202
  see also rituals in corruption
  see also tact and corruption
power 2, 3, 10, 14–19, 33, 39, 46, 48, 54–6, 62–72, 80, 83, 91–2, 95, 109, 110, 114, 125–40, 144–62, 171–3, 175, 181, 184–5, 192, 194, 205, 212
Piovra clan 106, 111, 115, 117
  see also Naples
public-private dichotomy 2, 5, 10, 14, 28
purity *see* discourses

Rais, Amien 56, 57–8, 59
Recruit scandal 78, 94
Roitman, Janet 7, 12
rituals in corruption 15–16, 18–19, 31, 65, 117, 161, 179, 180, 197

Schneider Jane and Peter Schneider 5, 191, 199, 204–5
Scott, James 9, 32, 56, 205
secrecy 12, 18, 19, 126, 130, 138–40, 177
Senegal 37, 39, 40–43
Shanghai 168, 183
Shōwa Emperor 79, 80
Singapore 175, 184, 185
social capital and corruption 167–9, 173–6, 183–6
Soekarno 54, 56, 68, 70–71
spectacle 18, 144, 154–5, 160–62
state, nation-state 2, 5, 8–10, 12, 32–6, 47–9, 58–60, 152, 171–3
  apparatus 9, 13, 137, 175, 192
  institutions 8–9, 56, 58, 72
  legal system 2, 12, 13, 14
  power 10, 144–5, 153, 161–2
  and society division 2, 8–10, 18, 47
Suharto 54–5, 56–8, 59, 64, 67, 68, 70–71

taboo 11, 12, 60, 63–5, 211
tact and corruption 17, 168, 177–83
taikasei 14, 83, 84, 85–95, 94–5
  see also Daishinin court
Tanaka, Kakuei 78, 92, 94
Taussig, Michael 4, 11–12, 30, 129–30, 144, 158
Tempo 56–7
Tianenmen Square protests 176, 182, 184
Toer, Pramoedya Ananta 56
  Korupsi 56
transaction and corruption 16–18, 32–4, 169–70
transparency 3, 5, 14, 16–18, 53, 103, 128–9
Transparency International 3, 6, 8, 17, 53, 175
transgression 1, 11–13, 28, 144, 158–9, 161, 204
trust 8, 13, 18, 86, 95, 102–3, 110, 131, 167–70, 186
Tutsi population 130–33, 134, 137–8, 139, 140

United States of America
  Border Patrol 196, 200–201, 203–5, 207, 211
  Drug Enforcement Agency (DEA) 201, 203

United States–Mexico borderlands 4, 16, 191–5, 214–15

Vendetta argument 108, 111

Weber, Max 9–10, 66, 73, 201
West, Harry and Todd Sanders 3, 5, 14, 128, 129, 130, 136

witchcraft and corruption 19, 28, 30–32, 126–9, 135, 138, 144
World Bank 3, 6, 8–9, 44, 54, 58, 71, 143, 150
World Trade Organization (WTO) 168, 173

Žižek, Slavoj 16–17, 19, 129–30, 161